Photo Steichen

Winston S. Churchill

TO

MY FATHER

"WITHOUT WHOSE HELP THIS BOOK
COULD NEVER HAVE BEEN WRITTEN"

PREFACE

MY father has consented to a suggestion I made him some time ago that I should compile a volume of his speeches on Foreign Affairs and National Defense. This book is the result. All except the first were delivered in the last six years, and all but two in the House of Commons. With Mr. Churchill's permission I have made some excisions to avoid repetition. And he himself has helped me in making certain minor verbal changes to meet the difference between the spoken and the printed word. But nowhere have I omitted any argument or statement on the ground that its republication today in vastly different circumstances might prove a source of political inconvenience to its author. That there should have been no temptation to do so may perhaps be thought a testimony to the integrity of the double theme—a strong Britain based upon the Covenant of the League which emerges as the author's plan for the defense of freedom and peace. Observant readers will note the many cases where Mr. Churchill's prescience has already been proved beyond dispute, and some will detect occasions when he was alone in giving advice which might have advanced the national cause if it had not been disregarded, or accepted only too late.

Mr. Churchill's advocacy of the League as an effective instrument for the maintenance of peace does not begin to emerge until November 1933.[1] The hope underlying the earlier speeches is that Britain will be able to steer clear of European commitments, and that France and her allies will be able to cope with any European dangers that may arise. He repeatedly points to the danger of urging France to disarm, and of thereby involving Britain more closely on the Continent. In these speeches, which cover the years 1932 and 1933, Mr. Churchill argues that Britain should confine her interventions in Europe to pressing for redress of the grievances of the

[1] See p. 81.

nations who lost the War. But even at this time he is constantly pointing out that, if Britain wishes to secure a real measure of detachment from the Continent and to preserve her full liberty of action, early rearmament is essential.

From November 1933 onwards Mr. Churchill has to face a changed situation. With none of her grievances redressed, Germany has begun to rearm. During this period he persists in exposing the unwisdom of the successive attempts to weaken France, intensifies his demand for a strengthening of British defenses, and (since Britain has meanwhile grown relatively weaker) begins to feel his way towards the establishment of a collective system to meet the arming German menace. But he continues to point out that, though this weakness must inevitably involve Britain more closely on the Continent, vigorous and timely rearmament still offers a hope of regaining a measure of detachment.

This mood underlies all the speeches from November 1933 to July 1936. Meanwhile the dangers which Mr. Churchill has foreseen have drawn nearer. By 1936 Germany has been rearming on a colossal scale for three and a half years, and still no substantial progress has been made in strengthening British defenses; and it is by now apparent that even if the British Government could be persuaded to make the necessary exertions, a long interval must elapse before Britain will once again be strong enough to maintain an independent position. Beginning with his speech "Collective Security," of November 5, 1936, Mr. Churchill presses with increasing resolution for a firm League policy to insure that a united stand may be made so that the various peaceful nations shall not be struck down one by one.

To mark the dynamics which produced these reactions in Mr. Churchill's arguments, I have divided the book into three parts—"Germany Disarmed," "Germany Rearming" and "Germany Armed." These, of course, are relative and not absolute divisions, but they conveniently serve to emphasize the crescendo of events to which his theme was responding.

In compiling this volume I have read most of the speeches made by the leading spokesmen of all parties, as well as those of Mr. Churchill, and I have reached certain conclusions which I trust it will not be thought unseemly, invidious, or unfilial for me to record. As a politician, Mr. Churchill suffers from the disadvantage of being strangely free from the prejudices and ideologies which constitute such a large part of the mental equipment of our more successful public men. He always finds it difficult to subordinate his views on public affairs to the current exigencies of party position. Such independence of thought and speech is a handicap in the days when party machines are steadily increasing their power.

One of the distinctions between a statesman and a politician is that the former indulges in the luxury of subordinating party interests to those of the State. It may be that this unfashionable spirit of detachment from Party dogma becomes a virtue when applied to what used to be the non-party fields of national defense and foreign affairs. Those who think that these speeches reveal a true picture of the European scene and point the path that Britain ought to follow may perhaps decide that Mr. Churchill's insight in these matters arises not so much from his wide experience as from his ability to look at foreign countries without the spectacles of class or party.

In the main these forty speeches are a sustained effort to maintain the peace of Europe and the safety of Britain. As dangers present themselves in different forms or from opposite quarters the arguments vary; but the purpose is always the same. If British interests are set in the foremost place, it is only upon the condition that they shall serve the cause of a free and progressive world.

Mr. Churchill's attitude towards foreign countries seems to be mainly influenced by whether their character and policy is likely to prove helpful or harmful to these larger conceptions. His natural liberalism is as much affronted by tyranny and cruelty in Nazi Germany as by similar acts in Communist Russia, but he does not allow the interior politics of foreign countries to cloud his judgment upon the practical question whether these countries are likely to prove themselves serviceable or dangerous to the high interests he sets himself to guard.

RANDOLPH S. CHURCHILL.

WESTMINSTER GARDENS,
May 28, 1938

CONTENTS

xi

PART III

GERMANY ARMED

PART I
GERMANY DISARMED

A DISARMAMENT FABLE

October 25, 1928

*Extract from a speech delivered at Aldersbrook Road,
in the West Essex (or Epping) Division*

A DISARMAMENT FABLE

ONCE upon a time all the animals in the Zoo decided that they would disarm, and they arranged to have a conference to arrange the matter. So the Rhinoceros said when he opened the proceedings that the use of teeth was barbarous and horrible and ought to be strictly prohibited by general consent. Horns, which were mainly defensive weapons, would, of course, have to be allowed. The Buffalo, the Stag, the Porcupine, and even the little Hedgehog all said they would vote with the Rhino, but the Lion and the Tiger took a different view. They defended teeth and even claws, which they described as honorable weapons of immemorial antiquity. The Panther, the Leopard, the Puma, and the whole tribe of small cats all supported the Lion and the Tiger. Then the Bear spoke. He proposed that both teeth and horns should be banned and never used again for fighting by any animal. It would be quite enough if animals were allowed to give each other a good hug when they quarreled. No one could object to that. It was so fraternal, and that would be a great step towards peace. However, all the other animals were very offended with the Bear, and the Turkey fell into a perfect panic.

The discussion got so hot and angry, and all those animals began thinking so much about horns and teeth and hugging when they argued about the peaceful intentions that had brought them together that they began to look at one another in a very nasty way. Luckily the keepers were able to calm them down and persuade them to go back quietly to their cages, and they began to feel quite friendly with one another again.

DISARMAMENT PROBLEMS

May 13, 1932

Debate on the Adjournment

1931

August 25   Formation of the first National Government.

September 18.   Japanese seize Mukden

September 20   Gold Standard suspended.

October 27   General Election

November 5.   Formation of the second National Government.

1932

February 18.   Japan proclaims establishment of Manchukuo.

April 6   Four-Power Conference (Britain, France, Germany and Italy) to discuss which Powers should be invited to the forthcoming Danubian Conference

April 8.   Conference adjourns indefinitely.

April 10.   German Presidential election (Field-Marshal von Hindenburg, 19,300,000 votes, Herr Hitler, 13,400,000 votes).

DISARMAMENT PROBLEMS

THE SPEECH of the Foreign Secretary [Sir John Simon] was depressing and disappointing to those who have attached high hopes to Disarmament Conferences. The Foreign Secretary began with an elaborate legal justification for holding the Conference at all—the Treaty of Versailles, the Treaty of Locarno, and so on. There is no need for legal justification. If by any means an abatement of the expense and sacrifice involved in maintaining large armies and navies could be achieved, we should not look back to the legal reasons which had brought the Conference into being. What we have to consider is whether any useful result is actually being obtained, or has been obtained. I confess I have always doubted the utility of these conferences on disarmament in the present condition of the world. I see that I said a year ago:

> I believe that the armaments of the world today would be positively even smaller, certainly no greater, if none of these discussions had taken place at Geneva.

I said also:

> They have been a positive cause of friction and ill-will, and have given an undue advertisement to naval and military affairs. They have concentrated the attention of Governments in all countries, many of them without the slightest reason for mutual apprehension or dispute, upon all sorts of hypothetical wars which certainly will never take place

The Foreign Secretary pointed out to the House that, when you come to discuss quantitative disarmament, every nation asks itself, not "What is it that I am actually going to have in military instrumentalities?" but "What is the claim that I must peg out for myself in circumstances which I cannot foresee, and which may come upon me at any time in the next

9

ten years?'" Consequently, the whole tendency of these conferences—and they have been going on ceaselessly for six or seven years in one form or another—has been to lead the Governments of all countries, and the military, naval and air authorities behind the Governments of all countries, to state their claims at a maximum. Undoubtedly, also, the governing minds of the different countries have been continually concentrated upon the prospects and conditions of wars, with the result that we have now an organized, regimented opinion in all the Governments that are met together at Geneva, and all mean to make sure that no diminution of armaments is effected which runs counter to the strong opinions that their military and naval experts have taken up.

I believe that there has been no diminution of naval expense through any of the agreements which have been made since, possibly, the first Treaty of Washington. Economic pressure has led to great slowings down. I still believe that we are greatly weakened by the Treaty of London, which was entered into last year. We have parted with our freedom of design. That is, to us, a very great loss, because having the leadership in design, we could ensure that such moneys as we could spare for naval defense were employed to the best possible advantage. We have parted with that, and we have also tied our hands in the defense of the Narrow Seas. I still hold that it would have been far better for us to have said to the United States, "Build whatever you will; your Navy is absolutely ruled out of our calculations except as a potential friend. Build whatever you will, and allow us to deal with our special problems."

I come now to the proposals of qualitative disarmament about which the Foreign Secretary was so insistent. He told us that it was difficult to divide weapons into offensive and defensive categories. It certainly is, because almost every conceivable weapon may be used either in defense or offense; it all depends upon the circumstances; and every weapon, whether offensive or defensive, may be used either by an aggressor or by the innocent victim of his assault. My right hon. Friend said that he wished to make it more difficult for the invader, and for that reason, I gather, heavy guns, tanks and poison gas are to be relegated to the evil category of offensive weapons. The invasion of France by Germany in 1914, however, reached its climax without the employment of any of these weapons at all. The heavy gun is to be described as an offensive weapon. It is all right in a fortress; there it is virtuous and pacific in its character; but bring it out into the field—and, of course, if it were needed it would be brought out into the field—and it immediately becomes naughty, peccant, militaristic, and has to be placed under the ban of civilization. Take the tank. The Germans, having invaded France, entrenched themselves; and in a couple of years they shot down 1,500,000 French and British soldiers who were trying to free the soil of France. The tank was invented to overcome the fire of the machine-guns with which the Germans were maintaining themselves in France, and it saved a lot of lives in the process of eventually clearing the soil of the invader. Now, apparently, the machine-gun, which was the German weapon for holding on to thirteen provinces of France, is to be the virtuous, defensive machine-gun, and the tank, which was the means by which these lives were saved, is to be placed under the censure and obloquy of all just and righteous men.

There is also the question of gas. Nothing could be more repugnant to our feelings than the use of poison gas, but there is no logic at all behind the argument that it is quite proper in war to lay a man low with high-explosive shell, fragments of which inflict poisonous and festering wounds, and altogether immoral to give him a burn with corrosive gas or make him cough and sneeze or otherwise suffer through his respiratory organs. There is no logical distinction between the two. A great many of our friends are here today because they were fired at by German gas shells, which inflicted minor injuries upon them. Had it been high-explosive shell, they would in all human probability have been killed. The whole business of war is beyond all words horrible, and the nations are filled with the deepest loathing of it, but if wars are going to take place, it is by no means certain that the introduction of chemical warfare is bound to make them more horrible than they have been. The attitude of the British Government has always been to abhor the employment of poison gas. As I understand it, our only procedure is to keep alive such means of studying this subject as shall not put us at a hopeless disadvantage if, by any chance, it were used against us by other people.

I wish submarines had never been invented. Everyone who has been connected with the Royal Navy or the Admiralty would take that view. But a small country, with seaport towns within range of bombardment from the sea, feels very differently about having two or three submarines to keep bombarding squadrons at a respectful distance.

I have only mentioned these details in order to show the House how absurd is this attempt to distinguish between offensive and defensive weapons and how little prospect there is of any fruitful agreement being reached by it. These illustrations that I have given will be multiplied a

hundredfold when the naval, military and air experts on the committees
to whom this subject is to be remitted get to work. I am sure that nothing will emerge from their deliberations, which no doubt will be prolonged, except agreements to differ in one form or another.

A much truer line of classification might have been drawn if the
Conference of all these nations at Geneva had set itself to ban the use
of weapons which tend to be indiscriminate in their action and whose
use entails death and wounds, not merely to the combatants in the fighting
zones, but to the civil population, men, women and children, far removed
from those areas There indeed would be a direction in which the united
nations assembled at Geneva might advance with hope. It may be said
that in war no such conventions would be respected, and very few were
respected in the Great War. We hope there will be no other wars, but
even if there are wars in the future, we need not assume that they will be
world wars involving all the Powers of the world, with no outside Powers
to impose a restraint upon the passions of the belligerents or to judge of
the merits of their cause. I do not at all despair of building up strong conventions and conceptions held by the great nations of the world against the
use of weapons which fall upon enormous masses of non-combatant persons. Still more should I like to raise my voice in abhorrence of the idea,
now almost accepted among so many leading authorities in different countries, that the bombing of open towns and the wholesale destruction of
civilian life is compatible with any civilized decency. We are all allowing
ourselves to be led step by step into contemplating such hideous episodes
as part of the ordinary give-and-take of war, should a war ever come.

This attempt to employ the energies of Geneva upon discriminating
between offensive and defensive weapons will only lead to rigmarole and
delay, and is in itself a silly expedient. The adoption of such topics for
discussion casts a certain air of insincerity over the proceedings at Geneva.
I do not believe that the naval or military experts who meet to discuss
these matters will have any doubt whatever that no practical advantage
can be gained. As for the French scheme of security, that certainly is a
logical proposition, and I do not know whether, in a quite different
world from that in which we live, the relegation of the Air arm to a
central police force might not conceivably be a means of providing a
higher organization of society than anything that we can achieve. Here,
again, is another one of these very complicated propositions which have
been put forward, the only purpose of which it would seem is to afford

for those fifty-three nations who have arrived together to discuss disarmament some provender upon which they could sustain themselves.

If you wish for disarmament, it will be necessary to go to the political and economic causes which lie behind the maintenance of armies and navies. There are very serious political and economic dangers at the present time, and antagonisms which are by no means assuaged. I should very much regret to see any approximation in military strength between Germany and France. Those who speak of that as though it were right, or even a mere question of fair dealing, altogether underrate the gravity of the European situation. I would say to those who would like to see Germany and France on an equal footing in armaments, "Do you wish for war?" For my part, I earnestly hope that no such approximation will take place during my lifetime or that of my children.[1] This does not in the least imply want of regard or admiration for the qualities of the German people, but I am sure that the thesis that they should be placed in an equal military position to France is one which, if it ever emerged in practice, would bring us within practical distance of almost measureless calamity.

We must also remember that the great mass of Russia, with its enormous armies and with its schools of ardent students of chemical warfare, its poison gas, its tanks and all its appliances, looms up all along the Eastern frontier of Europe, and that the whole row of small states, Finland, Estonia, Latvia, Lithuania, Poland—not a small state, but for this purpose in the line—and Rumania, are under the continued preoccupation of this gigantic, and to them in many ways unfriendly, Russian power. It may well be that there is no danger, but I expect that if we lived there we should feel rather uncomfortable about it. These grave political dangers must be faced and recognized.

All these small nations look to France, and the French Army, as giving them a kind of central support. Although I should like to see European peace founded upon a more moral basis, I am very anxious that the present foundation should not be deranged until at any rate we have built up something satisfactory in its place. I hope and trust that the Foreign Secretary will continue his pious labors at Geneva, and that he will be able at some future date to give us a more favorable account of

[1] Mr Churchill was too optimistic; both he and his children have lived to see this approximation of military strength achieved by Germany, and worse is now in store

them. For my part, I shall continue to build my hopes upon the strong and ceaseless economic pressure of expense which is weighing upon all countries, to the growth of a greater confidence which a long peace must ensure, and to the patient and skillful removal of the political causes of antagonism which a wise foreign policy should eventually achieve.

REPARATIONS ABANDONED

July 11, 1932

Second Reading of the Consolidated Fund Bill

1932

May 30. Resignation of Dr. Bruning.

June 1. Herr von Papen appointed Chancellor.

June 11. Mr. MacDonald and Sir John Simon leave London for Lausanne.

June 22. Hoover Disarmament Plan announced.

July 11. Mr. MacDonald returns from Lausanne Conference.

REPARATIONS ABANDONED

I CANNOT associate myself with the Socialist Opposition in applauding the settlement of Lausanne or joining in the apparent jubilation which that event has caused. Of course, anything which removes friction between Germany and France is to the good, and I congratulate the Prime Minister on that. But it seems to me that it is Germany which is most to be felicitated upon what has taken place. Within less than fifteen years of the Great War Germany has been virtually freed from all burden of repairing the awful injuries which she wrought upon her neighbors. True, there are 3,000,000,000 marks which are to be payable by Germany, but I notice that Herr Hitler, who is the moving impulse behind the German Government and may be more than that very soon, took occasion to state yesterday that within a few months that amount would not be worth three marks. That is an appalling statement to be made while the ink is yet damp upon the parchment of the Treaty. Therefore I say that Germany has been virtually freed from all reparations.

What, then, has become of the Carthaginian peace of which we used to hear so much? That has gone. Some of it may have been written down in the Versailles Treaty, but its clauses have never been put into operation. There has been no Carthaginian peace. Neither has there been any bleeding of Germany white by the conquerors. The exact opposite has taken place. The loans which Britain and the United States particularly, and also other countries, have poured into the lap of Germany since the firing stopped, far exceed the sum of reparations which she had paid; indeed, they have been nearly double. If the plight of Germany is hard—and the plight of every country is hard at the present time—it is not because there has been any drain of her life's blood or of valuable commodities from Germany to the victors. On the contrary, the tide has flowed the other way. It is Germany that has received an infusion of blood from the nations with whom she went to war and by whom she was decisively defeated. Even these loans, which are almost double the payments Germany has made in reparations, are now in jeopardy. They are subject to a moratorium.

Let me give one striking instance which came to my notice when I was crossing the Atlantic Ocean. We and America took under the Peace Treaty three great liners from Germany The Germans surrendered them at a valuation and then borrowed the money to build two very much better ones They immediately captured the Blue Riband of the Atlantic, and they have it still. Now the loans with which the Germans built these ships are subject to a moratorium, while we are unable to go on with our new Cunarder because of our financial crisis. That is typical of what I mean when I say that Germany has not nearly so much reason to complain as some people suppose.

Absolved from all the burden of reparations, with a moratorium upon all commercial debts, with her factories equipped to the very latest point of science by British and American money, freed from internal debt, mortgages, fixed charges, debentures and so forth, by the original flight from the mark, Germany only awaits trade revival to gain an immense mercantile ascendancy throughout the world. I think that we are entitled to felicitate Germany on what has taken place, and I am sorry to see, as far as any information has reached us, that her only reaction is to ask for more.

England has not done quite so well out of the whole business. As usual, it has been our part to make the sacrifices; and we seem to have done it most thoroughly and most cheerfully. Not only did we pay for every farthing of our war expenditure, but we lent £2,000,000,000 to various allies. We reduced this immense sum by a settlement, in which, when Chancellor of the Exchequer, I was much concerned, until we received £19,000,000 in reparations from Germany and £19,000,000 in war debts per annum from our allies. The principle of this settlement was the well-known principle of the Balfour Note—that we would take no more from Europe than was asked from us by those on the other side of the Atlantic. We nearly succeeded in achieving that annual balance of payments as between our debtors and creditors. There are, however, £134,-000,000 of arrears; that is, we have paid that much more to our creditors than we have received under this agreement.

I must pause to reflect on the extreme changeableness of public opinion.

Where are all those who used to demand that we should extract the last penny of war debts and reparations from Germany? There still rings in my ears the abuse and criticism to which I was subjected because I did not get more out of France and Italy. The spectacle rises in my imagination of the scene at Liverpool Street Station, less than three years ago, when the then Chancellor of the Exchequer [Mr. Snowden], who was supposed to be stark and stiff in comparison with his predecessor in reclaiming war debts and reparations, was received by rapturous crowds, who saluted him with tremendous cheers as the Iron Chancellor, and how he was conducted with the Prime Minister, the same Prime Minister, to the Guildhall to receive the freedom of the City. All this was because he was supposed to have secured half a million pounds more.[1] I well remember the calculations which Mr. Snowden when in Opposition used to make about the burden I had placed on British shoulders by my misjudged leniency to France and Italy. I have always held the view that these war debts and reparations have been a great curse. I was a cordial supporter of the Balfour Note from its inception, and I have always held the view that the sooner we could free ourselves from them and the less we exacted, the better for the whole world, always provided that we were not left in the position of shouldering the whole burden. I have not changed my view. Now we have the act of Lausanne. No longer returning from The Hague but from Lausanne, we have the same Prime Minister, a similar crowd, the same cheers, a different railway station, it is true, and a policy, so far as they can tell us, which is the exact opposite of the policy of The Hague.

[1] August 6, 1929; Hague Conference on Reparations. Mr. Snowden attacked the Young Plan and denounced the French delegate's interpretation of the Balfour Note as "grotesque and ridiculous."

EUROPEAN DANGERS

November 23, 1932

Debate on the Address

1932

July 31. Reichstag election. National Socialists poll 37 3 per cent

September 1. The German Government make a *démarche* to the French Ambassador in Berlin on the subject of equal rights with regard to armaments.

September 18. The British Government issue a memorandum dealing with Germany's claim to equality of armament status.

"His Majesty's Government can give no countenance or encouragement to the disregard of Treaty obligations Although His Majesty's Government do not understand the German memorandum to have stated a contrary view, they desire to associate themselves with the opinion that it could not be maintained as the legally correct construction of the Treaty of Versailles that Germany is legally entitled to the abrogation of Part 5 of the Treaty of Versailles by any disarmament treaty to be concluded, or by the failure to conclude any convention at all."

September 28. Resignation from Cabinet (as a result of the Ottawa Agreements) of Sir Herbert Samuel, Lord Snowden, and Sir Archibald Sinclair.

November 6 Reichstag election. National Socialists poll 33.1 per cent.

November 10. Mr. Baldwin places responsibility for aerial warfare on young men:

"I think it is well for the man in the street to realize that there is no power on earth which can protect him from being bombed. Whatever people may tell him, the bomber will always get through.... The only defense is in offense, which means that you have to kill more women and children more quickly than the enemy if you want to save yourselves.

"I do not know how the youth of the world may feel, but it is no cheerful thought to the older men that, having got that mastery of the air, we are going to defile the earth from the air as we have defiled the soil for nearly all the years that mankind has been on it. That is a question for the young men far more than it is for us. When the next war comes and European civilization is wiped out, as it will be and by no force more than that force, then do not let them lay the blame upon the old men. Let them remember that they principally and they alone are responsible for the terrors that have fallen on the earth." (Loud and prolonged cheers.)

November 17. Resignation of von Papen.

EUROPEAN DANGERS

•

IT IS ABOUT A YEAR now since I stood here and welcomed the National Government on its assumption of its great responsibilities It is not quite the same Government today. Two out of the three official parties and organizations in the country are tirelessly working against it, and, on the other hand, of course, the natural elements of Conservative strength and tradition are not developing the same degree of partisanship on its behalf as is usual in party government. We have had a year of conferences. There have been quite a number when one comes to think of them: the Lausanne Conference, the Danubian States Conference (dead almost as soon as it was born), the first Geneva Conference, the Ottawa Conference, the third Round Table Conference on India, and now Geneva again. Very little success, I think, has attended these conferences, except, of course, Ottawa. There may be a good many people who do not think much of Ottawa now, but perhaps their children may think more of it, and their grandchildren more still. That, at least, is our hope, ana it is in that hope that this act of faith and Imperial consolidation has been performed. But with regard to the other conferences I am bound to say that they all seem to me to fall under the criticism of trying to pay off realities with words.

Everything which has happened since July last shows how unwise it was to bring the Lausanne Conference to a conclusion,¹ and to trumpet its results all round the globe. If we look back on those July days, when the Prime Minister [Mr. Ramsay MacDonald] was welcomed in triumph on his return, with all the Cabinet and Under-Secretaries drawn up like a row of Grenadiers of varying sizes at the railway-station, we can see how absurd were the claims which were then advanced that Lausanne had "saved Europe," and that a "new era" had opened for the world.

There is quite a lot still to be done in Europe, and for many people it is very much the same old era in the world.

There is no doubt whatever that harm was done to the prospect of the settlement of the War debts by what happened at Lausanne. I ventured to warn the Government before this happened, in May or June of last year, of the extreme unwisdom of making the Debt Settlement an issue at the American elections. The consequences of Lausanne have been to force all the candidates for Congress and the Senate, on both sides of politics, to give specific pledges and to make definite declarations upon this subject. We all know what happens at elections.

If the House will be persuaded by me they will now embark upon a short voyage over a placid lake and come from Lausanne to Geneva What a scene awaits them there! They will walk through streets guarded by machine-guns, whose pavements are newly stained with blood [1]—I presume because of the conscientious scruples which prevented the use of the perfectly harmless tear gas—and they will enter those halls of debate where, with a persistency which rivals in duration the siege of Troy, the nations are pursuing the question of disarmament. It is a melancholy scene. I have sympathy with, and respect for, the well-meaning, loyal-hearted people who make up the League of Nations Union in this country, but what impresses me most about them is their long-suffering and inexhaustible gullibility. Any scheme of any kind for disarmament put forward by any country, so long as it is surrounded by suitable phraseology, is hailed by them, and the speeches are cheered, and those who speak gain the meed of their applause. Why do they not look down beneath the surface of European affairs to the iron realities which lie beneath? They would then see that France does not stand alone in Europe. France does not speak for herself alone when she speaks at Geneva. France is the head of a system of states, some large, others minor, including Belgium, Poland, Rumania, Czechoslovakia and Yugoslavia, comprising many millions of human beings, all of whom depend for their frontiers upon the existence of the present Peace Treaties, good or bad, all of whom are armed and organized to defend themselves and to defend their rights, and all of whom look to France and the French Army in very much the same sort of way as small nations before the War used to look to the British Navy in the days of its power. That is one side of the picture.

[1] On November 9, 1932, Swiss troops fired on Communist rioters in Geneva. Thirteen people were killed and seventy wounded.

On the other side there is Germany, the same mighty Germany which so recently withstood almost the world in arms; Germany which resisted with such formidable capacity that it took between two and three Allied lives to take one German life in the four years of the Great War; Germany which has also allies, friends and associates in her train, powerful nations, who consider their politics as associated to some extent with hers;[2] Germany whose annual quota of youth reaching the military age is already nearly double the youth of France; Germany where the Parliamentary system and the safeguards of the Parliamentary system which we used to be taught to rely upon after the Great War are in abeyance. I do not know where Germany's Parliamentary system stands today, but certainly military men are in control of the essentials.

Germany has paid since the War an indemnity of about one thousand millions sterling, but she has borrowed in the same time about two thousand millions sterling with which to pay that indemnity and to equip her factories. Her territories have been evacuated long before the stipulated time—I rejoice in it—and now she has been by Lausanne virtually freed from all those reparations which had been claimed from her by the nations whose territories have been devastated in the War, or whose prosperity, like ours, has been gravely undermined by the War. At the same time, her commercial debts may well prove ultimately to be irrecoverable. I am making no indictment of Germany. I have respect and admiration for the Germans, and desire that we should live on terms of good feeling and fruitful relations with them; but we must look at the fact that every concession which has been made—many concessions have been made, and many more will be made and ought to be made—has been followed immediately by a fresh demand.

Now the demand is that Germany should be allowed to rearm. Do not delude yourselves. Do not let His Majesty's Government believe—I am sure they do not believe—that all that Germany is asking for is equal status. I believe the refined term now is equal qualitative status, or, as an alternative, equal quantitative status by indefinitely deferred stages. That is not what Germany is seeking. All these bands of sturdy Teutonic youths, marching through the streets and roads of Germany, with the light of desire in their eyes to suffer for their Fatherland, are not looking for status. They are looking for weapons, and, when they have the weapons, believe me they will then ask for the return of lost territories and lost colonies, and when that demand is made it cannot fail to shake

[2] At this time Hungary and Bulgaria

and possibly shatter to their foundations every one of the countries I have mentioned, and some other countries I have not mentioned.

Besides Germany, there is Russia Russia has made herself an Ishmael among the nations, but she is one of the most titanic factors in the economy and in the diplomacy of the world. Russia, with her enormous, rapidly increasing armaments, with her tremendous development of poison gas, aeroplanes, tanks and every kind of forbidden fruit; Russia, with her limitless man-power and her corrosive hatreds, weighs heavily upon a whole line of countries, some small, others considerable, from the Baltic to the Black Sea, all situated adjacent to Russian territory. These countries have newly gained their independence. Their independence and nationhood are sacred to them, and we must never forget that most of them have been carved, in whole or in part, out of the old Russian Empire, the Russian Empire of Peter the Great and Catherine the Great. In some cases these countries are also in deep anxiety about Germany.

I am sure that I have not overdrawn the picture. I have marshaled the facts, but I have not overdrawn the picture. Can we wonder, can any reasonable, fair-minded, peace-loving person wonder, in the circumstances, that there is fear in Europe, and, behind the fear, the precautions, perhaps in some cases exaggerated precautions, which fear excites? We in these islands, with our heavy burdens and with our wide Imperial responsibilities, ought to be very careful not to meddle improvidently or beyond our station, beyond our proportionate stake, in this tremendous European structure. If we were to derange the existing foundations, based on force though they may be, we might easily bring about the very catastrophe that most of all we desire to avert. What would happen to us then? No one can predict. But if by the part we had played in European affairs we had precipitated such a catastrophe, then I think our honor might be engaged beyond the limitations which our treaties and agreements prescribe.

We must not forget, and Europe and the United States must not forget, that we have disarmed. Alone among the nations we have disarmed while others have rearmed, and we must not be expected to undertake a part larger than it is in our capacity to make good. For that reason the Memorandum which His Majesty's Government sent to Germany a couple of months ago was a wise, a prudent and a necessary document.[3] I think they might have prepared the public here and in Germany a little more for the terms of that Note, but that it was absolutely necessary I

[3] September 18 See p 22

have no doubt. If at that moment when General von Schleicher, one of the most powerful men in Germany, had openly said that in certain circumstances Germany would arm whatever the law and the League of Nations said, if at that moment when all parties in Germany were competing against each other as to which could put up the bravest front against the foreigner, in electioneering with foreign politics—a dangerous and delicate proceeding—if at that moment when it seemed, perhaps unwarrantably, that Italy was lending encouragement to the German view, we had added our approbation, or allowed it to be assumed that we approved of such a claim made by General von Schleicher, His Majesty's Government would have incurred the most serious responsibilities without any effective means of discharging them. I thank His Majesty's Government for their Note, and I should regret if anything has been said since which in any way weakens its effect.

Coming more closely to Geneva, I should like to say that I have watched the Disarmament Conferences which have now been going on for many years, and I have formed certain opinions about them. Disarmament divides itself into disarmament by scale and disarmament by ratio. Disarmament by scale is not so important, but disarmament by ratio, the altering of the relative positions of nations, is the part of the problem which excites the most intense anxiety and even passion. I have formed the opinion that none of the nations concerned in the Disarmament Conferences except Great Britain has been prepared willingly to alter to its own disadvantage its ratio of armed strength. I agree that there have been diminutions of armaments, but they have largely been produced, as they always will be produced, by the pressure of economic and political facts in a time when there is peace; and I do not think that any of these nations have intended to do anything which would destroy the *status quo;* and certainly they are not willing to impair their factor of safety. I prefer the expression "factor of safety" to another expression which has been used—insurance. Insurance is not a good word, because it does nothing to ward off a danger, and it only compensates, or attempts to compensate, after the evil or misfortune has occurred. "Factor of safety" is the expression which I prefer, and I do not think that any nation has been willing to impair that factor. Therefore, the first phase of the Disarmament Conferences, going on for four or five years, the Preparatory Commission and so on, consisted in every one of these nations trying to disarm some other nation, and a whole array of ingenious technical schemes were put forward by military experts, each of which was perfectly fair and reasonable until it was examined by the other side. Only in one case has this first phase of altering the ratio produced a success—when the United States wished to secure complete naval equality with Great Britain, and we complied with their request. For the rest, I do not think that anything so far has been achieved by the discussions.

But for some time a second phase has supervened at Geneva. The expectation of general disarmament upon a great scale has failed; the hope of one nation being able to disarm its rival has been frustrated by the very stout and stubborn resistance which every nation makes to that process. Now I am afraid that a large part of the object of every country is to throw the blame for an impending failure upon some other country while willing, if possible, to win the Nobel Peace Prize for itself. Again, we have had an elaborate series of technical maneuvers by military experts and by Governments and their advisers. I am not going to particularize, I am not going to put too sharp a point to my remarks, because I do not like to say anything which might be offensive to great nations who have put forward schemes for disarmament which place them in such a satisfactory light and cost them so very little in convenience. But every time one of these plans is launched the poor good people of the League of Nations Union clap their hands with joy, and every time they are disappointed—nay, I must say deceived. But their hope is unfailing. The process is apparently endless, and so is the pathetic belief with which it is invariably greeted. I repeat that we alone have been found willing to alter continually our ratio of armed strength to our disadvantage. We have done it on land, on sea, and in the air. Now His Majesty's Government have said that we have reached the limit, and I think we shall all agree with them in that statement.

I am sorry to be so pessimistic, but it is absolutely a duty to put the rugged facts as I conceive them before the House. I have constantly predicted, as the Prime Minister and the Lord President will bear me out, publicly and privately, that these Disarmament Conferences would not succeed in removing the danger of war, and I doubt if they will succeed in substantially reducing the burden of armaments. Indeed, I have held the view that the holding of all these conferences over the last seven or eight or nine years has had the opposite effect, and has actually prevented the burden from being lightened as it would have been if we had trusted to the normal and powerful working of economic and financial pressures. But these conferences have focused the attention of the leading men in all nations upon the competitive aspect of armaments, and upon technical questions which they never would have heard of. This process has intensified the suspicions and the anxieties of the nations, and has brought the possibilities of war nearer to us than they were some years ago. That, I fear, startling and unpleasant as it is, cannot be disputed by anyone who looks at the facts of the European situation today.

We have steadily marched backward since Locarno I am sorry that Sir Austen Chamberlain is not in his place Many criticisms have been applied to him. Since the War Locarno was the high-water mark of Europe. Look what a distance we have fallen since then. Compare the state of Europe on the morrow of Locarno with its condition today. Fears are greater, rivalries are sharper, military plans are more closely concerted, military organizations are more carefully and efficiently developed, Britain is weaker: and Britain's hour of weakness is Europe's hour of danger. The war mentality is springing up again in certain countries. All over Europe, except here, there is hardly a factory which is not prepared for its alternative war service; every detail worked out for its immediate transformation upon a signal. And all this has been taking place under Governments whose statesmen and diplomatists have never ceased to utter the most noble sentiments of peace amid the cheers of the simple and the good.

These are not pleasant facts, but I believe they are facts. I am sure they must be painful to the Prime Minister. Everyone knows how ardently he desires to work for peace, and everyone knows that there are no limits to his courage in such a calling. He said last month, to a deputation from the Churches which waited upon him, "I hope you will go on pressing and pressing and pressing. Do help us to do the broad, just, fundamental, eternal thing." We all admire such sentiments. Dressed in noble, if somewhat flocculent eloquence, they obtain the allegiance of all. But let it be noticed that there is just the same vagueness in this sphere of disarmament as is complained of in many quarters in the Government's utterances upon domestic matters, and particularly unemployment. There ought to be more precision. The question is: Have we gone the right way to achieve the purpose in hand? For more than three years my right hon. Friend has been Prime Minister and largely Secretary of State for Foreign Affairs. That is the sphere which he has chosen to make peculiarly his own. It must be very depressing for him to feel that the position has definitely got worse during his stewardship, and to see how much worse it has got since Locarno. Everyone would like to do the "broad, just, fundamental, eternal thing," whatever that may be, but they would like to do it in a way which made things better and not in a way that made them worse. I will not predict that no agreement will be reached at Geneva. Indeed, it would be disastrous if no agreement were reached there. But I do not believe that what is going to be done at Geneva is going to mean any great or decisive change in the condition of the world, or any real progress towards the consolidation of European and world peace. On the contrary, it may well be that the situation will be exacerbated by the termination of the Disarmament Conference.

I remember that after the Great War had begun a complaint used to be made by very upright men and women: "Why were we not told about this before? Why did we not hear before about all that was going on?" Everyone can remember that. And when the War was over there was a strong feeling in favor of what is called open diplomacy. In my experience, and interior knowledge of the working of Governments, which extends over nearly a quarter of a century, I cannot recall any time when the gap between the kind of words which statesmen used and what was actually happening in many countries was so great as it is now. The habit of saying smooth things and uttering pious platitudes and sentiments to gain applause, without relation to the underlying facts, is more pronounced now than it has ever been in my experience. Just as the late Lord Birkenhead used to say about India—I think it the beginning and end of wisdom there—"Tell the truth to India," so I would now say, "Tell the truth to the British people." They are a tough people, a robust people. They may be a bit offended at the moment, but if you have told them exactly what is going on you have insured yourself against complaints and reproaches which are very unpleasant when they come home on the morrow of some disillusion.

There is a certain amount of exaggerated talk of what is called French ascendancy. I do not like the present situation; no one does. But there is this to be said about French ascendancy, the French system in Europe, or whatever you like to call it—it gives stability. As Lord Grey has recently reminded us, France, though armed to the teeth, is pacifist to the core. All the countries associated with France have no wish to do anything except to maintain the *status quo*. They only wish to keep what they have got, and no initiative in making trouble would come from them. At the present time, and until or unless Germany is rearmed, France and her associates are, I believe, quite capable of maintaining themselves, and are in no immediate danger of being challenged by countries which are dissatisfied with the *status quo*. There is nothing wrong in that. I am not saying that it is the last word. It could be improved, but there is nothing wrong in it from a legal or public point of view. The case of France and her associates stands on exactly the same treaty foundations as the League of Nations itself. Not only have they ample military force, as I believe, at present, but they have the public law of Europe behind them until it is changed.

I think we ought to feel assurance that there is something equally solid with which we can replace the French system before we press them unduly to weaken the military factors of safety upon which their security depends. Europe might easily go farther and fare worse. I am not saying that I am pleased with the situation as it is. I am pointing out how easily we might, in trying to improve it too rapidly or injudiciously, bring about what of all things in the world we wish to avoid. I say quite frankly, though I may shock the House, that I would rather see another ten or twenty years of one-sided armed peace than see a war between equally well-matched Powers or combinations of Powers—and that may be the choice.

That I am a realist in these matters I cannot deny, but I am not an alarmist. I do not believe in the imminence of war in Europe. I believe that with wisdom and with skill we may never see it in our time. To hold any other view would indeed be to despair. I put my confidence, first of all, upon the strength of the French Army; secondly, upon the preoccupation of Russia in the Far East, on account of the enormous increase in the armaments of Japan; and, thirdly, I put it, in the general way, upon the loathing of war which prevails among the nationals of all the countries not dissatisfied with the late peace. I believe that we have a considerable breathing-space in which to revive again those lights of goodwill and reconciliation in Europe which shone, so brightly but so briefly, on the morrow of Locarno. We shall never do that merely by haggling about cannons, tanks, aeroplanes and submarines, or measuring swords with one another, among nations already eying each other with so much vigilance.

Are there no other paths by which we may recover the spirit of Locarno? I would follow any real path, not a sham or a blind alley, which led to lasting reconciliation between Germany and her neighbors. Here at this moment, if the House will permit me, I would venture to propound a general principle which I humbly submit to the Government and the House, and which I earnestly trust they will follow. Here is my general principle. The removal of the just grievances of the vanquished ought to precede the disarmament of the victors. To bring about anything like equality of armaments [between the vanquished and the victor nations] if it were in our power to do so, which it happily is not, while those grievances remain unredressed, would be almost to appoint the day for another European war—to fix it as if it were a prize-fight. It would be far safer to reopen questions like those of the Dantzig Corridor and Transylvania, with all their delicacy and difficulty, in cold blood and in a calm atmosphere and while the victor nations still have ample superiority, than to wait and drift on, inch by inch and stage by stage, until once again vast combinations, equally matched, confront each other face to face.

There is another reason why I commend this to the House. It must be remembered that Great Britain will have more power and will run far less risk in pressing for the redress of grievances than in pressing for disarmament We can only promote disarmament by giving further guarantees of aid. We can press for the redress of grievances by merely threatening, if our counsels are not attended to, to withdraw ourselves at the proper time from our present close entanglement in European affairs The first road of pressing for disarmament and offering more aid only leads us deeper and deeper into the European situation. The second either removes the cause of danger or leads us out of the danger zone.

Just look to where our present policy is leading us. Look at the situation into which we are apparently marching blindly and with a sort of helpless chorus of approval. When we say to France and to Poland, "Why do you not disarm and set an example, and respond to our gesture, and so on?" they reply, "Will you then help us to defend ourselves, supposing that you are wrong in your view of what our factor of safety ought to be?" Nobody keeps armaments going for fun. They keep them going for fear. "We would gladly reduce," they say, "provided we get you in line with us for certain. If you will take some of our burden off our shoulders there will be no hesitation on our part in transferring that burden." And what they say to us they say still more to the United States—or if they do not say it, they think it. But surely this is very dangerous ground for us. We are to persuade our friends to weaken themselves as much as possible, and then we are to make it up to them by our own exertions and at our own expense.

It is as if one said, "I will go tiger-hunting with you, my friend, on the one condition that you leave your rifle at home." That is not the kind of excursion on which our old men ought to send our young men. We have, of course, serious obligations, which we have no intention of discarding, under Locarno. But under Locarno we remain the sole and free judge of the occasion and of the interpretation put upon these obligations. Without our own vote on the Council of the League of Nations, which must be unanimous, we cannot be involved in war. But see now what the French propose in this latest scheme. They propose, quite logically and naturally, in responding to the pressure of Britain and the United States on disarmament, that the decision of the Council should be by a majority. That would mean that our fate would be decided over our head. We might find ourselves pledged in honor and in law to enter a war against our will, and against our better judgment, in order to preserve those very injustices and grievances which sunder Europe today, which are the cause of present armaments and which, if not arrested, will cause another war.

These are not the days when you can order the British nation or the British Empire about as if it were a pawn on the chessboard of Europe You cannot do it. Of course, if the United States were willing to come into the European scene as a prime factor, if they were willing to guarantee to those countries who take their advice that they would not suffer for it, then an incomparably wider and happier prospect would open to the whole world. If they were willing not only to sign, but to ratify, treaties of that kind, it would be an enormous advantage. It is quite safe for the British Empire to go as far in any guarantee in Europe as the United States is willing to go, and hardly any difficulty in the world could not be solved by the faithful co-operation of the English-speaking peoples. But that is not going to happen tomorrow. It is not in our power to anticipate our destiny. Meanwhile we ought not to take any further or closer engagements in Europe beyond those which the United States may be found willing to take.

I hope that the League of Nations is not going to be asked now to do the impossible. Those who believe, as I do sincerely, that the League of Nations is a priceless instrument of international comity, which may play as great a part as the most daring, hopeful founders ever forecast for it, should be especially careful not to put upon the League strains which in its present stage it is utterly incapable of bearing. I deprecate altogether the kind of thought that, unless the League can force a general disarmament, unless it can compel powerful nations in remote regions to comply with its decisions, it is dead—away with it. All that is as foolish as it is to grudge the small sums necessary to keep this precious international machinery in being He is a bad friend to the League of Nations who would set its tasks beyond its compass.

There is only one thing more to say before I sit down, and it is suggested to me by the speech which the Lord President of the Council [Mr. Baldwin] delivered recently.[4] I did not hear it, but from all accounts it was one which profoundly impressed the House, and revealed the latent and often carefully concealed powers which reside in my right hon. Friend. But that speech, while it deeply impressed the House, I have no doubt—and I have read it with great attention—led to no practical conclusion. It created anxiety, and it created also perplexity There was a sense of, what shall I say, fatalism, and even perhaps helplessness about it, and I take this opportunity of saying that, as far as this island is concerned, the responsibility of Ministers to guarantee the safety of the country from day to day and from hour to hour is direct and inalienable. It has always been so, and I am sure they will not differ from their predecessors in accepting that responsibility. Their duty is not only to try, within the restricted limits which, I fear, are all that is open to them, to prevent war, but to make sure that we ourselves are not involved in one, and, above all, to make sure that, if war should break out among other Powers, our country and the King's Dominions can be effectively defended, and will be able to preserve, if they desire to do so, that strong and unassailable neutrality from which we must never be drawn except by the heart and conscience of the nation.

[4] November 10. See p. 22.

AIR DEFENSE

March 14, 1933

Air Estimates

1932

December 2. General von Schleicher appointed Chancellor

1933

January 27. The British Government submit new proposals to the Disarmament Conference.

January 28. Resignation of General von Schleicher.

January 30. Herr Hitler appointed Chancellor in the Coalition Government, supported by Hugenberg and von Papen.

February 24. The League adopts Lytton Report on Manchurian situation and declares Japan to be aggressor.

February 27. Reichstag set on fire.
Sir John Simon announces embargo on export of arms to China and Japan.

March 5. Reichstag election. National Socialists poll 17 million votes—44 per cent. of total.

March 13. Mr. Baldwin announces withdrawal of arms embargo

March 14. Air Estimates introduced in the House of Commons. The services rendered by the Royal Air Force in combating the locust pest and in carrying blankets and other stores to certain flood-stricken areas were strongly emphasized.

AIR DEFENSE

IF OUR DISCUSSION this afternoon were confined solely to the topics upon which the Under-Secretary of State [Sir Philip Sassoon] thought it prudent to dwell, if, for instance, we were to go away, as we might easily go, with the idea that the Air Force exists to fight locusts and that it never drops anything but blankets, we should undoubtedly entertain incomplete impressions of some of the issues which are brought before the House when the Air Estimates for the year are introduced. I do not consider that the present state of Europe is comparable with the state of Europe in 1914. Although there is great unrest, and hatreds are as rife as ever, yet I feel that there is not the same explosive and catastrophic atmosphere as existed in 1914; and therefore we may discuss in cool blood and with calm hearts, or at any rate in tranquil circumstances, some of the technical issues which are raised by this Vote.

I must turn especially to the memorable speech which was delivered by the Lord President a few months ago. I agree with what I imagine were his feelings when he wished that neither aeroplanes nor submarines had ever been invented. I am sure they have both been deeply detrimental to the special interests and security of this island; and I agree also with his general theme that the air power may either end war or end civilization But we are bound to examine carefully the speech of the Lord President because of the feeling that he aroused alarm without giving guidance. My right hon. Friend swept away many important things in that half-hour. He did not believe there was never to be another great war; he thought wars would come again some day, but he hoped, as we all hope, they would not come in our time. He had apparently no real faith in the sanctity of agreements, such as the Kellogg Pact; neither had he any faith in the means of defense which are open to civilized communities when confronted with dangers which they cannot avoid. He led us up to a conclusion which was no conclusion. We were greatly concerned, and yet we were afforded no solace, no solution. So far as he made an appeal to youth, it was very difficult to see what was the moral which he inculcated, and as far as I can understand, reading in the current publications, his appeal to youth has been widely misinterpreted in some of our leading universities.[1]

There is a certain helplessness and hopelessness which was spread about by his speech from which I hope the House will endeavor to shake itself free. There is the same kind of helplessness and hopelessness about dealing with this air problem as there is about dealing with the unemployment problem, or the currency question, or the question of economy. All the evils are vividly portrayed, and the most admirable sentiments are expressed, but as for a practical course of action, solid footholds on which we can tread step by step, there is in this great sphere, as in other spheres of Government activity, a gap, a hiatus, a sense that there is no message from the lips of the prophet. There is no use gaping vacuously on the problems of the air. Still less is there any use in indulging in pretense in any form.

The spokesman for the Labour party, in a speech which certainly presented a definite point of view, spoke with much satisfaction of the proposals which the Government have been making at Geneva. The air forces of the world are all to be reduced to our level, and then we are all to take together another step down to the extent of 33⅓ per cent. Well, is there any reality at all in a proposal of that kind? We must not allow our insular pride to blind us to the fact that some of these foreigners are quite intelligent, that they have an extraordinary knack on occasion of rising fully up to the level of British comprehension. Of course, if all the air forces of the world were to be reduced to our level, as we are only fifth [2] in the list, that would be a great enhancement of our ratio of military strength; and the foreigners are bound to notice that. So I could not help feeling that the proposals which were made, and would sound very well while they were being unfolded, would give great gratification to the League of Nations Union, who, poor things, have to content themselves with so little. They would give the same kind of warm, sentimental,

[1] A reference to the Oxford Union's resolution "that this house will in no circumstances fight for its King and country."

[2] At this period the air strength of the leading Powers was as follows. France, U.S.A., Japan, Italy, and Great Britain.

generous feeling that we were doing the "broad, just, fundamental, eternal thing" that the recent arms embargo announcement [3] gave to so wide a circle. But I do not suppose that anyone would have been more surprised than the Under-Secretary of State or his Chief [Lord Londonderry] if, when they had made these specious suggestions at Geneva, all the Powers had suddenly risen and, with loud acclamations, said, "We accept them." I am sure that even the Prime Minister would have been, at any rate momentarily, disconcerted. In fact, there was no chance of these proposals being accepted, not the faintest chance—and no one knew it better than His Majesty's Government when they made them.

We ought not to deal in humbug. There are good people in this country who care about disarmament. In many ways I think they are wrong, but I do not see why they should be tricked. I think they should have the plain truth told them, and if they disagree they have their constitutional remedy. It is no kindness to this country to stir up and pay all this lip-service in the region of unrealities, and get a cheap cheer because you have said something which has not ruffled anyone, and then meanwhile do the opposite, meanwhile proceed on entirely pre-War lines, as all the nations of Europe are proceeding today in all the practical arrangements which they are making.

Another reason why these proposals had no chance of being accepted is their effect upon France. In the present temper of Europe can you ever expect that France would halve her air force and then reduce the residue by one-third? Would you advise her to do so? If she took your advice and did it, and then trouble occurred, would you commit this country to stand by her side and make good the injury? If we proceed to argue on lines which have no connection with reality, we shall get into trouble. You talk of secret diplomacy, but let me tell you that there is a worse kind of secret diplomacy, and it is the diplomacy which spreads out hope and soothing-syrup for the good, while all the time winks are exchanged between the people who know actually what is going on. That is a far worse situation. I am as a fact a member of the League of Nations Union. If I were one of their leading authorities I should be far more irritated with people who deceived me than with persons who, supposed to be lost souls, stated the blunt truth; because, unless the people know the truth, one day they are going to have a very surprising awakening.

These proposals which have been made by the Government at Geneva are not likely to be accepted, and I do not think there is a single man

[3] February 27. See p. 36.

in any part of the House who thinks, or who has ever thought, that they had the slightest chance of being accepted. You are not going to get an international agreement which will obviate the necessity of having your own defenses or which will remove the appalling dangers which have been so freely stated. I am most anxious that in anything that is said to France at Geneva upon air armaments or upon military armaments we should do nothing which exposes us to the French retort, "Very well; then you are involved with us." I would far rather have larger Estimates and be absolutely free and independent to choose our own course than become involved in this Continental scene by a well-meant desire to persuade them all to give up arms. There is terrible danger there.

I read in the newspapers today that the Prime Minister has been giving an ultimatum or making a strong appeal to France to disarm. Whether you deal with the Army or the Air, you are taking an altogether undue responsibility at a time like this in tendering such advice to a friendly nation. No; I hope and trust that the French will look after their own safety, and that we shall be permitted to live our life in our island without being again drawn into the perils of the continent of Europe. But if we wish to detach ourselves and lead a life of independence from European entanglements, we have to be strong enough to defend our neutrality. We are not going to preserve neutrality if we have no technical equipment That reason might again be urged if we were discussing Navy Votes. I am strongly of opinion that we require to strengthen our armaments in the air and upon the seas in order to make sure that we are still judges of our own fortunes, our own destinies and our own action.

I now come to the technical issue which was raised by Mr. Baldwin's speech—a famous speech, I must say, because how many speeches we make in this House and how few are remembered a week after! But here months ago my right hon. Friend made his speech and in this Air Debate it is the dominant theme. He was dealing with the bombing of open towns and the murdering of women and children as an orthodox and legitimate means of civilized war. I cannot follow him in two respects. First, he assumes that it would certainly be done. Secondly, he assumes that there is no remedy Neither of these impressions should guide public thought upon these matters. He said, with very great truth, that the only defense is offense. That is the soundest of all military maxims. But, as can be seen from the context of the phrase, my right hon. Friend had been led to believe that the only method of offense by which you could defend your own civil population from being murdered was to murder some of

the civil population on the other side. But that is nonsense. The true
defense would be entirely different.

In a war between two States with equal air forces it would not pay—I
put it no higher; leave out morality, humanity and the public law of
Europe—it would not pay, from the military self-preservation standpoint
of any Power engaged in an equal fight to waste its strength upon non-
combatants and open towns. To use an expression which I have heard,
they could not afford to waste their bombs on mere women and children.
Essentially a struggle of this kind—which I pray as much as any man we
shall never live to see, and which I am resolved to do my utmost to avert
—any struggle of this kind would resolve itself into a combat between
the two air forces. If all of a sudden two Powers with equal forces went
to war, and one threw its bombs upon cities so as to kill as many women
and children as possible, and the other threw its bombs on the aerodromes
and air bases and factories and arsenals and dockyards and railway local
points of the other side, can anyone doubt that next morning the one
who had committed the greatest crime would not be the one who had
reaped the greatest advantage?

[Mr. Maclean. What do you mean by that?]

What I mean is that this horrible, senseless, brutal method of warfare,
which we are told is the first military step that would be taken, the killing
of women and children, would not be comparable, as a military measure,
to an attack upon the technical centers and air bases of an enemy Power.

[Mr. Godfrey Nicholson: What about the moral effect on the people?]

The moral effect would be far greater if it were found the next day
that the hostile air forces were incapable of flying at all. That would
have not only a moral effect, but a physical effect of very remarkable
strength. But I must say this: While in the first instance in any conflict
the air forces would fight and would not be able, if equally matched, to
look elsewhere, yet once one side was decidedly beaten, this process
of torturing the civil population by killing the women and children might
well be used in order to extort abject surrender and submission from
the Power whose air defense had been broken down. Anyone can see
how that might be applied. If there were any Power in the world to
which it would not be applied, perhaps it would be our island, because so
much easier methods would be open for reducing us to submission. If
we were completely defenseless in the air, if we were reduced to a condition where we could not deal with this form of warfare, I doubt very
much whether even then the victorious Power would be well advised to

come and kill the women and children. By intercepting all the trade passing through the narrow seas and on the approaches to this island, they could employ the weapon of starvation which would probably lead to a peace on terms which they thought were desirable.[4]

Therefore, it seems to me that the possession of an adequate air force is almost a complete protection for the civilian population, not indeed against injury and annoyance, but against destruction such as was portrayed by the Lord President; and that, after all, is what we have to think of first. I cannot understand why His Majesty's Government and the representatives of the Air Ministry do not inculcate these truths, for truths they are, as widely as they possibly can. The only defense is an adequate air force, and the possession of an adequate air force will relieve the civil population from this danger until that air force is victorious or is beaten. If it is victorious then the danger is removed for a long period. Therefore, I do not think that we should be led by the Lord President into supposing that no means of safety are open to a vigorous, valiant race. There is a means of safety open. While I would not abandon hope of international agreement, I would not base the life of this country upon it in their present stage, but to cut us off from that, on the one hand, and to suggest on the other that no remedy is in our hands in the region of force, is indeed to expose us to a gloomy vision.

Not to have an adequate air force in the present state of the world is to compromise the foundations of national freedom and independence. It is all very well to suppose that we are masters of our own actions in this country and that this House can assemble and vote as to whether it wishes to go to war or not. If you desire to keep that privilege, which I trust we shall never lose, it is indispensable that you should have armaments in this island which will enable you to carry on your life without regard to external pressure. I regretted very much to hear the Under-Secretary state that we were only the fifth air Power. I regretted very much to hear him say that the ten-year program was suspended for another year. I was sorry to hear him boast that they had not laid down a single new unit this year. All these ideas are being increasingly stultified by the march of events, and we should be well advised to concentrate upon our air defenses with greater vigor. Certainly it looks curious that while our Army and Navy have been increased in expenditure this year— no doubt absolutely necessarily, because we had disarmed far below

---

[4] In later years Mr. Churchill has attached more importance to the dangers of a very short war ended by panic and an administrative breakdown.

what is reasonable—the Air Force, which is the most vital of all, should be the one subjected not to an increase but to an actual reduction [5]

Above all, we must not be led by the Lord President into this helpless, hopeless mood. Our island is surrounded by the sea. It always has been, and, although the House may not realize it, the sea was in early times a great disadvantage because an invader could come across the sea and no one knew where he would land; very often he did not know himself. On the Continent the lines of advance are fixed by the mountain passes, the roads, and the fertile plains and rivers. We were under a great disadvantage a thousand years ago in being surrounded by the sea, and we suffered terribly from it. But we did not give up; we did not evacuate the island and say that we must live on the mainland. Not at all. We conquered the sea; we became the mistress of the sea, and the very element which had given the invader access to the heart of our country, to our hearths and homes, became its greatest protection—became, indeed, the bridge which united us to the most distant parts of our Empire throughout the world. Now there is the air. The sea perhaps is no longer complete security for our island development; it must be the air too.

Why should we fear the air? We have as good technical knowledge as any country. There is no reason to suppose that we cannot make machines as good as any country. We have—though it may be thought conceited to say so—a particular vein of talent in air piloting which is in advance of that possessed by other countries. There is not the slightest reason to suppose that we are not capable of producing as good results for money put into aviation as any other country That being so, I ask the Government to consider profoundly and urgently the whole position of our air defense. I am not going to commit myself, without an opportunity of examining all the technical and financial details, to any particular standard, but this I say—that, in view of the significance which this subject has at the present time, in view of the state of the world, and in view of the speech of the Lord President of the Council, it is absolutely indispensable that the necessary program of air development should be carried out, and that our defenses in this matter· should be adequate to our needs.

[5] Army Estimates for 1933, £1,462,000 more than for 1932; Navy Estimates for 1933, £3,093,000 more than for 1932, Air Estimates for 1933, £340,000 *less* than for 1932, and over one million pounds *less* than for 1931.

THE MACDONALD DISARMAMENT PLAN

March 23, 1933

Third Reading of the Consolidated Fund Bill

March 16. Mr. MacDonald, submitting draft proposals to the Disarmament Conference at Geneva, says·

"The Five-Power Conference declared for equality with the co-operation of those who had it in their power, declaring that none of you here, no nation in Europe, be it a large nation or a small nation, be it a nation with enormous possibilities which tie up its Prime Minister to a caution which very often many of us would like to think was not binding our wrists or controlling our tongues, or a small nation with liberty of expression so that acceptance was very much easier because it meant so much less, whether large nations or small nations—all declared that by the granting of the principle of equality and security their safety would not be immediately endangered."

March 18. Signor Mussolini proposes Four-Power Pact to Mr. MacDonald and Sir John Simon in Rome

March 20. The British Government suspend negotiations for a commercial treaty with Soviet Russia as the result of the arrest of Metropolitan-Vickers employees.

THE MACDONALD DISARMAMENT PLAN

WE ALL DESIRE to see peace and goodwill established among the nations, old scores forgotten, old wounds healed, the peoples of Christendom united to rebuild their portion of the world, to solve the problem of their toiling masses, to give a higher standard of life to the harassed populations. We can all expatiate upon that. The differences which arise are those of method. They arise when our sentiments come into contact with baffling and extremely obstinate concrete obstacles.

Our first supreme object is not to go to war. To that end we must do our best to prevent others from going to war. But we must be very careful that, in so doing, we do not increase the risk to ourselves of being involved in a war if, unfortunately, our well-meant efforts fail to prevent a quarrel between other Powers. It is by this test that I wish to examine the foreign policy of the Prime Minister. During the whole of the last four years he has directed, and not only directed, but dominated, our foreign policy, and no one can pretend that the results are satisfactory. On the contrary, the state of Europe, the condition of the Far East, our relations with Japan, the authority and prestige of the League of Nations, the security of this island—all have in various degrees sensibly deteriorated. It may be that events have been too strong for the Prime Minister. There are tasks beyond the power of mortal man. It may well be so, and his friends will naturally like to adopt that view, but others may think that the course that he has adopted, from the highest motives, has actually aggravated the position.

The staple of the policy of the right hon. Gentleman has been disarmament. Of course, it is true that in that respect he was only following the policy to which all parties were committed and many nations committed by treaty. Nevertheless, the undue insistence upon disarmament, the prolonged attempts at Geneva of one nation to disarm another, and latterly of each nation to put some other nation in the wrong before public opinion—this prolonged process, which began before the Prime Minister was responsible for our affairs, but which he has impelled with all the resources at his disposal, has not had good results—in fact, it has in some respects worsened the relations between the Great Powers. I have held this view for some years, and I see it continually confirmed by events. I am very doubtful whether there is any use in pressing national disarmament to a point where nations think their safety is compromised, while the quarrels which divide them and which lead to their armaments and their fears are still unadjusted. The elaborate process of measuring swords around the table at Geneva, which has gone on for so many years, stirs all the deepest suspicions and anxieties of the various Powers, and forces all the statesmen to consider many hypothetical contingencies which but for this prolonged process perhaps would not have crossed their minds and would only have remained buried in the archives of some general staff.

I have always hoped and believed that the continuance of a long peace and the pressure of taxation would lead to a gradual, progressive neglect of armaments in all countries, as was the case after the conclusion of the great Napoleonic wars. I say nothing against private interchanges in secret diplomacy between the Foreign Offices of the different countries of a friendly character—"If you will not do this, we shall not have to do that," "If your program did not start so early, ours would begin even later," and so on—such as have always gone on, and may perfectly legitimately go on. I believe a greater advance and progress towards a diminution of expenditure on armaments might have been achieved by these methods than by the conferences and schemes of disarmament which have been put forward at Geneva. It is in this mood that I look at the Prime Minister's latest plan.

Taking a layman's view of these fact and figures, I cannot say that they are injurious to our own defensive interests, but I doubt very much indeed the wisdom of pressing this plan upon France at the present time. I do not think it is at all likely that the French will agree. They must be greatly concerned at what is taking place in Germany, as well as at the attitude of some others of their neighbors. I dare say that during this anxious month—we seem to have passed through a very anxious month— there are a good many people who have said to themselves, as I have been saying for several years, "Thank God for the French Army." When we read about Germany, when we watch with surprise and distress the tumultuous insurgence of ferocity and war spirit, the pitiless ill-treatment of minorities, the denial of the normal protections of civilized society to large numbers of individuals solely on the ground of race—when we see that occurring in one of the most gifted, learned, scientific and formidable nations in the world, one cannot help feeling glad that the fierce passions that are raging in Germany have not found, as yet, any other outlet but upon Germans. At a moment like this, to ask France to halve her army while Germany doubles hers—that is the scale of figures—to ask France to halve her air force while the German air force remains whatever it is—I am aware that there is no military air force permitted to remain—such a proposal, it seems to me, is likely to be considered by the French Government, at present at any rate, as somewhat unseasonable.

It seems unlikely, therefore, that these proposals will be found acceptable either by France or by various other countries concerned I do not mean that they will be rejected out of hand. On the contrary, all the nations at Geneva have developed a very elaborate technique in dealing with disarmament proposals which do not suit their needs or which they think are dangerous or inconvenient. They have learned very well to talk the language which is agreeable to the League of Nations Union. They think they do it very well there. They have had a lot of practice at it. They never refuse at first sight any proposal, however injurious, visionary or foolish they may think it. On the contrary, they make praiseworthy speeches They interchange agreeable compliments—"How interesting!" "How hopeful!" "What a meeting of our point of view is embodied in this!" "It is the first time we have really had a helping hand in this difficult situation." "What noble sentiments have inspired this theme for which we are indebted to the genius of England!" And then, having read it a second time, to use our Parliamentary forms, amid prolonged enthusiasm, they adjourn to the banqueting-hall and leave it to be killed in committee by a lot of minor objections to detail, or by putting forward counter-proposals which only make confusion worse confounded.

I understand that already there are fifty-six disarmament plans. Perhaps the Prime Minister has the right figure. It may be more now, because he has been two or three days away from Geneva. Fifty-six well-meaning plans, which certainly suited very well indeed the interests of the countries which proposed them, have already been disposed of by this machinery, and it seems not unlikely that the fifty-seventh will share the common fate. But although the plan of the Prime Minister may not be accepted, it cannot, I fear, fail to arouse distrust in the breasts of those from whom it asks the most hazardous sacrifices at the most inopportune time. Here I say very little of the Prime Minister's oratorical style We are familiar with it here. We know that he has, more than any other man, the gift of compressing the largest number of words into the smallest amount of thought. We have heard him on so many topics, from India to unemployment, providing us, apparently, with an inexhaustible flow of vague, well-sounding exhortation, the precise purpose of which is largely wrapped in mystery, and which, as far as it can be discerned, can be understood differently in different quarters, according to taste. The only comment I would make upon his eloquent speech at Geneva is that when he said to the assembled nations that if they would not adopt the proposals they would be mannequins—the functionaries who, I believe, are employed by French dressmakers to exhibit their wares to the best advantage—they would be mannequins, and not men, I cannot help thinking that he lapsed a little from those standards of international decorum which we expect in a representative of the British Empire in such circumstances. When I think of the figures which I have just been mentioning [*Laughter*]—I was dealing with statistics, and not with fashions—when I think of the statistics, I am not at all sure that the French will find such remarks even amusing.

All these considerations lead us to a very grave matter. I think that it is undoubtedly dangerous to press France at the present juncture to disarm, because of the effect which that must necessarily have upon our own obligations and our liabilities under the Treaty of Locarno. We have serious obligations under Locarno, but they are provided with various important safeguards which insure our having a wide discretion whether we should or should not engage, on one side or the other, in a European war. I am going to mention those safeguards because they are of the utmost consequence to all of us in this country who wish to be assured that we shall never see our men dragged into another tremendous Continental struggle.

The Council of the League of Nations must be unanimous. It would probably not be unanimous. In fact, in the grouping of the Powers it could hardly be unanimous, apart from the fact that we ourselves would be an indispensable factor in that unanimity. Then there is the emergency obligation under Clause IV. This operates in the case of what is called a flagrant violation of peace constituting an unprovoked act of aggression, which by reason of crossing the frontier, or the outbreak of hostilities, or the assembly of armed forces in the demilitarized zone requires immediate action.

"Immediate action" means before the Council of the League of Nations can be invoked. I know that that is often mentioned, but here again I think that a considerable latitude of judgment rests in the conditions of the Treaty. The word "flagrant" in this case not only embodies the idea of a grave breach of law, but it also involves the elements of magnitude, danger and urgency. It is of the utmost importance that those elements should be read into the meaning of the word "flagrant." We should be entitled to consider all these aspects before we felt ourselves bound to join in a European war without even having the opportunity to discuss the matter upon the Council of the League of Nations.

It must always be assumed, of course, that Great Britain will stand by her obligations. Probably she will be better than her legal word, but I do not admit that the Treaty of Locarno deprives us of the right to judge the facts and circumstances, even in an emergency, according to what we think right in our interests and for our duty. But many refinements, which may be of vital consequence to the people of this island and of the British Empire, will be swept away—I warn the Government—if we press France to disarm and encourage Germany to rearm to a point where dangerous conditions are created. If you press a country to reduce its defenses beyond its better judgment, and it takes your advice, every obligation you have contracted, however carefully it has been expressed, will be multiplied in force, and you will find your position complicated by fresh obligations of comradeship, honor and compassion which will be brought very prominently to the front when a country which has taken your advice falls into grave jeopardy, perhaps as a result of what you have pressed upon it.

I remember what happened before the Great War. The growth of the German Navy obliged us to concentrate all our battleships in the North Sea, and we withdrew our squadron of battleships from the Mediterranean. The French moved all their battleships into the Mediterranean. There was no bargain. The two operations took place independently. But although there was no bargain, when the peril of war came and all Europe was seen to be rushing towards catastrophe, the Ministers of the British Government who were the most resolved against participation in the War admitted the force of the argument that, since the north coasts of France were undefended in consequence of the French having moved their battleships, we should be bound to make sure that she did not suffer for that reason, and long before any agreement was reached as to whether we should participate in the War a general agreement was reached in the Government that the Germans should be forbidden to send any warships into the Channel. That shows the danger of pressing people to disarm beyond their better judgment, and of becoming too closely intermingled in their defensive arrangements. What terrible consequences this may have upon your freedom of choice at some future time! I am profoundly anxious that we should preserve and enjoy the full freedom to judge of our obligations under Locarno without any additional complications. Therefore, I urge the very greatest caution upon His Majesty's Government at the present time in pressing the French Government to weaken their strength relatively to Germany.

There is another and more obvious argument against our trying to weaken the armed power of France at this juncture. As long as France is strong and Germany is but inadequately armed there is no chance of France being attacked with success, and therefore no obligation will arise under Locarno for us to go to the aid of France. I am sure, on the other hand, that France, which is the most pacific nation in Europe at the present time, as she is, fortunately, the most efficiently armed, would never attempt any violation of the Treaty or commit an overt act against Germany without the sanctions of the Treaty, without reference to the Treaty, and, least of all, in opposition to the country with which she is in such amicable relations—Great Britain.

The Prime Minister spoke today of what he has put forward as the greatest effort for peace since the Great War. In this he did less than justice to the author of the Locarno Treaty, because certainly on the morrow of that we reached a position of far greater tranquillity and security than we have ever been able to obtain since. How glad we should be to go back to that shining morrow of Locarno and the hopes that were expressed there! It seemed to me at that time that as long as France was armed and Germany was disarmed we ran no great risks under the Treaty of Locarno, and we had an opportunity of bringing France and Germany together in friendly intercourse.

Although bringing France and Italy together in friendly intercourse is a most important work, yet the master key of Europe is some understanding and relationship between its two greatest nations, Germany and France. If we are now going to try to establish conditions of equality—the Prime

Minister used the word "equality" in a very loose way this afternoon, and I had to press him and make him add the important words "equality of status"—if we are now going to try to create conditions of equality between France and Germany in armaments, or even an approach thereto, because the potential alliances of Germany must be considered, we shall invest the whole situation under Locarno with a far graver, far more imminent and more practical character than it possesses today. If you are going to reduce the armies to the levels set out in the White Paper, then I say that before that result is achieved, Parliament ought to review the whole position of our responsibilities under the Treaty of Locarno. If the armies of Europe had been measured during the last month or the last six months, especially the last month, as they are set forth in this White Paper, those very horrors that it is our whole aim to avert from us would have leaped out upon us already. If Europe has enjoyed peace this year, it has been under the shield of France. Be careful not to break that shield. It is perhaps not the broad basis on which we should like to see the harmony of Christendom stand, but it is a shield. Beware that you do not lower it or weaken it by any action in your power before you have, at least, something which gives as good practical security erected behind it to put in its place.

Now I come to the proposals which the Prime Minister laid before us of a pact between the four Great Powers—no doubt, technically within the League of Nations—to preserve the peace and to plan a revision of the Treaties of Versailles and Trianon. I have always been attracted by this idea which Signor Mussolini has made so prominent. I have spoken for years of a pyramid of peace, which might be triangular or quadrangular—three or four great Powers shaking hands together and endeavoring to procure a rectification of some of the evils arising from the treaties made in the passion of war, which if left unredressed will bring upon us consequences we cannot name. The Prime Minister is, I think, a new convert to this idea. I have not had time to examine all his past utterances, but I had an impression that he had always condemned anything in the nature of a four-Power or a three-Power agreement and had considered that that was, as it were, inconsistent with the general authority of the League of Nations, on which so many Powers are represented. However, let that pass. Whether he was converted by the eloquence or by the strong personality of Signor Mussolini, or whether he had it in his mind before he went to Rome, are mysteries which are naturally hidden from us.

Although I have always been in favor of something of this character and have thought it the best line of approach to solid peace and to getting rid of the war peril, I am bound to say that the situation has deteriorated to such a point in the last year that such a plan is not nearly so hopeful now as it would have been some years ago, or as it might be perhaps at no distant date in the future. I am very doubtful whether the Prime Minister has been wise to launch it in the way in which he has done at the present moment. I should have thought that it was indispensable before this plan of a four-Power pact could have a fair chance to have got the Disarmament Conference laid to rest, and not to be assailing the nations involved with doubts as to their military strength and anxieties about their security at the same time that you are going to ask them to undertake the appallingly dangerous and difficult duty of endeavoring to get some revision of the peace treaties. I have always tried to urge upon the House that the redress of the grievances of the vanquished should precede the disarmament of the victors. This four-Power pact is a new idea, and you must revise your other procedure in relation to the new idea if you are to give it a chance.

The Prime Minister's interventions in foreign affairs have been—not through any fault or neglect on his part—remarkably unsuccessful. His repeated excursions have not led to any solid, good result. Where anything has been achieved it has nearly always been at British expense and to British disadvantage. On the whole, his four years of control of our foreign relations have brought us nearer to war, and have made us weaker, poorer and more defenseless. [Interruption]. Hon. Members say "No." You have only to study what is the position of Europe today. You have only to listen to what has been said from that Bench to know that we have been brought much nearer to war. [Hon. Members: "No." "By whom?"] I do not wish to place upon one man the responsibility for that, but at the same time when any one man has for four years held the whole power of this country in foreign affairs in his hands, and when he has pursued the lines of policy which I have indicated, you are making a profound mistake if you think the efficiency of our public service will be enhanced by pretending that there is no responsibility to be affixed anywhere.

I withdraw nothing. I repeat what I have said—that, with the best of endeavors, with the most praiseworthy exertions, the right hon. Gentleman's efforts have not been attended at any point with a measure of success. [Hon. Members: "Lausanne."] Lausanne. All right. Under

Lausanne we have now accumulated the gold to pay an additional install-
ment to the United States. Under Lausanne we have already told the
French and the Germans that they need not pay us anything. Is that a
great success? If eventually you reach good results and all War Debts
and Reparations are forgiven and forgotten, then will be the time for
these perfervid tributes to the Prime Minister. Then will be the time
for hon. Gentlemen to range themselves up on the platforms of railway-
stations, but that is not the position now. The position now is that we
have let everybody off, and we are going to pay everything ourselves.[1]

Then there was the Naval Treaty of London, which I am glad to
think the Conservative party voted against. It is cramping and fettering
our naval development, not merely the scale but the actual form and
shape of our naval expenditure, in a manner which is certainly detrimental. Then there is the Disarmament Conference at Geneva, a solemn
and prolonged farce, which has undoubtedly lowered the prestige of the
League of Nations and irritated many of the countries affected. Then,
to come to more recent times, there is the arms embargo. So little am I
prejudiced that I welcomed it in all the innocence of my heart, carried
away by the excellent speech of the Foreign Secretary. I said that I
thought it was the best thing to do. What happened to me? I had hardly
had time to turn round when the Government themselves had abandoned
this policy, which they had put forward not only on the grounds of
policy and expediency, but on those higher considerations of honor and
avoidance of blood-guiltiness which made such a very great appeal to
their audience.[2] Let me say that this treatment of the arms embargo has
seriously affected our relations with Japan We have abandoned the arms
embargo now. We have not the advantage of the high morality which
the Foreign Secretary [Sir John Simon] preached to us, and we shall
have to pay for it very considerably in after-years, if, as may well be the
case, some special intimacy should grow up in trade matters in that
part of the world between Japan and Germany. An hon. Member mentioned Lausanne. I have supplied him with other instances and illustrations of my theme.

Lastly, there is the visit to Rome. I do not wish to treat it too seriously.
No doubt it was a pleasant expedition. No doubt it gave Signor Mussolini
a great deal of pleasure; the same sort of pleasure that a thousand years

[1] The idea of repudiating Mr. Baldwin's Debt Settlement was not at that
time entertained.

[2] See p. 36

ago was given to a Pope when an Emperor paid a visit to Canossa. It was certainly a striking spectacle to see these two heads of Governments, the master of sentimental words and the master of grim and rugged action, meeting together in such friendly intercourse. I associate myself with my right hon. Friend in welcoming the Prime Minister back. We have got our modern Don Quixote home again, with Sancho Panza at his tail, bearing with them these somewhat dubious trophies which they have collected amid the nervous titterings of Europe. Let us hope that now the right hon. Gentleman is safely back among us he will, first of all, take a good rest, of which I have no doubt he stands in need, and that afterwards he will devote himself to the urgent domestic tasks which await him here, in this island, and which concern the well-being of millions of his poorer fellow-subjects, and leave the conduct of foreign affairs, at any rate for a little while, to be transacted by competent ambassadors through the normal and regular diplomatic channels.

THE DARKENING SCENE

April 13, 1933

Debate on the Adjournment

.

1933

March 27 Japan gives notice of resignation from the League of Nations.

April 1 One-day Jewish boycott in Germany.

April 6. Sir John Simon, the Foreign Secretary, moves the Second Reading of a Bill authorizing the Government to prohibit at its discretion imports from Russia as a reprisal for the conviction of the British engineers in Moscow.

THE DARKENING SCENE

I HAVE heard, as everyone has of late years, a great deal of condemnation of the treaties of peace, of the Treaties of Versailles and of Trianon I believe that that denunciation has been very much exaggerated, and in its effect harmful. These treaties, at any rate, were founded upon the strongest principle alive in the world today, the principle of nationalism, or, as President Wilson called it, self-determination. The principle of self-determination or of nationalism was applied to all the defeated Powers over the whole area of Middle and Eastern Europe. Europe today corresponds to its ethnological groupings as it has never corresponded before. You may think that nationalism has been excessively manifested in modern times. That may well be so. It may well be that it has a dangerous side, but we must not fail to recognize that it is the strongest force now at work.

I remember, many years ago, hearing the late Mr. Tim Healy reply to a question that he put to himself, "What is nationalism?" and he said, "Something that men will die for." There is the foundation upon which we must examine the state of Europe and by which we should be guided in picking our way through its very serious dangers Of course, in applying this principle of nationalism to the defeated States after the War it was inevitable that mistakes and some injustices should occur. There are places where the populations are inextricably intermingled. There are some countries where an island of one race is surrounded by an area inhabited by another. There were all kinds of anomalies, and it would have defied the wit of men to make an absolutely perfect solution In fact, no complete solution on ethnographical lines would have been possible unless you had done what was done in the case of Greece and Turkey—that is, the physical disentangling of the population, the sending

59

of the Turks back to Turkey and of the Greeks back to Greece—a practical impossibility.

I recognize the anomalies and I recognize the injustices, but they are only a tiny proportion of the great work of consolidation and appeasement which has been achieved and is represented by the Treaties that ended the War. The nationalities and races of which Europe is composed have never rested so securely in their beds in accordance with their heart's desire. It would be a blessed thing if we could mitigate these anomalies and grievances, but we can only do that if and when there has been established a strong confidence that the Treaties themselves are not going to be deranged. So long as the Treaties are in any way challenged as a whole it will be impossible to procure a patient consideration for the redress of the anomalies. The more you wish to remove the anomalies and grievances the more you should emphasize respect for the Treaties. It should be the first rule of British foreign policy to emphasize respect for these great Treaties, and to make those nations whose national existence depends upon and arises from the Treaties feel that no challenge is leveled at their security. Instead of that, for a good many years a lot of vague and general abuse has been leveled at the Treaties with the result that these powerful States, comprising enormous numbers of citizens—the Little Entente and Poland together represent 80,000,000 strongly armed—have felt that their position has been challenged and endangered by the movement to alter the Treaties. In consequence, you do not get the consideration which in other circumstances you might get for the undoubted improvements which are required in various directions.

The Prime Minister last year, in a speech at Geneva, used a very striking phrase when he described Europe as a house inhabited by ghosts. That is to misinterpret the situation. Europe is a house inhabited by fierce, strong, living entities. Poland is not a ghost: Poland is a reincarnation. I think it a wonderful thing that Polish unity should have re-emerged from long hideous eclipse and bondage, when the Poles were divided between three empires and made to fight one another in all the wars that took place. I rejoice that Poland has been reconstituted. I cannot think of any event arising out of the Great War which can be considered to be a more thoroughly righteous result of the struggle than the reunion of this people, who have preserved their national soul through all the years of oppression and division and whose reconstitution of their nationhood is one of the most striking facts in European history. Do not let us be led, because there are many aspects of Polish policy that we do not like or agree with, into dwelling upon the small points of dis-agreement, and forget what a very great work has been achieved, a work of liberation and of justice, in the reconstitution of Poland. I trust she will live long to enjoy the freedom of the lands which belong to her, a freedom which was gained by the swords of the victorious Allies.

We may look elsewhere. There is Bohemia, the land of Good King Wenceslas, which has emerged with its own identity re-established. There are the small countries on the Baltic, all holding tenaciously to their principles of nationhood. There are all those countries from the Baltic to the Black Sea, small individually compared to the greatest Powers, but comprising an enormous proportion of the European family. All these countries are armed and determined to defend the lands of their fathers and their new-gained independence, and it is most unwise to pursue any foreign policy which does not take account of these facts, which are not, as I have said, ghosts or memories of the past, but the living forces with which we have to cope at the present time.

New discord has arisen in Europe of late years from the fact that Germany is not satisfied with the result of the late War. I have indi-cated several times that Germany got off lightly after the Great War. I know that that is not always a fashionable opinion, but the facts re-pudiate the idea that a Carthaginian peace was in fact imposed upon Germany. No division was made of the great masses of the German people. No portion of Germany inhabited by Germans was detached, except where there was the difficulty of disentangling the population of the Silesian border. No attempt was made to divide Germany as between the northern and southern portions, which might well have tempted the conquerors at that time. No State was carved out of Ger-many. She underwent no serious territorial loss, except the loss of Alsace and Lorraine, which she herself had seized only fifty years before. The great mass of the Germans remained united after all that Europe had passed through, and they are more vehemently united today than ever before. We know what has happened to the War indemnity. They have lost their colonies, it is true; but these were not of great value to them, and it is not at all true for them to say that these colonies could ever have afforded any appreciable outlet for their working-class population. They are not suited for white colonization.

On the other hand, when we think of what would have happened to us, to France or to Belgium, if the Germans had won; when we think of the terms which they exacted from Rumania, or of the terms of the

Treaty of Brest-Litovsk; when we remember that up to a few months from the end of the War German authorities refused to consider that Belgium could ever be liberated, but said that she should be kept in thrall for military purposes forever, I do not think that we need break our hearts in deploring the treatment that Germany is receiving now. Germany is not satisfied; but no concession which has been made has produced any very marked appearance of gratitude. Once it has been conceded it has seemed less valuable than when it was demanded. Many people would like to see, or would have liked to see a little while ago— I was one of them—the question of the Polish Corridor adjusted. For my part, I should certainly have considered that to be one of the greatest practical objectives of European peace-seeking diplomacy. There again, however, we must think of the rights of Poland. The Polish Corridor is inhabited almost entirely by Poles, and it was Polish territory before the Partition of 1772 This is a matter which in quiet times, with increasing goodwill, Europe should have set itself—and might well some day set itself—to solve.

The question of the Germans regaining their colonies is being pressed by them, and the question of their rearmament—which, personally, I consider more grave than any other question—is being brought to the front. They demand equality in weapons and equality in the organization of armies and fleets, and we have been told, "You cannot keep so great a nation in an inferior position. What others have they must have." I have never agreed I think it is a most dangerous demand to make. Nothing in life is eternal, of course, but as surely as Germany acquires full military equality with her neighbors while her own grievances are still unredressed and while she is in the temper which we have unhappily seen, so surely should we see ourselves within a measurable distance of the renewal of general European war. If this process of rearmament or of equalization were actually to take place while the present conditions prevail, undoubtedly the nations who are neighbors of Germany and who fear Germany would ask themselves whether they would be well advised to postpone coming to a conclusion until the process of German rearmament has been completed. It is extremely dangerous for people to talk lightly about German rearmament and say that, if the Germans choose to do it, no one can stop them. I am very doubtful if Germany would rearm in defiance of the Treaty if there were a solidarity of European and world opinion that the Treaty could only be altered by discussion, and could not be altered by a violent one-sided breach.

I, therefore, do not subscribe to the doctrine that we should throw up our hands and recognize the fact that Germany is going to be armed up to an equality with the neighboring States in any period which we can immediately foresee. There may be other periods, but certainly we ought not to admit it at the moment.

I am not going to use harsh words about Germany and about the conditions there. I am addressing myself to the problem in a severely practical manner. Nevertheless, one of the things which we were told after the Great War would be a security for us was that Germany would be a democracy with Parliamentary institutions. All that has been swept away. You have dictatorship—most grim dictatorship. You have militarism and appeals to every form of fighting spirit, from the reintroduction of dueling in the colleges to the Minister of Education advising the plentiful use of the cane in the elementary schools. You have these martial or pugnacious manifestations, and also this persecution of the Jews, of which so many Members have spoken and which distresses everyone who feels that men and women have a right to live in the world where they are born, and have a right to pursue a livelihood which has hitherto been guaranteed them under the public laws of the land of their birth.

When I read of what is going on in Germany—I feel in complete agreement in this matter with hon. Gentlemen opposite—when I see the temper displayed there and read the speeches of the leading Ministers, I cannot help rejoicing that the Germans have not got the heavy cannon, the thousands of military aeroplanes and the tanks of various sizes for which they have been pressing in order that their status may be equal to that of other countries. The House has not always done justice to Sir Austen Chamberlain's conduct of foreign affairs. He was very much scolded and condemned at the close of the late Conservative Administration, but the Locarno Treaty and all that followed from it was a model of skillful peace-seeking diplomacy. Although other difficulties have come in other times, I cannot see that the handling of the Foreign Office since he left it should fill him with any particular feeling of humiliation.

I will leave Germany and turn to France. France is not only the sole great surviving democracy in Europe; she is also the strongest military Power, I am glad to say, and she is the head of a system of states and nations. France is the guarantor and protector of all these small States I mentioned a few moments ago; the whole crescent which runs right round from Belgium to Yugoslavia and Rumania. They all look to France. When any step is taken, by England or any other Power, to try to weaken the diplomatic or military security of France, all these small nations tremble with fear and anger. They fear that the central protective force will be weakened, and that then they will be at the mercy of the great Teutonic Power.

We should be very careful not to mix ourselves up too deeply in this European scene. Our desire to promote peace must not lead us to press our views beyond a point where those views are no longer compatible with the actual facts of the situation. It may be very virtuous and high-minded to press disarmament upon nations situated as these nations are, but if not done in the right way and in due season, and in moderation, with regard for other people's points of view as well as our own sentiments, it may bring war nearer rather than peace, and may lead us to be suspected and hated instead of being honored and thanked as we should wish to be. Even more vain is it for the United States to press indiscriminate disarmament upon the European States, unless, of course, the United States is prepared to say that those nations which take her advice will receive her aid if trouble should arise, and is prepared to envisage the prospect of sending millions of soldiers again across the ocean.

Our country has a very important part to play in Europe, but it is not so large a part as we have been attempting to play, and I advocate for us in future a more modest rôle than many of our peace-preservers and peace-lovers have sought to impose upon us. I remember when I was very young, before I came into this House, a denunciation by Dr. Spence Watson of what he called "the filthy Tory rag of a spirited foreign policy." In those days the feelings of the forerunners of those who sit opposite were directed against jingo policies of bombast and Palmerstonian vigor. But you may have another kind of spirited foreign policy which may also lead you into danger, and that is a policy in which, without duly considering the circumstances in which others are placed, you endeavor to press upon them disarmament or to weaken their security, perhaps with a view to gaining a measure of approbation from good people here who are not aware of the dangerous state of affairs in Europe. There you could have a peace policy which may be too spirited.

It is easy to talk about the moral leadership of Europe. That great prize still stands before the statesmen of all countries, but it is not to be achieved merely by making speeches of unexceptionable sentiments. If it is to be won by any nation it will only be by an immense amount of wise restraint and timely, discreet action which, over a period of years, has created a situation where speeches are not merely fine exhortations but record the unity and conciliation which have been achieved. There is the moral leadership of Europe It is not to be won by such easy methods as merely making speeches which will arouse the applause of every good-hearted person in this country.

The Prime Minister spread on the table at Geneva a few weeks ago a vast plan for bringing all armaments down and consequently improving relatively the military strength of Germany. The right hon. Gentleman made an extraordinary admission. He said he had not gone through the figures himself. But he took responsibility for them. It was a very grave responsibility. This proposal, which was put forward with the highest motives and with many good reasons behind it, touches all the most delicate and dangerous spots in Europe. If ever there was a document upon which its author ought to have consumed his personal thought and energy, it was this scheme of disarmament, prescribing for every country, great and small, what its military, air and naval forces should be. I have not heard it said with any assurance by the Government that the Committee of Imperial Defence were consulted upon these figures. I have not heard it said that the chiefs of the Fighting Services here have been consulted upon these figures. Unknown hands have prepared these figures, and the author of the document has admitted to us that he had not himself mastered them, either in scope or in detail.

Here in this country we know that no dark designs are harbored by our Government against the peace or well-being of any country. There may be mistakes, there may be muddles; but no dark designs are harbored by any British Prime Minister or Foreign Secretary. He could not live under the conditions of British Cabinet Government if it were otherwise. But foreign countries do not always attribute to us this innocence. I have been reading some of the comments in foreign newspapers lately, and in a Liberal newspaper of good standing in Switzerland I was surprised to see the interpretation that was put upon the proposals innocently and precipitately put forward by the Prime Minister. In that paper all is calculated out and worked up to give the impression that the Prime Minister was deliberately indulging pro-German sympathies and deliberately endeavoring to weaken France, and, seeing the detail with which the argument is set out, one could not help being impressed

But that is not by any means the whole story No sooner had this tremendous step been taken of prescribing to every country what its defenses should be than the Prime Minister left Geneva for Rome He arrived in Rome one day, and found himself with a new foreign policy the next. Signor Mussolini's proposal for a Four-Power pact or agreement has many arguments in its favor. I liked very much the language used by my right hon. Friend about the importance of the Great Powers who would have to bear the brunt of any serious conflict establishing good relations between themselves and being in close touch with each other, if only to enable them to spread those satisfactory relations wider among the larger number of smaller Powers. As I say, there are many arguments in favor of co-operation by the four Powers, but one does not always need to advertise the fact so very vigorously. There are many Cabinets in which an inner Cabinet grows up without any of the other members being offended, but it is only under the stress of war that we took the step of forming a War Cabinet, which definitely distinguished between those members and other persons in the Government. So it is in this European field.

As I say, there are arguments in favor of this policy, but at the present time there are two serious arguments against it. The first is this Of all times, this was not the time to make such a proposal with any prospect of success, and, secondly, nothing could be more unsuitable than to combine this Four-Power Pact with the disarmament proposals which had been laid before Geneva only two days before. By those proposals France was asked to reduce her army from 700,000 to 400,000; and at the same moment that this very serious demand was made upon her she was also invited, as the result of the Rome Conference, to take her seat at a table of four, with Herr Hitler and Signor Mussolini, the two Dictators, and with the Prime Minister, about whom France, of course, still has memories.

Putting this double pressure upon France at this moment, both from Geneva and from Rome, was calculated to court defeat for either or both of the schemes which the Government successively and, ultimately, simultaneously advanced. Such a procedure was to doom them to failure beforehand. It could not fail to aggravate suspicion, and not only to weaken the influence of our country, but to involve us more deeply in the Continental situation; for you cannot take the lead in this remarkable manner, presenting these successive policies to Europe with such rapidity, without being entangled to a very large extent as a consequence of the proposals that you have made.

Plans for disarmament so comprehensive should not have been put forward by the Prime Minister without his having studied them most carefully with all the highest technical experts here, nor should the proposals with which Signor Mussolini confronted the Prime Minister and the Foreign Secretary when they arrived in Rome have been even entertained on the spur of the moment. There may be all sorts of proposals put forward, with great ability, by a powerful personality which sound very well and look attractive at first sight, but in matters affecting the peace of so many countries and the lives and well-being of millions of men what harm would there have been in waiting till the Cabinet could have examined this proposal, till the trained officials of the Foreign Office could have examined it in all its aspects? They would not have taken very long to point out what the inevitable reactions would be. It astounds me that the Prime Minister, who has had such considerable opportunities of acquainting himself with European affairs, should not have mastered the real facts of the European situation or the articulation of the different countries which compose the system. At any rate, the results have been quickly apparent. France, confronted with this double, simultaneous demand, was deeply disturbed. But the French have learned to attune their language to the standard forms of phraseology which are highly in favor throughout the English-speaking world. They never on any account make abrupt or sharp contradictions of any proposals that are put to them. They say, "Most interesting, most helpful, and a great move forward," but they leave to their allies, the small nations—and not so small either—to say what France feels and thinks, but realizes had better be said by others.

What happened? Within one single week, if I may judge from the public prints, Poland, Czechoslovakia and Rumania at once made their appearance, and every one of them made in concert—no doubt with pre-arrangement—statements in which the danger of war was brutally referred to. Such a warning must never be disregarded. It is quite true that such warnings do not now bear the significance they would have borne in the days before the great struggle. But at the same time the statements made on behalf of these three Powers do constitute a definite and grave warning of the dangers of pursuing this policy. Thus all the small Powers, including the Scandinavian Powers, are making common

cause in the League of Nations in order to defend themselves against
what they think is a threatened overlordship of the four Great Powers.
What happens then? The Pact or Agreement so incontinently accepted
has to be amended, has to be modified to fit the views of the small nations
in the League. It has to be modified again to meet special claims. It
has to be modified again to meet the requirements of France, and it
very soon reaches the point where it loses the adherence of Germany.
It is no good saying it is merely "much ado about nothing." That is not
so Harm has been done, disturbance has been created, suspicion has
been spread, and English influence has lost a measure of its virtue
and added a measure to its responsibility. There may be days when all
our influence will be required to help to keep the peace of Europe, and
when all our detachment will be required to enable us to keep clear of
being involved in war.

I will say one word about the Prime Minister's visit to the United
States of America. It will be only a word. I do not understand how
any Prime Minister could have failed to take up, in the spirit of the
highest cordiality, the invitation tendered him in such striking terms
by the President of the United States at the beginning of his tenure of
power, and I am very glad indeed that the Government have decided
to send the Prime Minister upon this mission, described and limited as
it has been. For my part, I should not like to have spoken in this
Debate in a critical sense without wishing the Prime Minister, who is not
here now, a pleasant holiday and an agreeable conversation, a fruitful
result for his mission and a safe return to this country.

ENGLAND

April 24, 1933

Speech to the Royal Society of St. George

1933

April 15. Mr. MacDonald sails for the United States

April 16. Proclamation issued prohibiting importation from Russia of butter, wheat, petroleum and timber as a protest against conviction of Metropolitan-Vickers employees.

April 19. The United States abandon the Gold Standard.

ENGLAND

I AM A great admirer of the Scots. I am quite friendly with the Welsh, especially one of them. I must confess to some sentiment about Old Ireland, in spite of the ugly mask she tries to wear. But this is not their night. On this one night in the whole year we are allowed to use a forgotten, almost a forbidden word. We are allowed to mention the name of our own country, to speak of ourselves as 'Englishmen,' and we may even raise the slogan "St. George for Merrie England"

We must be careful, however. You see these microphones? They have been placed on our tables by the British Broadcasting Corporation. Think of the risk these eminent men are running. We can almost see them in our mind's eye, gathered together in that very expensive building, with the questionable statues on its front. We can picture Sir John Reith, with the perspiration mantling on his lofty brow, with his hand on the control switch, wondering, as I utter every word, whether it will not be his duty to protect his innocent subscribers from some irreverent thing I might say about Mr. Gandhi, or about the Bolsheviks, or even about our peripatetic Prime Minister. But let me reassure him. I have much more serious topics to discuss. I have to speak to you about St. George and the Dragon. I have been wondering what would happen if that legend were repeated under modern conditions.

St. George would arrive in Cappadocia, accompanied not by a horse, but by a secretariat. He would be armed not with a lance, but with several flexible formulas He would, of course, be welcomed by the local branch of the League of Nations Union. He would propose a conference with the dragon—a Round Table Conference, no doubt—that would be more convenient for the dragon's tail. He would make a trade agreement with the dragon. He would lend the dragon a lot of money for the Cappadocian taxpayers. The maiden's release would be referred to Geneva, the dragon reserving all his rights meanwhile. Finally St. George would be photographed with the dragon (inset—the maiden).

There are a few things I will venture to mention about England. They are spoken in no invidious sense. Here it would hardly occur to anyone that the banks would close their doors against their depositors. Here no one questions the fairness of the courts of law and justice. Here no one thinks of persecuting a man on account of his religion or his race. Here everyone, except the criminals, looks on the policeman as the friend and servant of the public Here we provide for poverty and misfortune with more compassion, in spite of all our burdens, than any other country. Here we can assert the rights of the citizen against the State, or criticize the Government of the day, without failing in our duty to the Crown or in our loyalty to the King. This ancient, mighty London in which we are gathered is still the financial center of the world. From the Admiralty building, half a mile away, orders can be sent to a Fleet which, though much smaller than it used to be, or than it ought to be, is still unsurpassed on the seas. More than 80 per cent. of the British casualties of the Great War were English. More than 80 per cent. of the taxation is paid by the English taxpayers. We are entitled to mention these facts, and to draw authority and courage from them.

Historians have noticed, all down the centuries, one peculiarity of the English people which has cost them dear. We have always thrown away after a victory the greater part of the advantages we gained in the struggle. The worst difficulties from which we suffer do not come from without. They come from within. They do not come from the cottages of the wage-earners. They come from a peculiar type of brainy people always found in our country, who, if they add something to its culture, take much from its strength.

Our difficulties come from the mood of unwarrantable self-abasement into which we have been cast by a powerful section of our own intellectuals. They come from the acceptance of defeatist doctrines by a large proportion of our politicians. But what have they to offer but a vague internationalism, a squalid materialism, and the promise of impossible Utopias?

Nothing can save England if she will not save herself. If we lose faith in ourselves, in our capacity to guide and govern, if we lose our will to live, then indeed our story is told. If, while on all sides foreign nations are every day asserting a more aggressive and militant nationalism by arms and trade, we remain paralyzed by our own theoretical doctrines or plunged into the stupor of after-war exhaustion, then indeed all that the croakers predict will come true, and our ruin will be swift and final. Stripped of her Empire in the Orient, deprived of the sovereignty of the seas, loaded with debt and taxation, her commerce and carrying trade shut out by foreign tariffs and quotas, England would sink to the level of a fifth-rate Power, and nothing would remain of all her glories except a population much larger than this island can support.

Why should we break up the solid structure of British power, founded upon so much health, kindliness and freedom, for dreams which may some day come true, but are now only dreams, and some of them nightmares? We ought, as a nation and Empire, to weather any storm that blows at least as well as any other existing system of human government. We are at once more experienced and more truly united than any people in the world. It may well be that the most glorious chapters of our history are yet to be written. Indeed, the very problems and dangers that encompass us and our country ought to make English men and women of this generation glad to be here at such a time. We ought to rejoice at the responsibilities with which destiny has honored us, and be proud that we are guardians of our country in an age when her life is at stake.

PART II

GERMANY REARMING

THE LEAGUE AND GERMANY

November 7, 1933

Motion for the Adjournment

1933

May 3.   Mr. Ramsay MacDonald returns from the United States.

June 7.   Britain, France, Italy and Germany initial a Four-Power Pact.

June 12.   Opening of the World Economic Conference.

June 27.   Hugenberg resigns from the German Government

July 27.   The World Economic Conference wound up

October 5   Meeting of National Union of Conservative Associations at Birmingham Lord Lloyd proposes, "That this Conference desires to record its grave anxiety in regard to the inadequacy of the provisions made for Imperial defense" Carried unanimously.

October 14.   Sir John Simon in a speech at Geneva charges Germany with having shifted her ground in the course of the preceding weeks Thereupon Germany leaves the Disarmament Conference and resigns from the League of Nations

October 20.   Publication of White Paper by British Government on Disarmament Conference

October 25.   Government lose East Fulham by-election on a wave of pacifism. Socialist vote increases by 8873. Conservative vote falls by 10,488.

THE LEAGUE AND GERMANY

MR. LLOYD GEORGE seems to suppose that he is entitled to some special claim to interpret the Treaty of Versailles and other treaties which ended the War. It is quite true that he had a great deal to do with the making of that Treaty, but once a treaty is signed it becomes an international instrument which everyone can judge, and I personally prefer the measured opinion of the jurists upon whom the Foreign Office relies.

I believe that the Treaty has been maintained in the letter and also in the spirit It is not true that this country or the great countries with whom we have been associated have violated the Treaty in the letter or in the spirit. So far as the letter is concerned, I rest upon the dispatch of the Government of September 1932, which laid out the whole case in a masterly manner.[1] So far as the spirit is concerned, it is well known that ever since the Treaty was signed mitigations have been constantly introduced—far more than the Treaty contemplated. The evacuations of German territory have been carried out with greater rapidity, while the whole scheme and structure of reparations has been swept away altogether, and the victors in the struggle have lent a thousand million sterling to Germany over and above anything they have been paid. It is altogether wrong, therefore, to suggest that the late Allies in the War have failed in the letter or in the spirit to carry out, broadly speaking, their Treaty obligations.

My right hon. Friend made tonight a deeply interesting speech, to which I listened, like everyone else, with admiration of the persuasive charm and skill with which he pressed his point. There is nothing that he can do so well as to draw one side of a picture in the most glowing manner and then reduce the other side to small and pitiable proportions.

[1] September 18, 1932

He gave an account of the state of Europe. He represented that Germany might have a few thousand more rifles than was allowed by the Treaty, a few more Boy Scouts, and then he pictured the enormous armies of Czechoslovakia and Poland and France, with their thousands of cannon, and so forth. If I could believe that picture I should feel much comforted, but I cannot. I find it difficult to believe it in view of the obvious fear which holds all the nations who are neighbors of Germany and the obvious lack of fear which appears in the behavior of the German Government and a large proportion of the German people. The great dominant fact is that Germany has already begun to rearm. We read of importations quite out of the ordinary of scrap iron and nickel and war metals. We read of the military spirit which is rife throughout the country; we see that the philosophy of blood lust is being inculcated into their youth in a manner unparalleled since the days of barbarism.

The Leader of the Opposition [Mr. Lansbury] said just now that he and the Socialist party would never consent to the rearming of Germany. I was very much pleased when I heard that. I agree with him. I should feel very much safer if I felt that that would not happen in my lifetime or in that of my children. But is the right hon. Gentleman quite sure that the Germans will come and ask him for his consent before they rearm? Does he not think that they might omit that formality and go ahead without even taking a card vote of the Trades Union Congress? Then the right hon. Gentleman said, "But in order to prevent them rearming I should like to see all the other countries, their neighbors, disarm," and that has been the burden of his speech and of many other speeches. But I doubt very much whether the other Powers are going to take any notice. I do not see why they should. In the next breath the right hon. Gentleman said that if they take his advice, and if it should turn out wrong and they find themselves exposed to attacks and getting into trouble, the first thing he will do will be to call a general strike in order to prevent any aid being sent them. If he is not going to take the slightest responsibility for these people, even if they do take his advice, I am inclined to think that they will be entitled to say to him, "Mind your own business."

But it is our own position that weighs upon us most of all here in this House. I am glad that an interval has been introduced into this dangerous process of disarmament in Europe, which has played a noticeable part in raising the temperature to its present level. If we wish to keep our freedom, we should forthwith recognize that our rôle in Europe is more limited than it has hitherto been considered to be. Isolation is, I believe, utterly impossible, but we should nevertheless practice a certain degree of sober detachment from the European scene. We should not try to weaken those Powers which are in danger, or feel themselves in danger, and thereby expose ourselves to a demand that we should come to their aid. I have deprecated these schemes which we have laid before the Disarmament Conference prescribing the size of all the armies and navies and air forces of Europe. I am not going to analyze the MacDonald Plan. I told the House in March that it never had the slightest chance of being accepted—never. How could you expect those countries that feel themselves in so great danger to make the very large reductions which were asked for in their armaments, their air forces and armies, while at the same time substantial increases were offered to the Germany with which we are now confronted?

I know that it is natural for Ministers, for the Prime Minister, to wish to play a great part on the European stage, to bestride Europe in the cause of peace, and to be as it were its saviors. You cannot be the saviors of Europe on a limited liability. I agree with the statement of the late Mr. Bonar Law, who said that we cannot be the policemen of the whole world. We have to discharge our obligations, but we cannot take upon ourselves undue obligations into which we shall certainly come if we are the leaders in compelling and pressing for a great diminution in the strength of France and other Powers which are neighbors of Germany. How lucky it is that the French did not take the advice that we have been tendering them in the last few years, or the advice which the United States has given them—advice tendered from a safe position 3000 miles across the ocean! If they had accepted it the war would be much nearer, and our obligation to come to their aid would be much more strictly interpreted. There should be recognition of the fact that we ought not to place ourselves continually in the most prominent position and endeavor to produce spectacular effects of disarmament in Europe, because as surely as we do a good deal of our discretionary power will be gradually whittled away.

There is a fairly general measure of agreement as to the course which we should now pursue. We should adhere to the League of Nations I did not agree with the Member for Carnarvon when he mocked and scolded the League in a speech in the country. Nor do I agree with those poor friends of the League who say that, just because the League was incapable of dealing with the situation in the Far East, on the other side of the world, it will have no efficacy in dealing with the European situation. What could you expect of the League in far-off Asia? China and Japan—what do they care for the League of Nations? Russia and the United States—neither of them members of the League. Those four countries comprise half the population of the globe. They form another world, a world in itself, and you should not judge of the success or power of a great international institution like this by the fact that it has not been able to make its will effective at the other side of the globe Very different is the case in Europe In Europe you have at least erected it upon the basis of the Treaties of Peace That is a foundation on which you can build, and not only is it erected on that foundation, but powerful nations stand fully armed to defend those Treaties and, if necessary, to make themselves the agents and authorities of the League of Nations.

I believe that we shall find our greatest safety in co-operating with the other Powers of Europe, not taking a leading part but coming in with all the neutral States and the smaller States of Europe which will gather together anxiously in the near future at Geneva We shall make a great mistake to separate ourselves entirely from them at this juncture Whatever way we turn there is risk. But the least risk and the greatest help will be found in re-creating the Concert of Europe through the League of Nations, not for the purpose of fiercely quarreling and haggling about the details of disarmament, but in an attempt to address Germany collectively, so that there may be some redress of the grievances of the German nation and that that may be effected before this peril of [German] rearmament reaches a point which may endanger the peace of the world.

I see in the House some of the Ministers responsible for Defence Departments I have been in that position myself in the years of baffling uncertainty through which we passed before the Great War, and I should like to tell those Ministers my own experience. In such circumstances every kind of pressure will be put upon them to reduce what they consider and what they are advised to be the necessary provision for our security. The papers will write leading articles. The Chancellor of the Exchequer and the Treasury are bound to put their case The economists will give their views, and in Parliament there will be pressure for cutting down this and that. But if trouble should come none of the able editors, none of the stern economists, will be at hand to defend the Ministers. When the Service Departments are found to be hopelessly lacking in the essentials of our safety it will be no use to turn round and say to a newspaper, "You wrote an article saying that there must be a great cut," or in saying to a Member of Parliament, "You voted against any increase." These people will be among the very first to say, "Oh, you took all this money, and yet you have not even provided what is necessary."

In these circumstances, proved as it is that we have disarmed to the verge of risk—nay, well into the gulf of risk—a very great responsibility rests upon the Ministers for the Defence Departments to assure us that adequate provision is made for our safety, and for having the power and the time, if necessary, to realize the whole latent strength of our country.

PREPARE!

February 7, 1933

On a private motion moved by Mr Clarry calling attention "to the inadequate defenses of Great Britain and the Empire from foreign attack"

1933

November 12. Reichstag election. No candidates except those endorsed by Hitler. Nazis obtain 95 per cent. of votes polled.

November 14. Government announce that "after anxious consideration and with much regret" two 9000-ton cruisers will be included in Naval program.

November 16. Samuelite Liberals withdraw support from Government.

1934

January 1. Mr. Anthony Eden, Under-Secretary for Foreign Affairs, appointed Lord Privy Seal.

January 26. German-Polish agreement. Hitler renounces for ten years all claims to Polish Corridor.

January 31. Publication of White Paper containing fresh British proposals for disarmament.

PREPARE!

I REMEMBER in the days of the late Conservative Administration, when I had the honor of serving under the Lord President, who is going to reply tonight, that we thought it right to take as a rule that there would be no major war within ten years in which we should be engaged. Of course, such a rule can only be a very crude guidance to the military and naval chiefs who have to make their plans, and it had to be reconsidered prospectively at the beginning of each year. I believe that it was right in all the circumstances With Locarno and the more mellow light which shone on the world at that time, with the hopes that were then very high, it was probably right to take that principle as a guide from day to day, and from year to year. No one could take that principle as a guide today. No Cabinet, however pacific and peace-loving, could base their naval and military organization upon such an assumption as that. A new situation has been created, mainly in the last three or four years, by rubbing this sore of the Disarmament Conference until it has become a cancer, and also by the sudden uprush of Nazi-ism in Germany, with the tremendous covert armaments which are proceeding there today. Everyone sitting on the Government Bench knows how seriously the position has been changed. Only yesterday we defined once again our commitments to other countries. They are very serious commitments. The White Paper which we discussed yesterday contains a grave sentence:

His Majesty's Government...have a right to expect that, if these provisions and pledges were solemnly entered into, they would not be lightly violated, and that any violation of them would be met in the most practical and effective way by immediately assembling Governments and States in support of international peace and agreement against the disturber and the violator.

I think that those are serious words to use in such a document, and it would be most unwise for us to proceed with our diplomacy in one direction, and not to make our necessary preparation in the other sphere. At Birmingham this year the Lord President went out of his way with great solemnity to issue a warning about the European situation, and he pointed out how strictly we should adhere to all the engagements into which we have entered. We must consider our military, naval and aviation defense in relation to facts of this character.

We are engaged in imposing equality of armies as far as we can upon the nations of the Continent—France, Germany, Poland and Italy Suppose it is asked in a few years that there should be equality of navies too? When the Government are asked about this, they say, "Oh, no, that would not apply; we should not agree to that." Suppose we are asked some time in the future to restore colonies for which we hold a mandate; the Government would say, "Certainly not; we should not open that question in any way." What do we back our opinions with; what armaments and what force have we behind these serious issues of opinion on which we declare our will and right? What happens, for instance, if, after we have equalized and reduced the army of France to the level of that of Germany, with all the reaction which will have followed in the sentiment of Europe upon such a change, and if Germany then proceeds to say, "How can you keep a great nation of 65,000,000 in the position in which it is not entitled to have a navy equal to the greatest of the fleets upon the seas?" You will say, "No; we do not agree. Armies—they belong to other people. Navies—that question affects Britain's interests, and we are bound to say, 'No.' " But what position shall we be in to say that "No"?

Wars come very suddenly. I have lived through a period when one looked forward, as we do now, with anxiety and uncertainty to what would happen in the future. Suddenly something did happen—tremendous, swift, overpowering, irresistible. Let me remind the House of the sort of thing that happened in 1914. There was absolutely no quarrel between Germany and France. One July afternoon the German Ambassador drove down to the Quai d'Orsay and said to M. Viviani, the French Prime Minister, "We have been forced to mobilize against Russia, and war will be declared. What is to be the position of France?" The French Prime Minister made the answer, which his Cabinet had agreed upon, that France would act in accordance with what she considered to be her own interests. The Ambassador said, "You have an alliance with Russia, have you not?" "Quite so," said the French Prime Minister. And that was the process by which, in a few minutes, the area of the struggle, already serious in the east, was enormously widened and multiplied by the throwing in of the two great nations of the west. But sometimes even a declaration of neutrality does not suffice. On this very occasion, as we now know, the German Ambassador was authorized by his Government, in case the French did not do their duty by their Russian ally, in case they showed any disposition to back out of the conflict which had been resolved on by the German nation, to demand that the fortresses of Toul and Verdun should be handed over to German troops as a guarantee that the French, having declared neutrality, would not change their mind at a subsequent moment.

That is how that great thing happened in our own lifetime, and I am bound to say that I cannot see in the present administration of Germany any assurance that they would be more nice-minded in dealing with a vital and supreme situation than was the Imperial Government of Germany, which was responsible for this procedure being adopted towards France. No, Sir, and we may, within a measurable period of time, in the lifetime of those who are here, if we are not in a proper state of security, be confronted on some occasion with a visit from an ambassador, and may have to give an answer in a very few hours; and if that answer is not satisfactory, within the next few hours the crash of bombs exploding in London and cataracts of masonry and fire and smoke will apprise us of any inadequacy which has been permitted in our aerial defenses. We are vulnerable as we have never been before. I have often heard criticisms of the Liberal Government before the War. All I can say is that a far graver complaint rests upon those who now hold power if, by any chance, against our wishes and against our hopes, trouble should come.

Not one of the lessons of the past has been learned, not one of them has been applied, and the situation is incomparably more dangerous. Then we had the Navy, and no air menace worth considering Then the Navy was the "sure shield" of Britain. As long as it was ready in time and at its stations we could say to any foreign Government, "Well, what are you going to do about it? We will not declare ourselves. We will take our own time, we will work out our own course. We have no desire to hurt anyone, but we shall not be pressed or forced into any hasty action unless we think fit and well." We cannot say that now. This cursed, hellish invention and development of war from the air has revolutionized our position. We are not the same kind of country we used to be when we were an island, only twenty-five years ago. That is borne in upon me more than anything else. It is not merely a question of what we like and what we do not like, of ambitions and desires, or rights and interests, but it is a question of safety and independence. That is involved now as never before.

It seems to me that there are three definite decisions which we should now take at once, and without any delay. The first affects the Army. We ought to begin the reorganization of our civil factories so that they can be turned over rapidly to war purposes. All over Europe that is being done, and to an amazing extent. This process is incomparably more efficient than anything that existed in the days of Prussian Imperialism before the War. Every factory in those countries is prepared to turn over to the production of some material for the deplorable and melancholy business of slaughter. What have we done? There is not an hour to lose. Those things cannot be done in a moment. The process should be started and the very maximum of money that can be usefully spent will be spent from today on—if we act with wisdom.

Then there is the question of the Navy. For the Navy, at any rate, we should regain freedom of design We should get rid of this London Treaty which has crippled us in building the kind of ships we want, and has stopped the United States from building a great battleship which she probably needed and to which we should have not had the slightest reason to object. It has forced us to spend some of our hard-earned money —the little there is for these purposes—unwisely. It has forced us to take great ships which would have been of enormous utility in convoying vessels bearing food to these islands and to sink them in the ocean, when they had ten to fifteen years of useful life in them [1] We must regain our freedom at the earliest possible moment, and we shall be helped in doing so by the fact that another of the parties to that Treaty [Japan] is resolved to regain her freedom too.

Then there is the air. I cannot conceive how, in the present state of Europe and of our position in Europe, we can delay in establishing the principle of having an Air Force at least as strong as that of any Power that can get at us. I think that is a perfectly reasonable thing to do. It would only begin to put us back to the position in which we were brought up. We have lived under the shield of the Navy. To have an Air Force as strong as the air force of France or Germany, whichever is the stronger,

[1] The *Tiger* and four *Iron Dukes*

ought to be the decision which Parliament should take, and which the National Government should proclaim.

There is only one other point which I will mention, and that is the co-ordination of the three Services. I doubt very much whether, at this stage, there is room for economy in any of them, but at any rate it would be advantageous, in my opinion, if the problem were studied from a central point of view, because things are changing very much. The emphasis should be thrown here or there, according to the needs of modern conditions, and there should be much more effective co-ordination than now exists. I ask that some time in this Session we can have a discussion on the three Services combined. It would be a valuable discussion—one such as has frequently been allowed in previous years, and was never more necessary than at the present time.

The responsibility of His Majesty's Government is grave indeed, and there is this which makes it all the graver. it is a responsibility which they have no difficulty in discharging if they choose. We are told they have to wait for public opinion, that they must bring that along and must be able to assure the good people here that everything is being done with the most pacific intentions—they must make a case. But nothing like that can stand between them and their responsibility to the Crown and Parliament for the safety and security of the country. The Government command overwhelming majorities in both branches of the Legislature. Nothing that they ask will be denied to them They have only to make their proposals, and they will be supported in them. Let them not suppose that if they make proposals, with confidence and conviction, for the safety of the country, their countrymen will not support them. Why take so poor a view of the patriotic support which this nation gives to those who it feels are doing their duty by it? I cannot feel that at the present time the Government are doing their duty in these matters of defense, and particularly in respect of the air. It seems to me that while we are becoming ever more entangled in the European situation, and while we are constantly endeavoring to weaken, relatively, our friends upon the continent of Europe, we nevertheless are left exposed to a mortal thrust, and are deprived of that old sense of security and independence upon which the civilization of our island has been built.

THE NEED FOR AIR PARITY

March 8, 1934

Air Estimates

1934

February 16. Anglo-Russian trade agreement signed in London.
Mr. Eden leaves London for Paris, Berlin and Rome.

February 24. The *Times* states that a reorganization of the Cabinet is regarded as "inevitable but not imminent," and hints that Sir John Simon's speech on the Blackshirt question may be meant to pave the way for his return to the Home Office in order to deal with this problem.

February 27. Sir John Simon states that he has no intention of retiring from the Foreign Office.

March 2. Publication of Air Estimates totalling £20,165,000 Provision made for four new squadrons—an increase of first-line air strength from 850 to 890

THE NEED FOR AIR PARITY

It is certain that the endeavors which have been made by the Government to procure a measure of disarmament from Europe similar to that which we have practiced ourselves as an example have failed. I have never thought that these efforts would succeed, and I have said so. Perhaps it was uncharitable to say it. I exceedingly regret that they have failed. The Government have admitted for more than a year past that in their desire to procure disarmament they have gone to the very edge of risk. Yes, Sir, and many of us think that they have gone beyond that edge. I have not been able to convince myself that the policy which the Government have pursued has been in sufficiently direct contact with the harsh realities of the European situation, but, of course, I admit most fully that they have made it clear before all the world, not only by words, which are so easy, but by actions, which are so hard, and by inaction, which is so questionable, how sincere has been, and still is, our desire to bring about a general measure of disarmament, especially in the air. That has failed, and nobody can deny it. You could not have chosen in this country anyone more qualified to bring success to his mission than the Lord Privy Seal [Mr. Eden]. It is not his fault that he has not met with success. No one could have stated our sincere case in a more agreeable manner, more simply and effectively, to the different countries which he has visited, but he has failed. In view of that failure we must now, from this moment, look to our own safety. That is the feeling which I believe is in the minds of all—that we must now betimes take measures to put ourselves in a state of reasonable security.

What are the measures that we can take? First of all, of course, there is the preservation of the peace of Europe. We should do everything that we can do to that end. I am astounded that this Government, which has labored far beyond the bounds of practical expectation in the cause of disarmament and peace, should be abused and insulted as if it were an administration that was anxious to plunge this country into another war. But, putting the preservation of peace in the first place, what is the next great object that we must have in view? It is to secure our national freedom of choice to remain outside a European war, if one should break out That I put as the more direct and more practical issue, subordinate to, but not less important than, the preservation of peace.

This is not the time, in this Debate, for us to argue about the duties and obligations which this country may have contracted or her interpretation of those obligations in regard to any Continental struggle that may arise.[1] We all hope it will never take place, and I am not at all prepared, standing here, to assume that it will inevitably take place. On the contrary, I still grasp the larger hope and believe that we may wear our way through these difficulties and leave this grim period behind. But there can be no assurance upon that, and we must have the effective right and power to choose our own path, in accordance with the wishes and resolves of the nation, in any contingency or emergency which may arise upon the continent of Europe; and for this purpose we must be safe from undue foreign pressure.

We cannot afford to confide the safety of our country to the passions or to the panic of any foreign nation which may be facing some desperate crisis. We must be independent. We must be free. We must preserve our full latitude and discretion of choice. In the past we have always had this freedom and independence. I have heard reproaches about the Liberal Government before the War, that they did not make enough preparations or look far enough ahead. But we were in a position where, at any rate, we had a complete freedom of choice; much might be lost by delay, but, as far as the safety of this country was concerned, we were not in any danger. We could hold our own here and take what time we chose to make up our minds, and what time we require to raise the whole vast might of the British Empire, month after month and year after year, from a peace to a war footing.

Nothing of that sort exists today, and unless we regain that freedom of choice, this is no longer integrally or characteristically the same kind of country in which we have always dwelt, and for hundreds of years have built up our own special, insular character and culture. We have never lived at anybody's mercy. We have never lived upon the good pleasure of

[1] See p 50

any Continental nation in regard to our fundamental requirements. We have never entrusted the home defense of this country to any foreign Power. We have never asked for any help from anyone. We have given help to many, but to make good the security of our own island we have asked for help from none. I recognize the strong ties of interest, of sentiment, and of modern sympathy which unite the two great still-remaining Parliamentary democracies of Western Europe. The French and British populations are profoundly bent on peace, and their Governments have nothing to gain by war, but everything to lose. There are great ties which we have in common with the French Republic, but, in spite of all that, we ought not to be dependent upon the French air force for the safety of our island home.[2] Although there may be no engagement, the mere fact that you cannot defend yourselves and that your friend across the Channel has additional power makes a whole series of implications which very nearly involve the condition of dependence upon overseas protection. All history has proved the peril of being dependent upon a foreign State for home defense instead of upon one's own right arm. This is not a party question, not a question between pacifists and militarists, but one of the essential independence of character of our island life and its preservation from intrusion or distortion of any kind.

Let us see what we mean by safety. It is a word easy to use, but somewhat difficult to explain. Now that the hideous air war has cast the shadow of its wings over harassed civilization, no one can pretend that by any measures which we could take it would be possible to give absolute protection against an aggressor dropping bombs in this island and killing a great many unarmed men, women and children. No Government can be asked to guarantee absolute immunity to the nation if we were attacked in this way by this new arm. It is certainly in our power, however, if we act in time, to guard ourselves, first of all, from a mortal blow which would compel us to capitulate; and, secondly, it is in our power, I firmly believe, to make it extremely unlikely that we should be attacked, or that we should be attacked by this particular method of terrorizing the civil population by the slaughter of non-combatants, which, to the shame of the twentieth century, we are now forced to discuss as a practical issue.

For this purpose we ought to use every method which is available. We cannot afford to neglect any. I am going to mention what I consider are the four simultaneous lines of defense which we should develop. The

[2] At this time the French air force ranked first in Europe in numbers.

first, of course, is a peaceful foreign policy. We must continue to strive, as we are striving, by every means, by every action, by every restraint and suppression of harsh feelings and expressions, to preserve the peace and harmony of Europe. No one, unless blinded by malice or confused by ignorance, would doubt that that has been the main desire of His Majesty's present Administration, just as it was of the Administration which preceded it.

What is the second line? We ought not to neglect any security which we can derive from international conventions. We must get all we can from them. I do not agree with those who say that these international conventions are not worth the paper on which they are written. It may well be that vague, general pious affirmations like the Kellogg Pact do not carry much practical conviction to people's minds, because everyone can see that, the right of self-defense being conceded, every country which plunges into war will allege that it is fighting in self-defense, and will probably convince its own people that it is doing so. It may be an extremely good thing in itself to make this wide, general affirmation that there will be no more war, but it undoubtedly has not carried conviction, and thus it has weakened the virtue of these international instruments. A greater measure of confidence can be reposed in more definite, limited and precise arrangements. At any rate, we should be very foolish to neglect them. Whatever may happen to the discussions, now going on about regulating the size of air fleets, we should strive to secure an international convention or a series of treaties confining air warfare to military and naval objectives and to the zones of field armies.

Such schemes would have to be drawn up in full detail, but I do not believe that this would be impracticable, and I hope the House is not going to be led by very easy arguments to suppose there is no validity or virtue in such arrangements. All the experience of the world shows that they have played their parts even in the most hideous quarrels of nations, and any nation that refused to enter into discussions of a convention to regulate air warfare would consequently be left in a position of grisly isolation, proclaiming its intention deliberately to make war as a scientific and technical operation upon women and children for the terrorization of the civil population. It would be a wise thing for us to get as many nations as possible to join in a convention which would exclude, on paper at any rate, this method from the arena of recognized warfare. I deprecate anything that is said to assume that such a method is compatible at all with any form of decent civilization. His Majesty's Government have been perfectly right to make it clear that no question of the convenience of using air warfare for police purposes in savage countries and barbarous regions should stand in the way of such an agreement of convention if that police measure becomes the sole obstacle to the conclusion of an arrangement otherwise generally satisfactory. We must not balance convenience against safety. Even if we were faced with the old difficulty of expense in maintaining order in the mountain valleys of India without the facilities of an air arm, provided there was a world consensus of opinion against the use of bombing undefended areas, it would be to our advantage to make the sacrifice in order to secure a much greater gain. Even taking the lowest view of human nature, nations in war do not usually do things which give them no special advantage, and which grievously complicate their own position.

No convention of the kind of which I have been speaking would be of the slightest use between the Great Powers unless it were based on parity [*i.e.* upon our having an Air Force equal to any other country within striking distance of our shores]. That is the key to any convention which may be negotiated. If one side had an all-powerful air force and the other only a very weak defense, the temptation to use the weapons of terror upon the civil population might far outweigh any detrimental effects on neutral opinion. If, however, the two sides were in an equality and in the position to do equal and simultaneous harm to each other, then the uselessness of the crime would reinforce its guilt and horror, and the effects upon the action of neutrals. I hold that we should make conventions to limit and regulate the use of the air arm, and these conventions should be made, and can only be made, on the basis of parity. If both sides feel that they would suffer equally from a breach of an international convention and neither side can see how it can gain an advantage over the other, it seems likely that these conventions will be respected. Not only would the danger of our being attacked be greatly diminished, but the character of the attack would be confined within the limits of the convention by breaking which neither side would have anything to gain.

That is the argument for parity, and for immediate parity. I believe that conventions based on parity are the best and only means of shielding the crowded populations of our great cities, and particularly of this enormous London, by making it certain that there will be no advantage to either side in departing from what has been agreed I do not see how the most sincere lover of peace or the most inveterate hater of war in this

House can dispute the good sense and reason of the argument for parity.[2]

There is, of course, one other and ultimate method of defense which we must also develop by every conceivable means. I mean the effective punishment and destruction, by an active and efficient home defense, of any invaders who may come to our shores. I do not pretend to deal with technical matters this afternoon. This is not the time for us to deal with them, nor do I think the House of Commons is the best place in which they can be ventilated, but I must express this opinion. It ought to be possible, by making good arrangements both on the ground and in the air, to secure very real advantages for the force of aeroplanes which is defending its own air and which can rise lightly laden from its own soil. I cannot believe that that advantage, properly organized, would not give an additional and important measure of protection. We should be able by these means to impose deterrents upon an invader, and even upon a potential declaration of war, and gradually to bring attacks upon us, by attrition, to smaller dimensions and finally to an end altogether. In these matters we have, of course, to trust our experts. I hope that they are busy, that they are tirelessly working out methods of defense; and we trust the Government and the Ministers concerned to guide the experts, and to make sure that the necessary funds and authority are supplied to carry out a complete scheme of home defense.

Therefore, there seem to me to be four lines of protection by which we can secure the best chance, and a good chance, of immunity for our people from the perils of air war—a peaceful foreign policy; the convention regulating air warfare; the parity in air power to invest that convention with validity; and, arising out of that parity, a sound system of home defense—in addition to all these other arrangements if they all fail. We must not despair, we must not for a moment pretend that we cannot face these things. Dangers come upon the world; other nations face them. When, in old days, the sea gave access to this island, it was a danger to this island. It made it liable to invasion at any point; but by taking proper measures our ancestors gained the command of the sea, and consequently, what had been a means of inroad upon us became our sure protection; and there is not the slightest reason why, with our ability and our resources, and our peaceful intentions, our desire only to live quietly here

[2] This argument for equal air strength applies only to one particular arm, and deals only with the position of Great Britain in relation to Continental Powers. It in no way contradicts the argument (see pp. 13, 31, 32) in which the dangers of a general equality of armaments between victor and vanquished nations are described.

in our island, we should not raise up for ourselves a security in the air above us which will make us as free from serious molestation as did our control of blue water in bygone centuries.

It is not to be disputed that we are in a dangerous position today. This is a very good White Paper. The opening paragraph sets forth a most admirable declaration, but what is there behind it? £130,000. Very fine words. It must have taken the Cabinet a long time to agree to them—with the Air Minister drafting them and passing them round. They give great paper satisfaction. But what is there behind them? £130,000. It is not the slightest use concealing the facts. The Under-Secretary has given some of them. The Liberal Member who spoke from the benches opposite gave some, as I thought, most disconcerting and alarming facts about air warfare and the growth of air armaments. And we are, it is admitted, the fifth air Power only,[3] if that. We are only half the strength of France, our nearest neighbor. Germany is arming fast, and no one is going to stop her. That seems quite clear. No one proposes a preventive war to stop Germany breaking the Treaty of Versailles. She is going to arm, she is doing it, she has been doing it. I have not any knowledge of the details, but people are well aware that those very gifted people, with their science and with their factories, with what they call their "Air Sport," are capable of developing with great rapidity a most powerful air force for all purposes, offensive and defensive, within a very short period of time.

Germany is ruled by a handful of autocrats who are the absolute masters of that gifted nation. They are men who have neither the long interests of a dynasty to consider, nor those very important restraints which a democratic Parliament and constitutional system impose upon any executive Government. Nor have they the restraint of public opinion, which public opinion, indeed, they control by every means which modern apparatus renders possible. They are men who owe their power to, and are, indeed, the expression of, the bitterness of defeat, and of the resolved and giant strength of that mighty German Empire. I am not going to speak about their personalities, because there is no one in the House who is not thoroughly aware of them and cannot form his own opinion after having read the accounts of what has been happening there, of the spirit which is alive there and of the language, methods and outlook of the leading men of that tremendous community, much the most powerful in the whole world. The German power is in their hands, and they can direct it this way or that by a stroke of the pen, by a single gesture.

[3] See p. 38 *n.* 2.

I dread the day when the means of threatening the heart of the British Empire should pass into the hands of the present rulers of Germany. I think we should be in a position which would be odious to every man who values freedom of action and independence, and also in a position of the utmost peril for our crowded, peaceful population, engaged in their daily toil. I dread that day, but it is not, perhaps, far distant. It is, perhaps, only a year, or perhaps eighteen months, distant. Not come yet—at least, so I believe, or I hope and pray. But it is not far distant. There is still time for us to take the necessary measures, but it is the measures we want. Not this paragraph in this White Paper; we want the measures. It is no good writing that first paragraph and then producing £130,000. We want the measures to achieve parity. The hon. Gentleman opposite who spoke so many words of wisdom seemed to me to mar the significance and point of his argument when he interposed in it the statement that he was not committing himself to any increase.

[Mr. MANDER: At this stage.]

But this *is* the stage. I do not say today, but within the next week or so. The turning-point has been reached, and the new steps must be taken. There are very special dangers to be feared if any Great Power possessing Dominions and connections all over the world falls into a peculiarly vulnerable condition. How many wars have we seen break out because of the inherent weakness of some great empire, such as the Hapsburg Empire or the Turkish Empire, when they fell into decay? Then all the dangerous forces become excited. No nation playing the part we play in the world, and aspire to play, has a right to be in a position where it can be blackmailed.

I said I would not dwell on the past, but I must repudiate the unfair attacks which have been made lately upon the Secretary of State for India [Sir Samuel Hoare]. He and I have very grave differences, and I, personally, shall carry them to their conclusion, but to charge him, or to charge Lord Trenchard, to whom our small but admirable Air Force owes so much, with having failed in their public duty is monstrous. At any rate, as Chancellor of the Exchequer responsible for five Budgets before 1929 I must entirely associate myself with the Secretary of State for India, then Minister for Air. Next to the Lord President of the Council, then Prime Minister, I shared the responsibility for what was done, or not done, in those years, and I am prepared to offer a detailed and, I trust, vigorous justification—or, I hope, vindication—if it should be desired in any quarter. But the scene has changed. This terrible new fact has occurred. Germany is arming—she is rapidly arming—and no one will stop her None of the grievances between the victors and the vanquished have been redressed. The spirit of aggressive nationalism was never more rife in Europe and in the world. Far away are the days of Locarno, when we nourished bright hopes of the reunion of the European family and the laying in the tomb of that age-long quarrel between Teuton and Gaul of which we have been the victims in our lifetime.

That hope is gone, and we must act in accordance with the new situation. Here I address myself particularly to the Lord President. I say nothing in derogation of the high responsibility of the Prime Minister, but I address myself particularly to the Lord President as he is in his place in the House. He alone has the power. He has the power not only because of the confidence which is placed by large numbers of people of the country in the sobriety of his judgment and in his peaceful intentions, but also because, as leader of the Conservative party, he possesses the control of overwhelming majorities of determined men in both Houses of the Legislature. My right hon. Friend has only to make up his mind and Parliament will vote all the supplies and all the sanctions which are necessary, if need be within forty-eight hours. There need be no talk of working up public opinion. You need not go and ask the public what they think about this. Parliament and the Cabinet have to decide, and the nation has to judge whether they have acted rightly as trustees. The Lord President has the power, and if he has the power he has also what always goes with power—he has the responsibility. Perhaps it is a more grievous and direct personal responsibility than has for many years fallen upon a single servant of the Crown. He may not have sought it, but he is tonight the captain of the gate. The nation looks to him to advise it and lead it, to guide it wisely and safely in this dangerous question, and I hope and believe that we shall not look in vain.

Mr. BALDWIN *in the course of his reply said:*

"If all our efforts for an agreement fail, and if it is not possible to obtain this equality in such matters as I have indicated, then any Government of this country—a National Government more than any, and this Government—will see to it that in air strength and air power this country shall no longer be in a position inferior to any country within striking distance of our shores."

THE MACDONALD PLAN REJECTED

March 14, 1934

Supply (Report Stage)

'

1934

March 14. Lord Londonderry, Secretary of State for Air, dismisses as impracticable any suggestion that a supreme Minister of Defense can be made responsible for the three Services.

THE MACDONALD PLAN REJECTED

I was taken to task the other day for saying that the Lord Privy Seal [Mr. Eden] in his mission, to the three capitals in Europe had failed. I have listened to his very agreeably delivered speech, so excellent in its phrasing and so well meant in its sentiments, and I am bound to say that the farthest I can go in altering my statement that his mission had failed is to say that up to the present at any rate it has not succeeded.

He was set an impossible task. Take one instance. He had to commend to France an elaborate scheme of disarmament which meant that the French would have to agree that their army in Europe, long the most famous in the history of the world, should be no stronger than the army of Poland, Germany or Italy. It seemed to me, even before he set out on his tour, extremely unlikely that France would agree to that at any time, least of all at a time like this. I ventured to say a year ago, when the Prime Minister's first scheme, prescribing in great detail to the countries in Europe exactly how large their armies, navies and air forces should be, was put forward, that there was no chance of it being accepted. And when this scheme had been received by the French with the greatest politeness, and with an ingenuity born of what is now a long and careful study of the Anglo-Saxon mentality and the character of public opinion in the United Kingdom and in the United States, when they accepted with great civility the scheme as a most valuable contribution to the progress of mankind and the consolidation of the peace of the human race, but mentioned that there were a few little reservations on this point and that which they might find it necessary to introduce, I predicted what the fate of the scheme would be.

The Lord Privy Seal has pointed out that the objections now are not the technical objections of experts as to the size of cannons, and so on; that is

107

not what is holding up agreement. For a long time we were told that this was the difficulty, but as the experts have now adjusted their views we have got back to where we started. Nations are not prepared to accept a great diminution of their individual security at this juncture, and they begin to raise new and fundamental opposition to the principles of the proposals put forward. Another proposal with which the Lord Privy Seal was charged was that France should reduce her air force to 500 machines. Actually at the moment she is proposing to spend, over a certain period, £40,000,000 to £50,000,000 in order to improve the character, quality and power of her air force, which already numbers three or four times that figure. Is she likely to agree? Will the French write back to us and say that they are entirely converted from their point of view and are ready to reduce their air force to 500 machines, while contemplating an improvement in the German air force at the same time?

Is it really worth while indulging in these illusions? Can we expect the French to write back to us agreeing to the proposal? We are not going to receive from this upstanding French Government anything which will meet the first MacDonald scheme or the second MacDonald scheme. I am reminded of a famous quotation from Dr. Johnson, which might well be read and pondered over by my hon. Friend:

> Ye who listen with credulity to the whispers of fancy, and pursue with eagerness the phantoms of hope, who expect that age will perform the promises of youth, and that the deficiencies of the present day will be supplied by the morrow; attend to the history of Rasselas, Prince of Abyssinia.

I did not find much in his most attractive and engaging speech that was reassuring. On the contrary, in the most correct phraseology which could possibly fall from the lips of a Minister of the Crown he painted for us a more somber picture of the deterioration which has been going steadily forward in Europe than any we have yet heard from that Bench I venture to suggest to my hon. Friend, in whose career the whole House has a common interest, because we do like to see new figures emerge, to be careful not to be too obliging in his departmental duties, and not to be too ready to do what is asked of him on all occasions, because he is very valuable, and we all hope that he will be associated with real success in the domain of foreign affairs.

False ideas have been spread about the country that disarmament means peace. The Disarmament Conference has brought us steadily nearer—I will not say to war because I share the repulsion from using that word, but nearer to a pronounced state of ill-will than anything that could be imagined. First of all, you were met with a competition among the different countries to disarm the other fellow, to take away the peculiar weapons of this or that other country, while safeguarding their own special military or naval interests. Then, in the second place, at Disarmament Conferences which were persisted in again and again year after year in spite of every failure, the desire was to throw the blame of the inevitable breakdown on some one country or another. "It was not me but that other country."

So in the end what have we got? We have not got disarmament. We have the rearmament of Germany. That is the monstrous offspring of this immense labor—the rearmament of Germany. Why, it is only a little while ago that I heard Ministers say and read diplomatic documents which said that rearmament was unthinkable—"Whatever happens, we cannot have that. Rearmament is unthinkable." Now all our hope is to regulate the unthinkable. Regulated unthinkability—that is the proposal now; and very soon it will be a question of making up our minds to unregulated unthinkability.

It is always an error in diplomacy to press a matter when it is quite clear that no further progress is to be made. It is also a great error if you ever give the impression abroad that you are using language which is more concerned with your domestic politics than with the actual fortunes and merits of the various great countries upon the Continent to whom you offer advice. Even suppose that the hon. Gentleman's mission shall be judged eventually to have failed, I am not so sure that we shall be so much worse off than if he had succeeded. Suppose France had taken the advice which we have tendered during the last four or five years, and had yielded to the pressure of the two great English-speaking nations to set an example of disarmament: suppose she had taken the advice of the Liberal newspapers! Only three or four years ago we noted the derision with which they wrote about the French barrier of fortresses which had been put up. Suppose the French had followed our example. Suppose they had made this gesture which is so much talked of today and had reduced themselves to allowing their defenses to fall into the kind of disarray to which we, out of the highest motives, for which we do not always get credit abroad, have reduced ours—what would be the position today? Where should we be?

I honor the French for their resolute determination to preserve the freedom and security of their country from invasion of any kind; I earnestly hope that we, in arranging our forces, shall not fall below their example. The awful danger, nothing less, of our present foreign policy is that we go on perpetually asking the French to weaken themselves And what do we urge as the inducement? We say, "Weaken yourselves," and we always hold out the hope that if they do it and get into trouble, we shall then in some way or other go to their aid, although we have nothing with which to go to their aid I cannot imagine a more dangerous policy. There is something to be said for isolation; there is something to be said for alliances. But there is nothing to be said for weakening the Power on the Continent with whom you would be in alliance, and then involving yourself further in Continental tangles in order to make it up to them In that way you have neither one thing nor the other; you have the worst of both worlds

The Romans had a maxim, "Shorten your weapons and lengthen your frontiers" But our maxim seems to be, "Diminish your weapons and increase your obligations" Aye, and diminish the weapons of your friends That has been the extraordinary policy of late years. Great hopes were set on the Disarmament Conference when it began, and after Locarno there were great hopes I am not going to pretend or suggest that the nagging and harping on disarmament have been the sole cause of the degeneration of European affairs. That would be unfair. Hideous new factors have rushed up at us from the gulf. Hideous new events have taken place which no one could have foreseen. Surely now we have reached a point where we ought to make an end of this effort to force disarmament upon countries which feel themselves in danger, and to put ourselves in a reasonable position of security. That will be better for peace, and much better for our own safety if peace should fail.

We now have an urgent duty. The Lord President made an important and welcome declaration in debate last week upon air policy—that if these attempts to obtain a Disarmament Convention failed, we should then place ourselves in a position of air parity, or words to that effect. I accept a statement of that kind without any hesitation, because I am certain that with his reputation and with his responsibility my right hon. Friend would not have made such a statement merely to get round a Parliamentary corner on a particular occasion, or to stave off the fulfillment of his undertaking by dilatory processes. Therefore, I did not share the anxiety of some Members at certain passages in his speech.

But there is one point on which anxiety might have arisen. When my right hon. Friend was making his speech and saying that if all failed, *then*—we all expected him to say, "Then we shall immediately take steps to put ourselves in a satisfactory position"; but after the "then" came something different. He said that then there would be an Air Convention. That was rather an anticlimax. It would be dangerous indeed if we had to begin again in regard to the Air Convention all those elaborate discussions with all the Powers, the tremendous procedure at Geneva, to go over the whole course again for one-third of the prize, as it were, and at the same time remain ourselves in this extremely dangerous position, while all the time the situation, for all we know, might be altering from week to week by the development of the aerial armaments and facilities of Germany. Therefore, one hopes that when the Minister who is to reply speaks he will say something to reassure us that this Air Convention which is to be entered upon if the main Convention fails, will not interpose a delay of more than a few weeks in the proper review and reconsideration of our domestic defense.

I made a proposal myself that we should endeavor to have an agreement with different Powers near us to limit the use of the air weapon. That is quite a different matter. There need be no delay in consequence of that —to confine air warfare as far as you can to the zones of the armies or military objectives There need be no delay in that, because the essence of it is that we have an equal air force. Therefore, every step we make meanwhile to secure parity would help an agreement if it could be reached on the limitations which should be imposed by either side on the use of aircraft.

There was one remark thrown out very tentatively and guardedly by the hon. Member for Caerphilly [Mr M. Jones], a remark which seemed to me to be pregnant. He said, in effect, why, if other things fail, should not the nations who are actually in agreement about keeping the peace and so forth reach out their hands to one another? Surely that is an idea which should be pursued, but it should be pursued through the League of Nations. It is to the League of Nations that France or Belgium or any of those countries who are alarmed by the proceedings of their powerful neighbor, Germany, should have recourse. There it is that they should make their case, and all consequential action should be taken under the authority of the League of Nations. If it be true that those countries are deeply alarmed by proceedings across their frontiers, and if no satisfaction is given to them and no explanation made of what is going on, then it seems to me that they should associate themselves one with another, under the ægis of the League of Nations. Thus you would have a large number of countries who agreed and who had powerful forces and who could stand there, armed to defend each other if necessary, but who would not be able to move in any way except by the sanction of the international body. You would thus have the strength of the individual armies plus the control and authority of a great world-wide international organization. I do not believe you will ever succeed in building up an international force in a vague and general manner, or that it can be created in cold blood. But it might well be that an international force would come into being by an alliance of national forces for a particular emergency or for particular purposes, and, once having been started, it might give the security to the world which would avert the approaching curse of war.

A MINISTRY OF DEFENSE

March 21, 1934

Second Reading of the Consolidated Fund Bill

1934

March 15. Introduction of Army estimates amounting to £39,500,000, an
increase of £1,600,000 over 1933.

A MINISTRY OF DEFENSE

THERE is a very general agreement in the House that a Ministry of Defense should be our ultimate aim. In no other way can the best arrangements be made for economy and efficiency. There are particularisms and what the Deputy-Leader of the Opposition [Mr. Attlee] described as the vested interests—the innocent and respectable vested interests—of the various Services, and they cause much waste and confusion. Our history books are full of the dissensions between the Army and Navy which have led to the loss of such fine opportunities in the past We are assured by the Prime Minister that everything is now brought into complete harmony from a central point of view at every moment, but when we come to look below the surface of this assurance one sees many things which do not square with this hopeful and desirable assumption.

One cannot help feeling that in the distribution of public money each Service naturally fights for its own hand There is nothing like leather, said the cordwainer, and each Service presses its own claims. In my experience, which is, I suppose, as long as anyone's, the Minister with most information and address and backed by the Department with the largest hold upon tradition and public goodwill gets the largest share, and a larger share than would be secured if the case for the three Services were presented to the Cabinet as a whole, and in relation to what is judged to be the chief danger of the times. That seems to me to be the first argument which can be adduced for a Ministry of Defense—that it would put us in a far better position for dealing with the changed conditions of high strategy and Imperial policy.

But there is a second argument that is novel and increasing. All the three Services in modern times have a new common factor which they never had in anything like the same degree until the present century, or, indeed, until after the recent Great War. I mean science and invention. Science and invention are sweeping all before them. The same science applies to all three Services alike, and its application must play a large part in all your plans and outlook. Nothing like this was known in the nineteenth century, and in those days the segregation of the Services seemed comparatively simple. The Navy, to quote Lord Fisher, was a dismal mystery surrounded by seasickness, and had nothing in common, except good conduct, with the barrack square and the red-coated Army of those days. The Air Force did not exist.

The new science has come along permeating all these Services—a solvent which disperses their differences. Science cares nothing for the professional particularisms or the established customs or the cherished traditions of any one of the Services. In the fires of science, burning with increasing heat every year, all the most dearly loved conventions are being melted down; and this is a process which is going continually to spread. In view of the inventions and discoveries which are being made for us, one might almost say every month, a unified direction of the war efforts of the three Services would be highly beneficial. We should have a greater chance of applying the gifts of science broadly to the whole texture of our defensive arrangements if there were a reception of all these new inventions and discoveries from a common elevated point of view, removed from the prejudice of any one particular uniformed profession. That is a second argument for a Ministry of Defense.

There is a third argument, which arises out of the other two, but which also affects the very important question of public economy—the expense, the burden upon this House and the taxpayer. There are many functions which are common to all three Services, but which are now managed as separate branches. There are separate medical services to succor the three separate Services of the Army, the Air, and the Navy. There are separate Departments of chaplains to minister to the spiritual needs of the airman, the soldier, and the sailor. Research—an enormous, vital field—has not been pooled; there must, surely, be great overlapping there. Above all, Intelligence has not been pooled, and this, I may point out, was recommended to a very considerable extent by the Weir Committee. They strongly urged a movement towards the pooling of the various, almost numerous, Intelligence branches which are at work at the present time in the body of our State. But nothing has been done about it. The Committee was appointed in 1923; it reported in 1926; we are now here in 1934, and nothing has been done about it. It was a very good

Committee. Their recommendations were modest. They pressed this, but nothing has been done about it in the interval.

Lastly, there is the great field of contracts, and here something has been done. I would go farther, and admit that much has been done. The Contracts Committee, which the Prime Minister mentioned, is at work, and even before that committee was set up I have never felt that it was true that the different Departments of the State have in time of peace been bidding against each other to any large extent in the common market so as to put prices up against one another. The Treasury take care of that. And our arrangements, as the Prime Minister has indicated, are often very much better in practice than they are in theory. But in the field of contracts there still is much that could be done, even in time of peace, and if ever we should be involved in a great war again it would be most important that the entire business of the purchase and manufacture of munitions and supplies of all kinds, possibly with certain highly technical exceptions, should be taken over by a central administration and unified.

When the Great War broke out, our Navy was by far the largest in the world, and its great supply departments of all kinds lay behind it in the same proportion. The Army, on the other hand, had to be multiplied twenty- or thirtyfold, but this took some time, and it was many months before the war pressure led the Navy and the Army even to impinge upon the real resources of British industry. But by the middle of 1915 we began everywhere to feel the frontiers of supplies of every kind; the bones began to appear through the skin; and thereafter, from that time onwards, there were lamentable collisions and dispute and friction between the Admiralty and the other two Services represented by the Ministry of Munitions. In the end, the Ministry of Munitions made everything for the Air Ministry and for the Army, but they had to fight with the Admiralty, who remained a separate enclave, almost a foreign Power, as it seemed, in the heart and center of our State. I hope that arrangements will be made in the future to ensure that nothing like that occurs again, for I have no doubt, from the experience which I have had—and I had opportunities of seeing a good deal—that the public did not get the best service or the best use of the available material during the opening years of the War, owing largely to the jealous clash which took place between the Admiralty and the other two Departments.

In organizing industry, not only actually but prospectively, surely we might learn something from our German friends, who are building up an entirely new army and other fighting Services, and who have the advantage of building them up from what is called a clean-swept table—starting fair in this respect, unhampered by past conventions, by customs or prejudices of any kind That is a great advantage indeed. I have been told that they have created what is called a "weapon office," or *Waffenamt,* which makes for all the three arms of the Service which they are so busily developing. It seems to me that this expression, "weapon office," is pregnant, and that it might well enter into and be incorporated in our thought at the present time. Not only in the current supplies of the three Services in time of peace, but still more in the organization of national industry in case war should come, it seems to me imperative that there should be one view and one control in this country.

To sum up, I urge, first of all, that the Government should affirm publicly and definitely the principle of a Ministry of Defense; secondly, that they should take forthwith every interim step towards the merging and the fusion which would render, after the passage of a number of years, such unification possible, and that this should be a steady policy pursued year after year. By doing this I believe we should increasingly fit ourselves for dealing with immediate practical problems. We should improve the value which we get for the taxpayers' money or, alternatively, we should get the same security for less money, according to whether the skies were dark or clear, and we should be moving steadily towards a sound, true organization of our resources.

THE VALUE OF THE LEAGUE

July 13, 1934

Supply (Foreign Office Vote)

1934

April 9. The Foreign Secretary in reply to a question states that there has been a considerable increase in the expenditure allocated to all three arms of the German defense in 1934.

April 17. The French Government inform the British Government that Germany has made clear her determination to "continue every form of rearmament within limits of which she claims to be the sole judge in contempt of the provisions of the Treaty." She has thus "made impossible the negotiations the basis of which she has by her own act destroyed."

May 18. Mr. Baldwin tells the House of Commons, "There is no such thing as a sanction that will work that does not mean war."

June 14 German Reichsbank declare that Germany will be unable to pay interest on long-term foreign loans as from July 1.
Hitler visits Mussolini in Venice.

June 27. Lord Londonderry, Secretary of State for Air, in the House of Lords states that the Government are making preparations in ample time to secure parity in the air.

June 30. Assassination of Roehm, Heines, Strasser, Schleicher and several hundred others. Von Papen dismissed from office of Vice-Chancellor and sent as Ambassador to Vienna.

July 8. M. Barthou (French Foreign Minister) visits London and proposes to Sir John Simon the negotiation of an Eastern Locarno. The French proposal contemplates a pact between Russia, Poland, Czechoslovakia, Germany and the Baltic States. Barthou urges that Russia must join the League of Nations if she is to take part in the pact Sir John Simon gives the proposed pact Britain's moral support, concurs in Russia joining the League, but refuses to commit Britain to any new responsibilities.

THE VALUE OF THE LEAGUE

I HAVE never listened to a debate upon foreign affairs where there has been such a deep, wide measure of agreement upon many of the most difficult and fundamental points. There is agreement, of course, in the object. The object that we all seek is peace. We all wish to prevent war. We all wish that the horrors into which we were plunged twenty years ago may never be repeated in our time. There is always agreement on the object, but there has been today, I think, a nearer approach to agreement upon the method than anything I have seen in our recent debates.

The leader of the Opposition [Mr. Lansbury] re-stated the Labour view in regard to war and upon the present situation. His re-statement faces many of the realities and dangers in a courageous manner, and I believe that the new definition of the Labour attitude will undoubtedly be a help in preserving the peace and security of this country in the difficult times which lie ahead. Then I was very glad also to hear the tribute which Sir Herbert Samuel paid to France. He spoke of French militarism as being at an end. He spoke of the ties of sympathy and agreement which exist between us and what is now almost the only great democracy in Europe. I am not quoting him; I am carrying his thoughts forward—I trust into fields where he would not be unwilling to venture.

Those are very important declarations When the Labour party definitely state that their abhorrence of war does not extend to passive recognition of flagrant wrongdoing, and when a member of the Liberal party, taking a very different course from that advocated some time ago by the Archbishop of York, goes out of his way to express his sympathy for France, there are the elements of a more general body of agreement than any we have seen hitherto.

I have been trying to seek out for myself what would be the best way of preventing war, and it has seemed to me that the League of Nations should be the great instrument upon which all those resolves to maintain peace should center, and that we should all make our contribution to the League of Nations. If there be Powers alarmed at the behavior of their neighbors, they should refer to the League, and lay their anxieties before that body It has seemed to me perfectly legitimate that the League of Nations should encourage with the sanction of international authority the formation of regional pacts between nations who may fear danger, and who seek to join hands together for mutual security against aggression. Therefore, I had the hope that the Government would nòt hesitate to further such developments. I could not see how better you can prevent war than by confronting an aggressor with the prospect of such a vast concentration of force, moral and material, that even the most reckless, even the most infuriated, leader would not attempt to challenge those great forces. It seemed to me that if a number of agreements, all under the sanction and authority of the League of Nations, grew up between Powers who have anxieties, those Powers would naturally maintain forces which were adequate to enable them to discharge their duties and their obligations, and not try to weaken each other, because there is no greater danger than equal forces If you wish to bring about war, you bring about such an equipoise that both sides think they have a chance of winning. If you want to stop war, you gather such an aggregation of force on the side of peace that the aggressor, whoever he may be, will not dare to challenge.

This process of agreements under the sanction of the League of Nations might eventually lead to a state which we should never exclude—namely, the ultimate creation of some international force, probably particularly in aviation, which would tend to place the security of nations upon a much higher foundation than it stands on at present; and it seems to me you will never get such a development by arguing on purely general grounds. If there were, over a prolonged period of time, some general cause of anxiety, which all nations, or many nations, felt, then possibly forces might come together for that purpose which, after that danger had happily been tided over, might still subsist permanently in amity. Therefore, I was very much interested to hear the lucid statement which the Foreign Secretary has made to us upon what is called the Eastern Locarno.[1] I understood that what had been done in the east was in the same sense and spirit as that which was done in the Treaty of Locarno, and that the

[1] See page 120.

spirit of mutuality and reciprocity which is so important in the Locarno Treaty is, indeed, one of the principal features in this Eastern Pact for the Guarantee of Mutual Security. That brings us to a very important consideration. It involves the reassociation of Soviet Russia with the Western European system. Remember that it is an historic event. I must say that I do not see how anyone who wishes to induce Germany to come back to the League, as she has a perfect right to do at any moment, can possibly find reasons for objecting to Russia also joining that body. The statement which the Foreign Secretary has made about the welcome which would be extended to Soviet Russia in the League of Nations is one about which there will be no dispute in this country, even among those who have the greatest prejudice against the political and social philosophy and system of government which the Russian people have, I will not say chosen for themselves, but found it necessary to adopt.

I notice that for some time the speeches of M. Litvinoff have seemed to give the impression, which I believe is a true one, that Russia is most deeply desirous of maintaining peace at the present time. Certainly she has a great interest in maintaining peace. It is not enough to talk about her as "peace-loving," because every Power is peace-loving always. One wants to see what is the interest of a particular Power, and it is certainly the interest of Russia, even on grounds concerning her own internal arrangements, to preserve peace. If Russia is to become a stabilizing force in Europe and to take her part with other countries whose danger she feels herself to share, it seems to me that that would possibly have a favorable reaction upon Russian propaganda in those other countries. There certainly would be no incentive, nothing that could be reconciled with a logical process, for Russia to make the arrangements suggested in this Eastern Pact, and at the same time to seek to weaken those countries with whom she was associated Events have their effects upon all our minds as time passes and as they present themselves to us in new forms and in different ways, and while I certainly did not expect to find myself supporting the step which has been taken, I can do so with natural feeling and without the slightest doubt that that step is in all the circumstances right and wise.

I am also very glad that the Disarmament Conference is passing out of life into history. One of the greatest mistakes that can be made is to point to the failure of the Disarmament Conference as if it were really the failure of the League of Nations, and to mix up disarmament with peace. When you have peace you will have disarmament. But there has been during these years a steady deterioration in the relations between different countries and a rapid increase in armaments that has gone on in spite of the endless flow of oratory, of well-meaning sentiments, of perorations, and of banquets. Europe will be secure when nations no longer feel themselves in danger as many of them do now. Then the pressure and the burden of armaments will fall away automatically, as they ought to have done in a long peace, and it might be quite easy to seal a movement of that character by some general agreement.

I hope, indeed, that we have now also reached the end of the period of the Government pressing France—this peaceful France with no militarism—to weaken her armed forces. I rejoice that the French have not taken the advice which has been offered to them so freely from various quarters, because I am sure that if they had done so, and if France were as weak on the land as we are weak in the air, dangers which we may now succeed in averting, dangers which we can by patience, sanity and coolness succeed in sweeping away from the lifetime of this generation, would be on top of us at the present time.

What is the dominant fact of the situation? Germany is arming. That has been the great result of the Disarmament Conference. Out of it has emerged the rearmament of Germany. Germany is arming, particularly in the air. They have already a civil aviation which is called "Air Sport" and which is, I believe, on a gigantic scale, with aerodromes, trained pilots and so forth. All they have to do is to give that vast plant a military character. It may take some time, but it will not take anything like as long as it would take us, with our very limited aviation, to develop our air armaments. I have no special knowledge of these matters, but it may well be that by this time next year German aviation will be definitely stronger than ours whatever we do. I hope that on a suitable occasion we may hear more from the Government on that point, because if that be so, it seems of the utmost importance, not only that we should lose no time in putting ourselves in an adequate position of defense, but that we should keep close relations with other Great Powers of a friendly character who have not fallen into the error which has overtaken us of late years of neglecting the essentials of our own security.

It is no use disguising the fact that there must be and there ought to be, deep anxiety in this country about Germany. This is not the only Germany which we shall live to see, but we have to consider that at present two or three men, in what may well be a desperate position, have their grip on the whole of that mighty country with its wonderful scientific, intelligent, docile, valiant people of 70,000,000. We must remember that there is no Parliament where anything can be discussed, that there is no dynastic interest such as Monarchy brings as a restraint upon policy, because it looks long ahead and has much to lose, and that there is no public opinion except what is manufactured by those new and terrible engines of broadcasting and a controlled Press. We have to consider also the risks these men run, because politics in Germany are not what they are over here. There you do not leave Office to go into Opposition. You do not leave the Front Bench to sit below the Gangway. You may well leave your high office at a quarter of an hour's notice to drive to the police-station, and you may be conducted thereafter, very rapidly, to an even harder ordeal.

Men in that position might very easily be tempted to do what even a military dictatorship would not do, because a military dictatorship, with all its many faults, at any rate is one that is based on a very accurate study of the real facts; and there is more danger in this new kind of [party] dictatorship than there would be in a military dictatorship, because you have men who, to relieve themselves from the peril which confronts them at home, might easily plunge into a foreign adventure of catastrophic character to the whole world. People may say that we have no quarrel with Germany and that Germany has no quarrel with us, but do not doubt that there is very sharp resentment against England in Germany at the present time. We may find ourselves in a position in which, if offense is taken against anything we say or do in this country, we may be confronted with an ultimatum, or very grievous action even before an ultimatum is delivered. We ought not to be in a position where we are dependent upon assistance which France could give. It is our duty to place this Empire in security at the heart and center, and to rely upon our own strength; and, believe me, we should be far more likely to keep out of trouble, and to keep the world out of trouble, if we put ourselves in that position.

I do not at all understand the line which Sir Herbert Samuel took in his carefully thought-out remarks about my being a Malay run amok,[2]

---

[2] Mr. Churchill, speaking at Wanstead on July 7, 1934, said:

"We are told that plans are being made and that paper work is proceeding. All that ought to have been done long ago. We ought to have a large vote of credit to double our Air Force; we ought to have it now, and a larger vote of credit as soon as possible to redouble the Air Force."

Commenting on this in the House of Commons on July 13, Sir Herbert Samuel said:

"Utterly regardless of any question of what parity really means in terms which arose, possibly, from an imagination lately stimulated by contact with Oriental lands. He spoke of the pre-War Cabinet of which we were both members, and of how measures had been taken then to put our naval forces into a state of adequate preparedness, and he was proud, and rightly proud, of that. Though it was extremely obnoxious, as the Foreign Secretary [Sir John Simon] reminded us, to the members of the Government of that day, yet they did their duty, and what had to be done was done; but the situation now is in many ways more dangerous than it was then. I am not to be understood to mean that the possibilities of a gigantic war are nearer, but the actual position of Great Britain is much less satisfactory than it was this time twenty years ago, for then at least we had a supreme Fleet; nobody could get at us in this island; and we had powerful friends on the continent of Europe, who were likely to be involved in any quarrel before we were. But today, with our aviation in its present condition, we are in a far worse position. The Disarmament Conference has been carried out year after year, *ad nauseam*. It must no longer delay our taking the necessary measures ourselves.

I was also very glad to hear from His Majesty's Government that a statement is now to be made, in a few days, before Parliament rises, which will proclaim without any further delay the beginning of steps to create a powerful Air Force in this country. Never mind the details. It certainly should be an effort to double the existing Air Force, and that alone would take a long time; and it is open for us to consider the situation when we have done that. Hoping and believing that that statement will be made, and will be found satisfactory, I feel entitled to congratulate the Government on at once taking the diplomatic steps which are appropriate to collective security at the present time, and also informing us of their intention to propose the military and financial measures which are required for our own safety.

of aeroplanes and other equipment, utterly regardless of any needs of the situation, he [Mr Churchill] comes forward and tells the nation that we ought straightaway to double and redouble our Air Force, that we ought to have an Air Force four times as big as we have now, without giving the smallest reasons why this colossal expenditure should immediately be undertaken That is rather the language of a Malay running amok than of a responsible British statesman. It is rather the language of blind and causeless panic."

GERMANY APPROACHING AIR PARITY WITH BRITAIN

July 30, 1934

*Socialist Vote of Censure condemning Government's
Rearmament Program*

1934

July 19. Mr. Baldwin announces a new five-year air program by which R A F. will be increased by 41 squadrons, or about 860 machines (including those already announced in the 1934 program). Of these 41 squadrons 33 will be allotted to home defense, raising the existing force at home to a total of 75 squadrons comprising 880 machines.

July 25. Assassination of Dr. Dollfuss in Vienna.

July 30. Mr. Baldwin in the House of Commons·
"Let us never forget this, since the day of the air the old frontiers are gone. When you think of the defense of England you no longer think of the chalk cliffs of Dover, you think of the Rhine. [Hon. Members: "Hear, hear."] That is where our frontier lies."

GERMANY APPROACHING AIR PARITY
WITH BRITAIN

THE position which has been unfolded to us today and the state of the world leave us in no doubt that Europe is moving ever more rapidly into a tightly drawn condition. Hatreds are rampant, disorder is rife, almost all the nations are arming, and everyone feels, as the Lord President of the Council has admitted, that the danger which we dread most of all and which we seek most of all to avert is drawing nearer to us If this be the state of Europe, what is our position in relation to Europe? We are deeply involved in Europe. We are more deeply involved, much more precisely and formally involved, in Europe than we were twenty years ago I think that is indisputable. We have signed the Treaty of Locarno. There is no doubt that we are at the present moment under obligations in regard to acts of aggression by Germany which are far more precise than any which bound us twenty years ago.

Ministers, with the full assent of Parliament, have repeatedly affirmed the sanctity, reality and modernity of these obligations. There is the Eastern Pact, which the Houses approved so generally and warmly, which does not add to our obligations but which certainly increases the contingencies in which existing obligations might become effective. Only last week we had a declaration from the Foreign Secretary reaffirming our interest in maintaining the neutrality of Belgium, in terms even stronger than before the Great War. Then there have been declarations, made, as far as I can gather, with the assent of Parliament, both sides as far as there are two sides, which have associated us with other great and friendly Powers in earnestly desiring to maintain the independence of Austria. We are to hear more about that tomorrow. Lord Halifax,[1] on Saturday, in a public speech which no doubt will be studied with great

---

[1] At that time President of the Board of Education.

care abroad, made it clear that we were not to be excluded as a factor in a possible European conflict, and, finally, the Lord President of the Council uses a phrase which I am sure by now has traveled from one end of the world to the other when he said, with his customary directness, that our frontier is the Rhine. If the Socialist Opposition had their way I gather that we should now have added the cold, unforgetting, unforgiving hostility of Japan to all these other serious preoccupations, and that the acting Leader of the Opposition would be reminding us that our frontier was the Yangtse.

What are the measures which the Government propose? We have a general scheme to spend an extra £20,000,000 in five years upon increasing our Air Force, of which we should spend £4,000,000 or £5,000,000 before the end of this Parliament. That probably means an addition to our fighting aeroplanes of perhaps fifty machines in the lifetime of the present Parliament. Instead of five hundred and fifty, which is our present home defense air strength, we shall have about six hundred by the end of the financial year 1935-6. At the present time we are the fifth or sixth air Power in the world.[2] But every State is rapidly expanding its air force. They are all expanding, but much more rapidly than we. It is certain, therefore, that when the Government, this National Government and this National House of Commons, go in 1936 to the country and give an account of their stewardship, we shall have fallen farther behind other countries in air defense than we are now.

If we extend our view over the five years' program, I believe it is also true that, having regard to the increases which are being made and projected by other countries, we shall, at the end of the period, if there is continuity of policy between the two Parliaments, be worse off in 1939 relatively than we are now—and it is relativity that counts. By that time France, Soviet Russia, Japan, the United States, and Italy, if they carry out their present intentions, will be farther ahead of us than they are now. There is no dispute about this, just in the same way as there is no dispute about the gravity of the European situation or the manner in which we are involved in it. Yet even for this tiny, timid, tentative, tardy increase of the Air Force, to which the Government have at length made up their mind, they are to be censured by the whole united forces of the Socialist and Liberal parties here and throughout the country.

---

[2] It had recently become known that Soviet Russia had constructed a large air force, second only to that of France. Britain consequently declined from fifth to sixth position in the list.

One would have thought that the character of His Majesty's Government and the record of its principal Ministers would have induced the Opposition to view the request for an increase in the national defense with some confidence and some consideration. I do not suppose there has ever been such a pacifist-minded Government. There is the Prime Minister who in the War proved in the most extreme manner and with very great courage his convictions and the sacrifices he would make for what he believed was the cause of pacifism. The Lord President of the Council is chiefly associated in the public mind with the repetition of the prayer, "Give peace in our time" One would have supposed that when Ministers like these come forward and say that they feel it their duty to ask for some small increase in the means they have of guaranteeing the public safety, it would weigh with the Opposition and would be considered as a proof of the reality of the danger from which they seek to protect us

Then look at the apologies which the Government have made. No one could have put forward a proposal in such extremely inoffensive terms. Meekness has characterized every word which they have spoken since this subject was first mooted We are assured that we can see for ourselves how small is the proposal. We are assured that it can be topped at any minute if Geneva succeeds—on which, of course, we all have expectations; I beg pardon, official expectations. We are assured of that And we are also assured that the steps we are taking, although they may to some lower minds have associated with them some idea of national self-defense, are really only associated with the great principle of collective security.

But all these apologies and soothing procedures are most curtly repulsed by the Opposition. Their only answer to these efforts to conciliate them is a Vote of Censure, which is to be decided tonight. It seems to me that we have got very nearly to the end of the period when it is worth while endeavoring to conciliate some classes of opinion upon this subject. We are in the presence of an attempt to establish a kind of tyranny of opinion, and if its reign could be perpetuated the effect might be profoundly injurious to the stability and security of this country. We are a rich and easy prey. No country is so vulnerable and no country would better repay pillage than our own. With our enormous Metropolis here, the greatest target in the world, a kind of tremendous, fat, valuable cow tied up to attract the beast of prey, we are in a position in which we have never been before, and in which no other country in the world is at the present time.

Let us remember this. Our weakness does not only involve ourselves; our weakness involves also the stability of Europe. I was very glad to hear some admission from the Lord President of the Council of how he had found himself hampered, or his representatives had found themselves hampered at Geneva, by our weakness. If it is thought that there is nothing behind your words, when you are in fact in a position of great danger yourself, not much attention is paid to what you say; the march of events takes place regardless of it. That march has been set in motion. Who can say that we shall not ourselves be dragged into it? There is also a European duty and talk about our being good Europeans. The best way in which a British Member of Parliament or statesman can be a good European is to make sure that our country is safe and strong in the first instance. The rest may be added to you afterwards, but without that you are no kind of European. All you are is a source of embarrassment and weakness to the whole of the rest of the world.

Then we are told that this might be all right for some other time, but not now. That was dwelt on by both the Opposition speakers this afternoon. Sir Herbert Samuel begged that, at any rate, we might put these measures off for at least a few more weeks in order to see what would happen at Geneva. Eight years ago we were told that disarmament had been discussed at Geneva. For two and a half years the actual conference has been proceeding. The Leader of the Liberal Opposition has, therefore, had a good run for his experiment. His hope has been abounding. It has preserved him at every stage from seeing the facts. Now, when even those who have worked as no other Government has ever worked for disarmament, when even they say that they cannot take the responsibility of remaining in the present condition, the right hon. Gentleman gets up and asks for a few more weeks' delay.

I should have thought that the time had come when Ministers must not complicate the problems that already have to be solved by endeavoring to square the discharge of their duty with the particular formulas which have gained such popularity during the course of the Disarmament Conference. If they are only doing what is their duty they have no need to apologize to the House, and still less to the public out of doors. Of course, no one wants to spend money on armaments needlessly. But the electors of all parties in the country expect a Government to provide for the safety of the Homeland. That is what the ordinary man regards as the Government's first duty, and that is what he considers they are paid for—to make sure that the country is safe. If Ministers, especially with the record and temperaments of these, come forward and demand a certain measure of additional force and personnel, they have only to put that forward with courage and conviction to gain an enormous measure of support throughout the country.

I cannot think of anything more likely to rally their forces than that we should see the two Oppositions presenting themselves on the ground that they will not support the necessary defense of the country and that they intend to utilize all the prejudice and the cry of unpopularity which they suppose may be brought against a Government which has to propose an increase of armaments. If they do that they will only be making another of those historic miscalculations upon large issues for which they have so often been severely chastised but from which they seem incapable of learning the wisdom of silence. It is a source of wonder to me that public men who have filled high office and who aspire to fill it again should be prepared, like the leaders we see opposite, to vote for either of the Motions which are put forward from the Opposition side. Such an act is of a far-reaching character. It will not affect the decision of Parliament, but by so doing hon. Members opposite place themselves in an invidious position as to which they may be required to give an answer, in circumstances which no human being can foresee.

The need and the interest which the Government have in doing their duty turn upon whether the measures which they propose are really a contribution to our security or not. If they are not, then the Government run the risk of falling between two stools. Their duty is to provide adequate measures of defense before it is too late. Whatever they propose, they are going to be assailed by the pacifists throughout the country with all that interested and unscrupulous vituperation which we saw in the squalid election at Fulham some time ago and which finds an echo in these Votes of Censure this afternoon. Whatever the Government do, they are going to have that thrown at them, and it is vital therefore that they should so shape their course as to gather around them and behind them all the forces upon which they would naturally rely and to which they would look for support upon a question of this character. To encounter all this storm for something which is insufficient to meet the need is to have the worst of both worlds. The Government will get their abuse, but we shall not get our defense.

We must assume, of course, that Ministers have considered this aspect of the matter and that they see where their duty and their interest lie, but I must point out that there are no grounds whatever for suggesting that it is not possible to increase the Air Force more rapidly than is now proposed. I conceive that there are many ways of rapidly augmenting our Air Force which the Government have not adopted at present. The decision which they have just taken is a deliberate decision, and I confess I find it difficult to believe that it makes adequate provision against the dangers which we have to face and which are admitted.

It is no use examining national defense in the abstract and talking in vague and general terms about hypothetical dangers and combinations which cannot be expressed. Before the War the Liberal Government of those days did not hesitate to specify the quarter from which they expected danger, and they did not hesitate to specify the navy against which we were determined to maintain an ample superiority. We measured ourselves before the War publicly and precisely against Germany. We laid down a ratio of 16 to 10 against existing programs and of 2 to 1 against any additions to those programs. Such calculations are perfectly well understood abroad. They were stated publicly, and they bred no ill-will and caused no offense. As a matter of fact, the contrary was the case, and I think I shall be borne out in that statement by those who remember what happened in those days. As the preponderance of our Navy grew stronger our relations with Germany steadily improved, and they were never better than in the last few months before the War. [*Laughter.*] It is a fact that the relations between Great Britain and Germany were never better than on the eve of the War, which arose from troubles entirely outside our relations with the German Government. The fact that our Navy was measured against the German Navy played no part in bringing about that struggle, and therefore I propose to speak quite plainly about Germany.

My question to the Government is this What is their view about the German military air force? The Lord President used some sentences upon this point which I think were not cast by him with the intention of achieving any special degree of clarity. I understand, of course, that officially Germany has no air force at all. She is prohibited by the solemn treaties which she signed after the War from having any military aviation. But the right hon. Gentleman said that the worst crime is not to tell the truth to the public, and I think we must ask the Government to assure us that Germany has observed and is observing her treaty obligations in respect of military aviation. If so, I shall be greatly relieved, and I think the House will be greatly relieved. But if that assurance cannot be given—

and, of course, it cannot be given—then I say we are bound to probe and examine what is taking place as far as we are in a position to do so. It was different when we were talking about Dreadnoughts You could not build Dreadnoughts in boat-houses on the Elbe, and what Admiral von Tirpitz said before the War was found to be true—that nothing outside the regular program was being embarked upon. It is a different matter with regard to aeroplanes which can be so easily constructed and their component parts assembled. Military aviation shades into civil aviation by such indefinable graduations that I dare say the Government are right in not making statements which would in fact be charges and no doubt would be capable of being rebutted or denied.

I will venture, however, to assert some broad facts. I shall be delighted if the Government are able to contradict them. I first assert that Germany has already, in violation of the Treaty, created a military air force which is now nearly two-thirds as strong as our present home defense air force. That is the first statement which I put before the Government for their consideration. The second is that Germany is rapidly increasing this air force, not only by large sums of money which figure in her estimates, but also by public subscriptions—very often almost forced subscriptions—which are in progress and have been in progress for some time all over Germany. By the end of 1935 the German air force will be nearly equal in numbers and efficiency—and after all no one must underrate German efficiency, because there could be no more deadly mistake than that—it will be nearly equal, as I say, to our home defense air force at that date even if the Government's present proposals are carried out.

The third statement is that if Germany continues this expansion and if we continue to carry out our scheme, then some time in 1936 Germany will be definitely and substantially stronger in the air than Great Britain. Fourthly, and this is the point which is causing anxiety, once they have got that lead we may never be able to overtake them If these assertions cannot be contradicted, then there is cause for the anxiety which exists in all parts of the House, not only because of the physical strength of the German air force, but I am bound to say also because of the character of the present German dictatorship If the Government have to admit at any time in the next few years that the German air forces are stronger than our own, then they will be held, and I think rightly held, to have failed in their prime duty to the country.

I ask, therefore, for a solemn, specific assurance from the Government that at no moment for which they will have responsibility will they fail to have a substantially superior military air force at home to that which they have reason to believe has been set on foot in Germany. Can that assurance be given? Will it be given? I think it will make a great difference to the judgment which must be passed upon these proposals if the Government are in a position to say that that is their resolve.

But in this connection we must face some of the facts about German civil aviation and British civil aviation. I am assured that the German civil aviation is three or four times as large as our civil aviation, but that is only part of the story. The British civil aviation is in its character purely commercial, and the machines cannot be converted for military purposes without falling far below the standard of war machines. Our civil machines would have little war value if they were to be converted. We are the only country whose civil aviation is so completely divorced from the technical military aspects. The German machines, on the other hand, have been deliberately and scientifically planned by the Government for the express purpose of being converted into war machines. Not only have they a speed and a design suited for this purpose, going at over 200 miles an hour, but the whole scheme of conversion has been prepared and organized with minute and earnest forethought. I am perfectly ready to be corrected, and no one will be more pleased than I to hear a convincing, an overwhelming, answer on the subject, but I am informed that the bomb-racks which would be substituted for the passenger accommodation in a great number of these fast German civil machines have already been made and delivered, and it would be a matter of only a few hours to unbolt the one and fasten in the other.

The same story can be told about the pilots Germany has a trained personnel of pilots which is many times more numerous than our own. Gliders are a wonderful means of training pilots, giving them air sense, and there are, I believe, over 500 qualified glider pilots in Germany, whereas we have only about fifty in this country. If, therefore, you have to add to the regular increase in German military aeroplanes, which we have to expect and which, I imagine, the Government are well informed about, and which alone will bring the forces almost to equality by the end of 1935—if you have to add to that an enormous and indefinite transference of pilots and machines from civil to military aviation, it would seem that there is a very obvious danger that before the end of next year we shall be definitely weaker than the German aviation. I have tried to state these facts with moderation, and, as I say, nothing would give me greater pleasure than to learn that I have discovered another mare's nest.

I shall rejoice at my own discomfort if these facts are able to be over-turned or superseded by other more reassuring facts. But unless these facts can be contradicted, precisely and categorically, it seems to me that our position is a very serious one, and that not only should we brush aside a Vote of Censure on this small increase, but that we should urge a much greater degree of action, both in scale and speed, upon the responsible Ministers.

Our weakness in the air has a very direct bearing on the foreign situation, and on those foreign obligations to which I ventured to refer at the beginning of my remarks. So long as our policy harmonized with that of France and that of other countries who were the allies or associates of France, the preponderance against Germany, if Germany became an aggressor, would be so large as to constitute a deterrent against any action other than action so desperate as to be almost insane. But a new series of questions arises. We must ask ourselves whether we wish to be dependent on France for our domestic safety. We must ask ourselves whether we can accept the protection of a foreign country for any long period of time without losing that freedom to place our own interpretation upon our Continental obligations which, it seems to me, is absolutely vital to the sound conduct of our affairs. We have these obligations, but we still have the right to judge according to our sense of justice and the circumstances of the time.

I should have thought that the pacifists and the isolationists would have joined with His Majesty's Government in urging that we should at least make our island independent of foreign protection for its safety. If, however, owing to the long delays to which we have agreed in the hope of arriving at some arrangement at Geneva, we have fallen behind and are not able to put ourselves in a secure position, it seems to me that we must harmonize our policy with that of France and of the other powerful countries who are associated with France. That, it seems to me, is absolutely necessary. But what is the course of those who now urge us to pass this Vote of Censure? They have been doing all that they could to urge France to disarm and have pleaded for German equality of armaments.

[Mr. COCKS: The Government have done that.]

The hon. Gentleman and his followers are the driving force. What I have regretted so much is the attention that has been paid to these evil counsels. The hon. Gentleman has shown more sanity than many of those among whom he sits, but undoubtedly the course which hon. Gentlemen opposite have adopted would have the effect of weakening France, and if France had disarmed and Germany rearmed I shudder to think what the state of Europe might be at this very moment. The hon. Gentlemen opposite are very free-spoken, as most of us are in this country, on the conduct of the German Nazi Government. No one has been more severe in criticism than the Labour party or that section of the Liberal party which I see opposite. And their great newspapers, now united in the common cause, have been the most forward in the severity of their strictures But these criticisms are fiercely resented by the powerful men who have Germany in their hands. So that we are to disarm our friends, we are to have no allies, we are to affront powerful nations, and we are to neglect our own defenses entirely. That is a miserable and perilous situation. Indeed, the position to which they seek to reduce us by the course which they have pursued and by the vote which they ask us to take is one of terrible jeopardy, and in voting against them tonight we shall hope that a better path for national safety will be found than that along which they would conduct us.

THE GERMAN AIR MENACE

November 28, 1934

Debate on the Address

1934

August 2. Death of President von Hindenburg. By new law the offices of Chancellor and President are united, and Hitler appoints himself "Leader and Chancellor."

August 19. German plebiscite (38 4 millions vote for Hitler, 7 millions abstain or vote against him).

October 4. Conference of the National Union of Conservative Associations unanimously carry resolution moved by Lord Lloyd expressing "grave anxiety at the inadequacy of the provision made for Imperial Defense."

November 23. Mr. Baldwin states at Glasgow that a "collective peace system is impracticable."

THE GERMAN AIR MENACE

I BEG to move, at the end of the question, to add the words:

> But humbly represent to Your Majesty that, in the present circumstances of the world, the strength of our national defenses, and especially of our air defenses, is no longer adequate to secure the peace, safety and freedom of Your Majesty's faithful subjects [1]

To urge the preparation of defense is not to assert the imminence of war. On the contrary, if war were imminent preparations for defense would be too late. I do not believe that war is imminent or that war is inevitable, but it seems very difficult to resist the conclusion that, if we do not begin forthwith to put ourselves in a position of security, it will soon be beyond our power to do so. What is the great new fact which has broken in upon us during the last eighteen months? Germany is rearming. That is the great new fact which rivets the attention of every country in Europe—indeed, in the world—and which throws almost all other issues into the background. Germany is rearming, that mighty power which only a few years ago, within our own experience, fought almost the whole world, and almost conquered. That mighty Power is now equipping itself once again, 70,000,000 of people, with the technical apparatus of modern war, and at the same time is instilling into the hearts of its youth and manhood the most extreme patriotic, nationalist and militarist conceptions. According to what we hear, according to what we are told and what comes in from every quarter, though little is said about it in public, Germany has already a powerful, well-equipped army, with an excellent artillery, and an immense reserve of armed, trained men. The German munition factories are working practically under war conditions,

[1] The Amendment stood in the names of Mr. Churchill, Sir Robert Horne, Mr. Amery, Captain F. E. Guest, Lord Winterton, and Mr. Boothby.

and war material is flowing out from them, and has been for the last twelve months in an ever broadening flow Much of this is undoubtedly in violation of the treaties which were signed. Germany is rearming on land; she is rearming also to some extent at sea; but what concerns us most of all is the rearmament of Germany in the air.

In my Amendment other aspects of defense besides the air are comprised, but I shall confine myself absolutely to the danger from the air. I shall be specially careful not to exaggerate. Indeed, I hope that every statement that I make will be admitted to be an under-statement I shall try my utmost to keep within the limits of what is really known and proved.

Let us, first of all, look at the dimensions of the danger as it affects this country at the present time. However calmly surveyed, the danger of an attack from the air must appear most formidable I do not accept the sweeping claim of the extreme votaries of the air. I think that a great many statements which are made are calculated to frustrate the purpose of reasonable precautions by presenting the problem as if it were one which was insoluble. But, without accepting these claims, no one can doubt that a week or ten days' intensive bombing attack upon London would be a very serious matter indeed. One could hardly expect that less than 30,000 or 40,000 people would be killed or maimed.

The most dangerous form of air attack is the attack by incendiary bombs Such an attack was planned by the Germans for the summer of 1918, I think for the time of the harvest moon. The argument in favor of such an attack was that if in any great city there are, we will say, fifty fire-brigades, and you start simultaneously one hundred fires and the wind is high, an almost incalculable conflagration may result. The reason why the Germans did not carry out that attack in 1918 must be stated. It was not at all, as Lord Mottistone suggested in another place, that our air defense had become so excellent that we were protected against it. It was because the advance of the Allied Armies, with the British Army in the van, already confronted the Imperial Government of Germany with the prospect of impending defeat, and they did not wish to incur the fury of retribution which would follow from such a dreadful act of power and terror as would have been involved in such a raid. Since those days the incendiary thermite bomb has become far more powerful than any that was used in the late War. It will, in fact, I am assured by persons who are acquainted with the science, go through a series of floors in any building, igniting each one practically simultaneously.

Not less formidable than these material effects are the reactions which will be produced upon the mind of the civil population. We must expect that under the pressure of continuous air attack upon London at least 3,000,000 or 4,000,000 people would be driven out into the open country around the Metropolis. This vast mass of human beings, numerically far larger than any armies which have been fed and moved in war, without shelter and without food, without sanitation and without special provision for the maintenance of order, would confront the Government of the day with an administrative problem of the first magnitude, and would certainly absorb the energies of our small Army and of our Territorial Force. Problems of this kind have never been faced before.

Then there are the docks of London and the estuary of the Thames. Everyone knows the dependence of this immense community, the most prosperous in the whole world, upon the eastern approaches by water. We studied it very carefully in the War, and I have not the slightest doubt that it has weighed very much on the minds of His Majesty's Government. It ought not to be supposed that the danger of an air attack, assuming that such a thing occurred, would necessarily be confined to London or the area around it. Birmingham and Sheffield and the great manufacturing towns might all be made the subject of special study, and every part of the country is equally interested in whatever measures of security can be taken to provide against such a peril. Not less dangerous than the attack upon the cities and the great working-class areas and upon the manufacturing centers would be that directed upon the dockyards and the oil-fuel storage, which unless proper precautions are taken, as I trust they have been or are being taken, might actually paralyze the Fleet, with consequences which no one can fail to perceive.

The danger which might confront us would expose us not only to hideous suffering, but even to mortal peril, by which I mean peril of actual conquest and subjugation. It is just as well to confront those facts while time remains to take proper measures to cope with them. I may say that all these possibilities are perfectly well known abroad, and no doubt every one of them has been made the subject of technical study. I have therefore stated to the House as briefly as possible—and I trust I have not overstated the case—the kind of danger which reasonably ought to be taken into consideration should, unhappily, a breakdown in European peace occur.

I come to the more difficult and much more debatable question of what remedy can be applied. What measures can we take to provide against these very great perils, or at any rate to mitigate and minimize their effects? I do not think, to give a personal opinion, that it is much use planning to move our arsenals and factories over to the west side of the island. When one considers the enormous range of modern aeroplanes and the speeds at which they travel—230 and 240 miles an hour—it is evident that every part of this small island is almost equally within range of attack. If vast sums of money were spent in displacing our arsenals from their present position, it might well be found that before this cumbrous process was completed improvements in aeroplanes would have more than discounted any advantage which might have been gained. The flying peril is not a peril from which one can fly. It is necessary to face it where we stand. We cannot possibly retreat. We cannot move London. We cannot move the vast population which is dependent on the estuary of the Thames. We cannot move the naval bases which are established along our southern coasts with the great hereditary naval populations living around them. No doubt where new factories were being created the factor of distance would be an important consideration, but in the main I am afraid we shall have to face this peril, whatever it may be, where we stand.

It would be a great mistake to neglect the scientific side of defense against aircraft attack—of purely defensive action against aircraft attack. Certainly nothing is more necessary, not only to this country but to all peace-loving and peace-interested Powers in the world and to world civilization, than that the good old earth should acquire some means or methods of destroying sky marauders. It is a matter which is of interest to us all that we should be able to meet this present menace which no generation before our own has faced, which shakes the very fabric and structure of all our civilized arrangements, and, by spreading fear and danger far and wide, makes it more and more difficult to preserve security and tranquillity in the minds of the different great States. If anything can be discovered that will put the earth on better terms against this novel form of attack—attack by spreading terror throughout civil populations—anything that can give us relief or aid in this matter will be a blessing to all.

I hope that the Government will not neglect that aspect of the question. There is a committee, I have no doubt, studying it. It ought to be the strongest committee possible, it ought to have the greatest possible latitude, and it ought to be fed with the necessary supplies to enable experiments of all kinds to be made against this danger. I have heard many suggestions with which I would not venture to trouble the House now, but they ought to be explored and explored thoroughly, and with all the force of the Government behind the examination. It ought to be not merely a question of officers of a Department doing their best, but of the force of the Government, and I do hope that the Lord President when he replies will tell us that steps of this kind will be taken, that there will be no danger of service routine or prejudice or anything like that preventing new ideas from being studied, and that they will not be hampered and subjected to so many long delays as were suffered in the case of the tanks and other new ideas during the Great War.

The fact remains that when all is said and done as regards defensive methods, pending some new discovery the only direct measure of defense upon a great scale is the certainty of being able to inflict simultaneously upon the enemy as great damage as he can inflict upon ourselves. Do not let us undervalue the efficacy of this procedure. It may well prove in practice—I admit you cannot prove it in theory—capable of giving complete immunity. If two Powers show themselves equally capable of inflicting damage upon each other by some particular process of war, so that neither gains an advantage from its adoption and both suffer the most hideous reciprocal injuries, it is not only possible but it seems probable that neither will employ that means. What would they gain by it? Certainly a Continental country like Germany with large foreign armies on its frontiers, would be most unwise to run the risk of exposing itself to intensive bombing attacks from this island upon its military centers, its munition establishments and its lines of communication, at a time when it was engaged or liable to be engaged by the armies of another first-class Power.

We all speak under the uncertainty of the future which has so often baffled human foresight, but I believe that if we maintain at all times in the future an air power sufficient to enable us to inflict as much damage upon the most likely potential aggressor as he can inflict upon us, we may shield our people effectually in our own time from all those horrors which I have ventured to describe. If that be so, what are £50,000,000, or £100,000,000 raised by tax or by loan, compared with an immunity like that? Never has so fertile and so blessed an insurance been procurable so cheaply.

Observe the reverse of the picture. Assume that one country has a powerful air force and that the other has none, or that the other country has been so decisively beaten in the air that it has hardly any air force left. Then not only war machines but almost any flying machine that can be fitted to carry bombs will be employed to go over and to torture every part of the State and the community in that other country until it surrenders all that is asked from it. Absolute subjugation could in the end be enforced by such air attack, once a country had lost all power to fight in the air. Once complete ascendancy in the air had been secured, the victor Power might almost at leisure pick out any aircraft factory and make an intensive attack upon it, and thus there could be no recovery. It is almost the only form of war that we have seen in the world in which complete predominance gives no opportunity of recovery. That is the odious new factor which has been forced upon our life in this twentieth century of Christian civilization.

For all these reasons we ought to decide now to maintain, at all costs, in the next ten years, an Air Force substantially stronger than that of Germany, and that it should be considered a high crime against the State, whatever Government is in power, if that force is allowed even for a month to fall substantially below the potential force which may be possessed by that country abroad. That is the object with which I have put this Amendment on the Paper. I am not going into other questions than those with which I am specially concerned today, but I must just mention that if, to this provision which I have suggested, you add those measures towards collective security [i e , regional pacts] by placing, as it were, special constables upon the dangerous beats in Europe and perhaps later on elsewhere, under the ægis and authority of the League of Nations, I firmly believe that we may have it in our power to avert from this generation the supreme catastrophe of another war. The idea that we can intervene usefully in sustaining the peace of Europe while we ourselves are the most vulnerable of all—are the beggars, in fact—is one which cannot be held firmly by any man who looks at this in the faithful discharge of his duty.

I have now spoken of the danger, and I have indicated, as far as I can see, what is the only remedy or mitigation which is in our power, and I have suggested that it is a good and effective mitigation and a very reasonable security. I now come to compare the actual strengths, present and prospective, of Great Britain and Germany, as far as I have been able to form an opinion about them. Here again there is no reason to assume that Germany will attack us. In fact, the German people have very friendly feelings in many ways towards us, and there is no reason at all why we should expect that they would attack us; but it is not pleasant for us to feel that it may soon be in the power of the German Government to do so unless we act.

I will not dwell this afternoon on the character of the present German Government, because the House knows it well, and there is no need to repeat all that. I will content myself by saying that the decision of a handful of men, the men of the 30th of June, is all that is required to launch an attack upon us, if such an attack were possible, and that only the shortest notice or no notice at all could be counted upon Never in our history have we been in a position where we could be liable to be blackmailed, or forced to surrender our possessions, or take some action which the wisdom of the country or its conscience would not allow. It is a danger to all Europe that we should be in that position and I do not think His Majesty's Government ought to put us or leave us in such a plight, where we, with our wealth and Empire, exist on the good behavior and good faith, which may not be lacking, but which may not endure, of the present rulers of Germany. I am sure our people are not willing to run such risks, and yet, as I am going to show, I think indisputably, this is the kind of danger which is coming upon us in a very short time unless we act upon a great scale and act immediately.

According to the Treaty of Versailles, the German Government are not allowed to build any military aircraft or to organize any military air force Now this stipulation was intended to be a protection to the other countries and for their greater security and assurance, but it has in fact become an additional danger. What was meant for a safeguard for the Allies has in fact become only a cloak or a mask for a potential aggressor. With any other country, the facts about its air development would have been stated quite promptly. We could have put a question on the Paper as to the strength of the air force of France, or the United States, or any other country. In fact, the League of Nations collects these figures It is part of the process of waging war against war that there shall be full disclosure, that people shall know where they stand, so that at any rate, if you cannot remove fear, at least you can remove suspicion.

But the time has come when what was meant to be a protection for others must no longer be a cloak or a mask for Germany. The time has come when the mystery surrounding the German rearmament must be cleared up. We must know where we are. The House naturally in these matters leaves the main responsibility to the Executive, and that is quite right, but at the same time it cannot divest itself of responsibility for the safety of the country, and it must satisfy itself that proper measures are being taken. I will therefore this afternoon assume the duty of stating what, to the best of my belief, are the strengths and programs of the German military air force which is being built up in contravention of the Treaty, and I invite the Lord President to confirm, correct, or contradict me when he speaks, as I believe he is going to do immediately after I sit down. If he does not contradict me or correct me, the House should assume that the statements which I make are true or that they are understatements. In order that my right hon. Friend might be able to deal effectively with these issues and might not be confronted with them abruptly in the House, I sent him last week a précis of the exact points which I propose to put to him, and I understand that he has had an opportunity of consulting with the high expert authorities upon this matter.

I therefore assert, first, that Germany already, at this moment, has a military air force—that is to say, military squadrons, with the necessary ground services, with the necessary reserves of trained personnel and material—which only await an order to assemble in full open combination—and that this illegal air force is rapidly approaching equality with our own. Secondly, by this time next year, if Germany executes her existing program without acceleration, and if we execute our existing program on the basis which now lies before us without slowing down, and carry out the increases announced to Parliament in August last, the German military air force will this time next year be in fact at least as strong as our own, and it may be even stronger. Thirdly, on the same basis—that is to say, both sides continuing with their existing programs as at present arranged—by the end of 1936—that is, one year further on, and two years from now—the German military air force will be nearly 50 per cent. stronger, and in 1937 nearly double. All this is on the assumption, as I say, that there is no acceleration on the part of Germany, and no slowing down on our part.

I come to civil aircraft which are capable of being used for military operations, the dual-purpose machines, as they are called in Germany. Here the story is very much worse for us. Germany has already between 200 and 300 machines of long range with great speed, 220 to 230 miles an hour, which are now ostensibly or actually employed in carrying mail-bags and to some extent in carrying passengers; these machines can be converted into long-distance bombers of the highest efficiency

in a few hours. All that is necessary is to remove some parts of the passenger accommodation and fit bomb-racks in their place. These bomb-
racks, I told the House five months ago, are already made and kept
in close proximity to the machines. That is the position at the present
time. Germany has already between 200 and 300 of these machines. This
time next year the number will have risen to at least 400 of these machines, which in the case of war will be a direct addition to the German
military air force.

Against that we, as I understand, can set nothing that is in the slightest
degree comparable for military purposes. Our civil aviation is valueless for
war purposes. Indeed, it has been the custom of Ministers and others to
boast of this fact as proof of our pacific intentions—if, indeed, proof were
needed. Everyone knows that we have built for comfort and for safety,
and without the slightest contemplation of convertibility. Therefore, I
assert—and I invite the Government to contradict the statement if they
can—that by this time next year, taking both the military and the convertible civil air craft into consideration, Germany will have a substantially stronger air force than Great Britain. Frankly, I do not think that the
country has prepared itself to realize this fact. The conditions in 1936
and 1937, if the German convertible machines are added to the military
machines, will be that the figures of the German air force will be far
more adverse to this country than the purely military figures, which are
bad enough, that I gave a few moments ago.

I come to ordinary civil aviation. It is difficult to compute the value
of this for war, but it represents reserve pilots, mechanics, landing-grounds,
factories, aerodromes and a general familiarity with the flying art, which
is, indirectly, of great importance. I think you may say that civil aviation
bears the same relation to the fighting force as the mercantile marine
has for so many generations borne to the Royal Navy. It is quite certain
that the German pool of civil aviation, from which a military air force
can be expanded and developed, is already far larger and far more
closely related to military purposes than ours. The principle underlying
German civil aviation, and all the regulations and subventions, point to
their commercial machines being made efficient for rapid transformation
into military or training machines.

Nor is Germany neglecting defensive preparations. Air alarm arrangements, gas drill and so forth are taking place all over Germany
as well as in many other parts of the continent of Europe. The House
must not miss the bearing of this upon retaliation, upon the protection

one can get from the power of retaliation, because if of two populations, both exposed to attacks of this kind, one has all kinds of protection which enable it to avoid loss of life, it is perfectly obvious how great will be the injury to the one unprepared. I know that the Government have been considering this matter, and I understand the reason why nothing has been done is the fear of frightening the population. It is much better to be frightened beforehand than when the danger actually comes to pass. It is much better to be frightened now than to be killed hereafter.

I am assured that many of the German aerodromes are proof against air attack. They build concrete embankments round the shelters where the aeroplanes are stored, so that the place is quite safe; whereas you have only to look at the aerodromes of our Air Force to see that they are vulnerable to any attack, and might be put out of action altogether. Anyone, however pacific he may be, must surely admit that there is no proper protection of our aerodromes. I think that this is a primary and an urgent duty of the Government. I heard the Debate the other day upon the devastated areas of our country. Many suggestions were made for remedying the situation. Suppose there is a great deal of work to do in earthing up these aerodromes which will have to be constructed; why not give it to those unemployed people? Recruit twenty or thirty thousand men from those areas on good wages, and let them go about the country and do this necessary work, instead of being employed on relief work and so forth. Let them act, not as unemployed, but as a labor reserve, and let them go forward and revivify their own homes by sending back the wages which they earn by doing the most necessary and urgent of public tasks.

I have now completed my review of the two countries, and I invite my right hon. Friend the Lord President to state, if I am wrong, where I am wrong, and to what extent I am wrong. But I cannot leave this subject without also referring to another cause of anxiety. So far I have dealt with what, I believe, is the known, but beyond the known there is also the unknown. We hear from all sides of an air development in Germany far in excess of anything which I have stated today. As to that, all I would say is: Beware. Germany is a country fertile in military surprises. The great Napoleon, in the years after Jena, was completely taken by surprise by the strength of the German army which fought the War of Liberation Although he had officers all over the place, the German army which fought in the campaign of Leipzig was three or four times as strong as he expected. Similarly, when the Great War broke out the French general staff had no idea of the reserve divisions which would be brought immediately into the field They expected to be confronted by twenty-five army corps; actually more than forty came against them.

It is never advisable to underrate the military qualities of this remarkable and gifted people, nor to underrate the dangers that may be brought against us. I only say it does not follow that, in the figures I have given today, I am not erring grievously on the side of understatement. It sounds absurd to talk about 10,000 aeroplanes, but, after all, the resources of mass production are very great, and I remember when the War came to an end the organization over which I presided at the Ministry of Munitions was actually making aeroplanes at the rate of 24,000 a year, and planning a very much larger program for 1919 Of course, such numbers of aeroplanes could never be placed in the air at any one moment, nor a tenth of them, but the figures give an idea of the scale to which manufacture might easily rise if long preparations have been made beforehand, and a great program of production is launched.

The danger I have dealt with. I have mentioned the remedy so far as it can be described, and I have compared the two air forces. But what have we done in the last year? This is the last aspect with which I wish to deal. We had a Debate last March, and there was a good deal of anxiety expressed. The Lord President made a very weighty declaration, and he overwhelmed the Debate. But in the evening the Debate revived, and a great deal of anxiety was expressed for a more explicit statement, and my right hon. Friend showed a little less than his usual urbanity and patience, and said, "If you are not satisfied, you can go to a Division." What was the use of going to a Division? You might walk a majority round and round the Lobbies for a year, and not alter the facts by which we are confronted. What happened after the March Debate? Very little —so far as I can see, nothing happened for five months. Then we came to July. In July the right hon. Gentleman came down to the House with the full authority of the Government and announced the program of the forty-two new squadrons to be added to the Air Force in five years. I pointed out there and then that this scheme did not propose to strengthen the Air Force even by one additional squadron before the 31st of March next, and only by fifty machines—that is to say, fifty machines in their proper squadrons with all their reserves—by 31st March, 1936. Another five months have passed, and we now know that nothing has been done, and that nothing will be done before the 31st of March which would involve a Supplementary Estimate. I am well aware of all that has been rightly said of the complication of this service and the necessity of preliminary preparation, and so forth. I will deal with that not now, but when an opportunity occurs upon the Air Estimates. To continue this dilatory process in the present situation, even for a few more months, and certainly for another year, will deprive us of the power ever to overtake the German air effort. I therefore invite His Majesty's Government to tell us, firstly, what are the facts; and, secondly, when the facts are established, what will be their action.

I have not always found myself in full agreement with this House of Commons, but I have never lost all hope that it will prove itself to be what its creators hoped for it, a great House of Commons in the history of the country. The election which brought this House into power was one in which the greatest number of voters ever called upon to exercise the franchise in this country voted, above all things, for the maintenance of the strength and the security of their native land. That was the emotion which brought us into power, and I would venture to say: Do not, whatever be the torrent of abuse which may obstruct the necessary action, think too poorly of the greatness of our fellow-countrymen. Let the House do its duty. Let the Government give the lead, and the nation will not fail in the hour of need.

Mr. BALDWIN *in the course of his reply said:*

"Even now, when things look at their blackest, I have not given up hope either for the limitation or for the restriction of some kind of arms. . . .

"I think it is correct to say that the Germans are engaged in creating an air force. I cannot give the actual number of service aircraft, but I can give two estimates between which probably the correct figure is to be found. The figures we have range from a figure, given on excellent authority and from a source of indisputable authority, of 600 aircraft to the highest figure that we have been given, also from good sources, of something not over 1000. The probability is that the actual figure ranges between those two. . . .

"The first-line strength of the regular units of the Royal Air Force today, at home and overseas, is 880 aircraft. Of these, including those of the Fleet Air Arm, 560 are at present stationed in the United Kingdom. There are also at home the Auxiliary Air Force and the Special Reserve squadrons, with an establishment of 127 aircraft, making a total of just under 690 aircraft available today in the United Kingdom that could be put into the first line. But the House must realize that behind our regular first-line strength of 880 aircraft there is a far larger number either held in reserve to replace the normal peace-time wastage or in current use in training and experimental work. Therefore I say that there is no ground at this moment for undue alarm and still less for panic. There is no immediate menace confronting us or anyone in Europe at this moment— no actual emergency....

"We propose to form in the years 1935 and 1936 22 squadrons for home defense and, in addition, three squadrons for the Fleet Air Arm. These 25 squadrons are additional to the four already forming in the current year. That means that by 1936 our first-line strength will be increased by some 300 aircraft over its present figure....

"I think the House will see ... that no time has been lost in giving effect to the desire of the House that the program should be proceeded with. In view of the rapid progress we are making we find it will be necessary to bring in a Supplementary Estimate in February....

"It is not the case that Germany is rapidly approaching equality with us. I pointed out that the German figures are total figures, not first-line strength figures, and I have given our own first-line figures and said they are only first-line figures, with a considerably larger reserve at our disposal behind them. Even if we confine the comparison to the German air strength and the strength of the Royal Air Force immediately available in Europe, Germany is actively engaged in the production of service aircraft, but her real strength is not 50 per cent. of our strength [2] in Europe today. As for the position this time next year, if she continues to execute her air program without acceleration, and if we continue to carry out at the present approved rate the expansion announced to Parliament in July, so far from the German military air force being at least as strong as, and probably stronger than, our own, we estimate that we shall still have a margin in Europe alone of nearly 50 per cent. I cannot look farther forward than the next two years. Mr. Churchill speaks of what may happen in 1937. Such investigations as I have been able to make lead me to believe that his figures are considerably exaggerated."

[2] In reply to Lord Winterton, who asked whether Mr Baldwin included the Mediterranean in Europe, Mr. Baldwin said, "I referred to machines available for home defense which are stationed in the United Kingdom."

MR. BALDWIN'S MISTAKES

March 19, 1935

Air Estimates

1935

January 13. Saar Plebiscite. Nine-tenths vote for return to Germany.

March 4. Publication of White Paper on Imperial Defense calling attention to the accumulation of "serious deficiencies in all the Defense Services," and incidentally referring to German rearmament

March 6. The German Government notifies the British Government that the Chancellor is suffering from a severe cold and that therefore Sir John Simon's visit must be postponed.

March 16. German conscription proclaimed.

March 19 The Under-Secretary of State for Air tells the House of Commons:
"If I may take the figure of the current year, the figure of 1020, that represents the first-line strength of the British Air Force all the world over, including the Fleet Air Arm and auxiliary squadrons, but not including any reserve machines or any machines used for training purposes If you deduct the first-line machines overseas it will give you 690 this year, 810 for 1935, and 950 for 1936....
"We have no official statistics, but, according to the latest information in our possession, it is not correct that Germany is already stronger than this country. Even confining comparison to the number of machines we have in this country in terms of first-line strength, we believe that, including the Auxiliary Air Force and the special reserves and the Fleet Air Arm squadrons based on home waters, we have a substantially stronger force It is also not correct to say that at the end of the present calendar year the German air force will be 50 per cent. stronger than ours, either on the basis of first-line strength or on the basis of total aircraft So far as we can at present estimate we shall still, at the end of this year, possess a margin of superiority."

MR. BALDWIN'S MISTAKES

IN THE comparisons of air strength we suffer very much because there is no accurate knowledge and definite terminology by which it can be compared Happily this difficult matter is not complicated by any differences about the standard towards which we should work. The Lord President of the Council in March 1934 laid down, in the most plain and solemn manner, his view of what our air-power standard should be. I must read what he said from the Official Report:

> ...Any Government of this country—a National Government more than any, and this Government—will see to it that in air strength and air power this country shall no longer be in a position inferior to any country within striking distance of our shores.[1]

Therefore, those of us who accept that statement have no need to go into questions of alliances, or difficult aspects of foreign policy, or questions of international morality and pacifism which have played, and ought to play, a part in these various debates. We have a perfectly definite objective proclaimed in March last by the highest authority on a most serious occasion, and I take that as the starting-point of the argument that I wish to put before the House. In November of last year, supported by some friends of mine, I moved an Amendment to the Address representing that

> In the present circumstances of the world the strength of our national defenses, and especially of our air defenses, is no longer adequate to secure the peace, safety and freedom of your Majesty's faithful subjects.[2]

[1] See p. 103.
[2] See p. 141.

I do not think that the course of events has in any way stultified those who put down that Amendment. I must apologize for quoting what I said in that Debate, but it is necessary to my argument today. I said:

> I therefore assert, first, that Germany already, at this moment, has a military air force—that is to say, military squadrons, with the necessary ground services, with the necessary reserves of trained personnel and material—which only await an order to assemble in full open combination— and that this illegal air force is rapidly approaching equality with our own.[3]

In reply to that statement the Lord President made a momentous announcement, and confirmed the fact that Germany was forming, or had formed, a military air force.[4] Hitherto the official view had been that Germany was observing the Treaty which precluded her from having a military air force. But, as a result of that Debate in November, the statement of the Lord President to which I have referred was made. Subsequent events have shown how true it was. In reply to the further statements which I made my right hon. Friend uttered very definite contradiction, and it is with those contradictions that I wish to deal. He said:

> It is not the case that Germany is rapidly approaching equality with us. ... Her real strength is not 50 per cent. of our strength in Europe today.

That is to say, half our strength in Europe. That directly contradicted the assertion which I had made. My right hon. Friend further proceeded to say, "As for the position this time next year" (that would be November 1935),

> ... so far from the German military air force being at least as strong as, and probably stronger than, our own, we estimate that we shall still have in Europe alone a margin of nearly 50 per cent. I cannot look farther forward than the next two years.

Does my right hon. Friend adhere to that statement today? I wonder whether he will tell us when he speaks whether further information has led him to modify those very striking statements. Certainly, if they are true they are enormously reassuring. If, by any chance, my right hon. Friend has been misled into making an understatement or an erroneous statement I am sure that he would wish to correct it at the first oppor-

[3] See p. 148.
[4] See p. 152

tunity. At any rate, I propose to examine and analyze those two statements. But before I do so I must say a word on the question of terminology. The Lord President warned us on that same 28th of November of the danger of making false comparisons. He said:

> The total number of service aircraft which any country possesses is an entirely different thing from the total number of aircraft of first-line strength. The total number, of course, includes the first-line strength and all the reserve machines used in practice and many things of that kind. I would like the House to remember that one may get a wholly erroneous picture in making comparisons, just to mention the aircraft of our own country, when perhaps the figures that have been mentioned are but the figures of first-line strength.

That is perfectly true, and we are indebted to my right hon. Friend for establishing these definite categories, so that we can carry on something like intelligent discussion upon air matters. Military aircraft and first-line strength are two different categories. I wish, therefore, this afternoon to examine the air power of Great Britain and Germany in both categories—that of military aircraft and that of first-line strength. I will deal with the position last November, when, dealing with the German position, the Lord President said:

> The figures we have range from a figure, given on excellent authority, of 600 aircraft—600 military aircraft altogether—to the highest figure that we have been given, also from good sources, of something not over 1000. The probability is that the actual figure ranges between those two, near which limit I cannot say; but it is interesting to note that in the French Chamber the French Government—and I do not think their tendency would be to minimize figures—gave the figure of the military aircraft at 1100.

I believe it will be found that my right hon. Friend, or those who advised him, mixed up the two classes that we were asked to keep separate in our minds. Instead of saying that Germany had 600 military aircraft, he should have said that Germany had 600 first-line air strength. However, taking the basis of those figures for comparison, let us see what are the comparable figures given by my right hon. Friend for Great Britain. The Lord President said:

> The first-line strength of the regular units of the Royal Air Force today, at home and overseas, is 880 aircraft. Of these, including those of the Fleet Air Arm, 560 are at present stationed in the United Kingdom. There are also at home the Auxiliary Air Force and the Special Reserve squadrons,

with an establishment of 127 aircraft, making a total of just under 690 aircraft available today in the United Kingdom that could be put into the first line. But the House must realize that behind our regular first-line strength of 880 aircraft—

my right hon. Friend seems to have used the total figure for the British Empire in dealing with home defense—

there is a far larger number either held in reserve to replace the normal peace-time wastage or in current use in training and experimental work

I must draw the attention of the House to certain defects in that statement. My right hon. Friend says that 560 first-line air strength aircraft were available for the defense of the United Kingdom, and in order to make those figures look larger 127 auxiliary aircraft were added to produce a total of 687 Those auxiliary aircraft are not fairly comparable to the whole-time regular units of the Royal Air Force. There is the same kind of gap between them and the Royal Air Force as there is between the Territorial Army and the whole-time professional Army.[5]

The actual facts are perfectly well known abroad. If those 127 auxiliary aircraft are to be added to the British first-line strength, then at least 300 fast commercial dual-purpose bombing machines which exist in Germany, ready and available for immediate conversion, will have to be added on the other side, which would alter the count even more to our disadvantage. Therefore, from a study of all that has been said it is apparent that in November on a comparable basis the German first-line air strength was 600 and the British home defense, including the Naval Air Arm, was 560.

Now I come to military aircraft. The 1000, or 1100, military aircraft then possessed by Germany no doubt include 300 fast dual-purpose bombing machines. What is the comparable British figure? The Lord President did not mention it in November; he left it veiled. But the Under-Secretary has told the House this afternoon that the military machines at the present time consist of 890, plus 130 of the auxiliary force, which makes exactly 1020. On this basis the British and German air forces at the end of November would appear to have been as follows: first-line strength, Great Britain 560, Germany 600; military aircraft, Great Britain 1020, without training machines, and Germany 1100. Beyond all question these are much the most favorable figures from our point of view which could

[5] Mr. Churchill was not at this time fully appreciative of the efficiency of the Territorial Squadrons.

possibly be cited. But even taking them as they are, they altogether dis-
prove the first assertion of the Lord President of the Council on the 28th
of November, because they show the two countries virtually on an
equality, neck and neck, whereas the Lord President said:

> It is not the case that Germany is rapidly approaching equality with
> us....Her real strength is not 50 per cent. of our strength in Europe today.

I come to the second and more disquieting stage of my argument
Since our Debate in November four months have passed, and during
that period our position has sensibly changed for the worse. The German
Government have announced, formally and publicly, that on the 1st of
April—that is, in thirteen days' time—it is their intention to constitute
a military air force. They are going to assemble all those elements which
have hitherto been altogether unofficial in strong units of the German
regular air force. It involves no great change. It only means officers
putting on their badges of rank which have hitherto been tacitly understood. We do not know what proportion of the vast pool of their military, commercial and sporting aviation Germany will declare as their
first-line air strength, but I have no doubt that they will declare the
lowest figure—that is, 600 first-line air strength—and it may easily be
doubled, and more than doubled. I must point out that I have been using
only the minimum figures, but although they are minimum figures, they
are amply sufficient to prove the case. I do not wish to use alarmist
figures unless they are forced upon me by the fact that one cannot close
one's eyes to them. But I take no responsibility—and I wish to make this
clear in case there is any inquest afterwards into all these statements. I
must not be understood to be giving even as a private Member any
assurance that the actual truth may not be much worse than the figures
I have cited.

Last November in the same Debate the Lord President of the Council
gave the figures of the German army which has been formed contrary
to the Treaty as 300,000 men in 21 divisions. Only four months after,
Germany declared on Saturday last, what we knew—that there are
500,000 men in barracks, for compulsory universal service to sustain 36
divisions. The 21 has grown to 36. It may be—indeed, it is—only natural
to assume that the expansion of the German air force will bear the same
proportion of the new German army as the air forces of other conscript
countries bear to the armies of those countries; it will undergo the same
expansion; and it may be that an even more unpleasant surprise awaits

His Majesty's Government on the 1st of April than occurred when the German army scheme was declared on Saturday last.

But what will be the relative position a year from now—that is, at the end of the next financial year? We are to add during the year 11 squadrons of nine machines each—let us say 100 machines to our first-line air strength. Eleven new squadrons will come into being with all their appurtenances and reserves. The Under-Secretary said, evidently with great pleasure, that the Air Ministry were ordering over 1000 new machines. We want to know how many new machines are being delivered. The machines may be ordered so late in the year as not really to be anything but paper decisions; and we must deal with realities in this matter. When I looked at Vote 3 I found that only £1,000,000 more was being taken for this part of the construction vote—that is, £6,800,000 instead of £5,800,000—and I do not see how the addition of £1,000,000 can possibly make such a very large addition to our Air Force. Nor does it in fact, because the Under-Secretary, with complete candor, has shown exactly the amount of the advance in British military aircraft during the year, and has told us that we now possess 1020, and that at the end of the year we shall have 1170—that is, an increase of 150 machines.

We know that the financial provisions only permit of an addition of 150 machines of this type and the addition of 11 squadrons, which will raise our first-line air strength for home defense to 659 and our military aircraft to 1170, exclusive of training machines. What, then, will be the German first-line air strength at the end of this year? We cannot tell. We shall learn officially on the 1st of April, and it is no use speculating on what they will declare as their first-line air strength. I must confine myself to the other factor, German military aircraft.

Here, again, mystery shrouds all German preparations. At various points facts emerge which enable a general view to be taken. Enormous sums of money are being spent on German aviation and upon other armaments. I wish we could get at the figures which are being spent upon armaments. I believe that they would stagger us with the terrible tale they would tell of the immense panoply which that nation of nearly 70,000,000 of people is assuming, or has already assumed. But there are certain things which strike one. For instance, the population of Dessau increased during last year by 13,000. Dessau is a center of the great Junkers aeroplane works, but it is only one of four or five main factories of Germany. There are at least twenty others of a secondary but important character; and 13,000 people are known to have entered the town of

Dessau—I do not say that they are all workers—in the course of last year. One can see what the scale of production must be. Further, owing to the fact that the Germans had to prepare their air force in secret and unofficially, there has grown up a somewhat different method of producing aircraft from that which obtains in this country and in France. Much smaller elements are actually made outside the main factories than over here. Nuts and bolts and small parts are spread over an enormous producing area of small firms, and then they flow into the great central factories. The work which is done there consists in a rapid assembly, like a jig-saw puzzle or Meccano game, with the result that aeroplanes are turned out with a speed incomparably greater than in our factories, where a great deal of the earlier stages of the work is done on the spot.

I must set forth these facts because they are very important. According to yesterday's *Daily Telegraph,* between 250 and 300 military aircraft have been added to Germany's total since November. I fear it will be found that the German factories are working up from their present rate of output of more than 100 a month to some unknown monthly increase. It may be 100, 120 or 140 a month; I do not pretend to be able to say. Nothing I have gathered from the newspapers enables me to judge what the ultimate result will be, but it seems to me that if you take the next twelve months at an average output of 125 machines a month—I am sure there are a great many people who will scoff at such a low figure, and I may be only making myself ridiculous by using it and may afterwards be mocked at for doing so—even if you take that moderate figure of 125, it will mean an addition to Germany's military aircraft in the financial year 1935–36 of 1500, of which a portion will go to replace wastage, and the rest will be a net addition to their total military aircraft strength. That is many times larger than any program of deliveries provided in this Estimate, which we see is concerned with an increase of 150, plus the natural wear and tear and wastage. Therefore, I am unable to accept the second statement of my right hon. Friend the Lord President in November last, which I have read to the House and will read again:

> As for the position this time next year...so far from the German military air force being almost as strong as, and probably stronger than our own, I estimate that we shall have in Europe alone a margin of nearly 50 per cent.

On the contrary, I must submit to the House that the Lord President was misled in the figures which he gave last November, quite unwittingly no doubt, because of the great difficulty of the subject. At any rate, the true position at the end of this year will be almost the reverse of that which he stated to Parliament. We must remember also that Germany's scale of reserves, judging by the lectures which are being delivered at different times by those who have been presiding over German aviation development, is 200 per cent. The reason is this: it will take them three months to get their peace-time industry working at full blast on a war-time basis, and they calculate on a loss of 100 per cent. of aeroplanes per month in time of war. They hope to transfer the whole of the civilian industry to maintain their air force on a wastage of 100 per cent. a month. They have, of course, made preparations for converting the entire industry of Germany to war purposes by a single order of a detail and refinement which is almost inconceivable. I am certain that Germany's preparations are infinitely more far-reaching than our own. So that you have not only equality at the moment, but the greater output which I have described, and you have behind that this enormous power to turn over, on the outbreak of war, the whole force of German industry.

It is admitted at the present time that the only effective means of defense against air attack is retaliation and counter-attack, and, from the point of view of counter-attack, the Germans seem to have a great advantage over us. Although they declare that their force is purely defensive, it has a much larger percentage of long-distance bombing machines than any other force—far larger than we have ourselves.

The next point is a matter of geography. The frontiers of Germany are very much nearer to London than the sea-coasts of this island are to Berlin, and whereas practically the whole of the German bombing air force can reach London with an effective load, very few, if any, of our aeroplanes can reach Berlin with any appreciable load of bombs. That must be considered as one of the factors in judging between the two countries. We only wish to live quietly and to be left alone. If it is thought that the power to retaliate is a deterrent—I believe it is—to an outrageous attack, then it seems that we are at a disadvantage in that respect, quite apart from any numerical disadvantage. I was very glad indeed that the Prime Minister today, in answer to Sir Austen Chamberlain, spoke about the committee which is to examine defensive measures against aeroplane attacks. That is a matter in which all countries, in my opinion, have a similar interest—all peaceful countries. It is a question not of one country against another, but of the ground against the air, and unless the dwellers upon earth can manage to secure the air above their heads it is almost impossible to forecast the misfortunes and fears which this invention, of which the world has proved itself so utterly unworthy, may bring upon them.

One of the factors to be remembered is the preparation made by the civilian population on either side to guard themselves against an air raid. Obviously if one side has made good preparations the loss inflicted upon it will be very much less than that inflicted on the side which has made no preparation at all. Great panics may arise if this is not foreseen. Up to the present what has been done on the Continent is incomparably ahead of anything that has been even presented on paper publicly here. It takes a frightfully long time to get anything done in this country. We move like a slow-motion picture in all these matters.

I do not think my right hon. Friend's solemn pledge, that we are not inferior to any country within striking distance, is being kept, or that it will be kept, because the efforts which are being made will not be made by this country alone. The great advance of German aviation is only now beginning to assume its full force. The program which was announced in this country in August last was hopelessly inadequate. Its leisurely, stinted execution has so far made no appreciable addition to our strength. The provision for this year is hopelessly inadequate. We are told that we are expanding as fast as we can, but that the preparations have to be made, that aerodromes have to be bought, the training schools enlarged, and that all this takes time. There are many arguments which the Government can use to show how slow and difficult the work is. I do not accept those arguments at their face value.

I am sure that if the vigorous measures that the situation requires were adopted to put ourselves in a position of defensive security, very much more rapid progress could be made in every branch But even if the argument were true and there is to be this great delay, if we can only proceed by such very gradual stages, then I say that the responsibility of the Government and of the Air Ministry will be all the greater. If the necessary preparations had been made two years ago when the danger was clear and apparent, the last year would have seen a substantial advance, and this year would have seen a very great advance. Even at this time last year, if a resolve had been taken, as I urged, to double and redouble the British Air Force as soon as possible—Sir Herbert Samuel described me as a Malay run amok because I made such a suggestion— very much better results would have been yielded in 1935, and we should not find ourselves in our present extremely dangerous position.

Everyone sees now that we have entered a period of peril. We are faced, not with the prospect of a new war, but with something very like the possibility of a resumption of the War which ended in November, 1918. I still hope, and I believe—the alternative would be despair—that it may be averted. But the position is far worse than it was in 1914, and it may well be found to be uncontrollable. We are no longer safe behind the shield of our Navy. We have fallen behind in the vital air defense of this island. We are not only far more deeply and explicitly involved in Continental affairs than we were in 1914, but owing to the neglect of our own defenses we have become dependent upon other countries for our essential security.

From being the least vulnerable of all nations we have, through developments in the air, become the most vulnerable, and yet, even now, we are not taking the measures which would be in true proportion to our needs. The Government have proposed these increases. They must face the storm. They will have to encounter every form of unfair attack. Their motives will be misrepresented. They will be calumniated and called war-mongers. Every kind of attack will be made upon them by many powerful, numerous and extremely vocal forces in this country. They are going to get it anyway. Why, then, not fight for something that will give us safety? Why, then, not insist that the provision for the Air Force should be adequate, and then, however severe may be the censure and however strident the abuse which they have to face, at any rate there will be this satisfactory result—that His Majesty's Government will be able to feel that in this, of all matters the prime responsibility of a Government, they have done their duty.

MR. BALDWIN'S CONFESSION

May 2, 1935

Supply (Foreign Office Vote)

1935

March 23. Sir John Simon leaves for Berlin.

March 27. Sir John Simon tells the Cabinet that his discussions with Herr Hitler have disclosed considerable divergences of view between the two Governments. Hitler rejects proposed Eastern Pact, and has no interest in collective system of peace and security, though not unwilling to return to the League of Nations on his own terms. He would give no guarantee with regard to Austria. He would not hear of withdrawing the conscription order, and he stated that Germany has now achieved parity with Great Britain in the air.

April 12. Stresa Conference. France, Italy and Britain agree to co-operate to secure independence of Austria.

April 17. League Council takes note of the French accusation that Germany's reintroduction of conscription and creation of military air force is a deliberate repudiation of Treaty obligations, and condemns Germany's action.

May 2. Franco-Soviet Pact signed in Paris.

MR. BALDWIN'S CONFESSION

WE have before us in the sphere of foreign policy three new and separate documents of importance. We have the League of Nations resolution;[1] we have the declarations of the Stresa Conference;[1] and we have the Prime Minister's article in his own organ, the *News-Letter*. I find myself— I think in common with the great majority of the House, not in one party but in all parties—in very general agreement with the Prime Minister and His Majesty's Government upon the measures taken by the Government in these three documents. The sentiments set forth in the *News-Letter* about the dangers of German rearmament are akin to those which I myself have expressed several times in the last two or three years, beginning in the autumn of 1932. The Stresa declaration, including the statement that the three Powers, Great Britain, Italy and France, will keep in touch with one another and are pledged to study the maintenance of peace in common, seems to be no more than national safety or national survival requires. There remains the Resolution of the Council of the League of Nations complaining of the growth of German armaments and of the unilateral violation of treaties. I have seen a great deal of criticism in quarters where one would least expect it of France for appealing to the League of Nations against Germany, and of the League of Nations for giving a faithful verdict upon the questions submitted for their judgment.

When I hear extreme pacifists denouncing this act of the League of Nations I am left wondering what foundation these gentlemen offer to countries for abandoning individual national armaments. We are reminded how in a state of savagery every man is armed and is a law unto himself, but that civilization means that courts are established, that

[1] See p. 168.

men lay aside their arms and carry their causes to the tribunal. This presupposes a tribunal to which men, when they are in doubt or anxiety, may freely have recourse. It presupposes a tribunal which is not incapable of giving a verdict. Personally, I admire greatly the self-restraint and courage with which France addressed herself to the League of Nations. It was far better surely than that she should have dealt in ultimatums or should have seized territories as hostages, as would have been the practice in former generations. She appealed to the tribunal which has been set up, and I do also admire the spirit of that tribunal and of these different countries, some great and some small, drawn from different parts of the world, who showed themselves, according to their lights, prepared to give justice. If we are to be told now it was very wrong for France to go to the League of Nations, and how foolish and tactless of the League to give its opinion, if that view is to be held by those who have hitherto told us to look to this international procedure, then they have absolutely stultified all their arguments, for never again, if that is the case, will nations be prepared to abandon the security which resides in strong national armaments. All that prospect—the only prospect which opens itself before our eyes—of establishing a reign of law and building up a great international structure to which all nations will accede—that prospect and hope will dwindle and die away. Therefore, I am in general agreement with His Majesty's Government upon all these three steps which have been taken by them in the last few months in company with other nations.

If I criticize these measures it is not at all because of their character, but because of their tardiness. Why was all this not done two or three years ago? If the Prime Minister two years ago had thought what he now says in his *News-Letter* about the German danger, he need perhaps never have published his thoughts to the world. Instead of lecturing the German nation, now already so heavily armed, he could have imparted his ideas as wise guidance to our own Cabinet. If only the French Government two and a half years ago, when the German process of rearmament began, had laid their much-talked-of dossier before the League of Nations and demanded justice or protection from the concert of Europe; if only Great Britain, France and Italy had pledged themselves two or three years ago to work in association for maintaining peace and collective security, how different might have been our position. Indeed, it is possible that the dangers into which we are steadily advancing would never have arisen. But the world and the Parliaments and public opinion would have none of that in those days. When the situation was manageable it was neglected, and now that it is thoroughly out of hand we apply too late the remedies which then might have effected a cure. There is nothing new in the story. It is as old as the Sibylline Books. It falls into that long, dismal catalogue of the fruitlessness of experience and the confirmed unteachability of mankind Want of foresight, unwillingness to act when action would be simple and effective, lack of clear thinking, confusion of counsel until the emergency comes, until self-preservation strikes its jarring gong—these are the features which constitute the endless repetition of history.

All this leads me to the principal matter—namely, the state of our national defenses and their reactions upon foreign policy. Things have got much worse, but they have also got much clearer. It used to be said that armaments depend on policy. It is not always true, but I think that at this juncture it is true to say that policy depends, to a large extent, upon armaments. It is true to say that we have reached a position where the choice of policy is dictated by considerations of defense. During the last three years, under the Government of Herr Hitler, and before him under that of Chancellor Bruning, Germany worked unceasingly upon a vast design of rearmament on a scale which would give the Germans such a predominance in Europe as would enable them, if they chose—and why should they not choose?—to reverse the results of the Great War. The method should be noted. The method has been to acquire mastery in the air, and, under the protection of that mastery, to develop—and it is fortunately a much longer process—land and sea forces which, when completed, would dominate all Europe. This design is being completed as fast as possible, and the first part of it—German ascendancy in the air—is already a fact. The military part is far advanced, and the naval part is now coming into view.

For the last two years some of us have been endeavoring to convince His Majesty's Government of the scale and pace at which German aviation was progressing. We debated it in March 1933, on the Air Estimates of 1934, in August 1934, in November 1934, and quite recently —in March 1935. On all these occasions the most serious warnings were given by private Members who spoke on this subject, of whom I was one. The alarm bells were set ringing, and even jangling, in good time if only they had been listened to. This afternoon I am not concerned with what private Members said in giving their warning, but I am bound to address myself to the main statements and promises which were elicited on these occasions from His Majesty's Government. In March 1934 we had the first declaration of the Lord President:

> Any Government of this country—a National Government more than any, and this Government—will see to it that in air strength and air power this country shall no longer be in a position inferior to any country within striking distance of our shores.

That declaration was considered of high importance. That was in March, but nothing happened until August, when, under the pressure, not, indeed, of those hon. Gentlemen in this House who were raising this matter, for their pressure could easily have been disdained—but under the pressure of events, the Government produced a five years' program for increasing the home defense portion of the Royal Air Force to 75 squadrons, comprising 880 machines, by 1939. Anyone could see that that was utterly inadequate, and that it bore no relation whatever to the pace at which German aviation was developing and to the military character which it was assuming. At that time, nine months ago, I urged that without a day's delay measures should be taken, first to double, and then to redouble the Royal Air Force. Anyone can see now, and most of all the Ministers responsible, that the policy of doubling and redoubling the Air Force which I then proposed was the least which should have been set on foot. If nine months ago these measures had been begun you would today have been beginning to reap the harvest and beginning to obtain results, and very different would have been the position. In November some of us moved an Amendment to the Address, and I took the responsibility then of making some definite statements, or rather understatements, about the German air menace. In order that the Government should have an opportunity of consulting their expert advisers, I supplied the Lord President with a précis in advance, and upon this he made a series of strong declarations. I must read these to the House.

> It is not the case that Germany is rapidly approaching equality with us. ...Her real strength is not 50 per cent. of our strength in Europe today. As for the position this time next year—

that is, November of this year—

> ...so far from the German military air force being at least as strong as, and probably stronger than, our own, we estimate that we shall still have in Europe alone a margin of nearly 50 per cent.

It is quite true that my right hon. Friend in that second statement said, "Provided that there is no acceleration in Germany." But it is very difficult to know what is acceleration when the original speed at which the German air force was constructed is not known and when the final limit at which they are aiming is known. Then came this declaration, the most important that we have had—the Prime Minister has repeated it today:

> His Majesty's Government are determined in no conditions to accept any position of inferiority with regard to what air force may be raised in Germany in the future.

Here we have an assertion that the Government, with all their sources of information, were convinced that they had, and would continue to have for many months, a large air superiority over Germany, and that in no case would they fail to maintain what has been called air parity with Germany. These assurances were accepted. Mr. Lloyd George spoke in that debate. I remember his speech well. He declared himself completely reassured. He declared himself in agreement with the principle that we should maintain our parity, and said that he was completely reassured by the fact that we still had this air superiority and that the Government intended to maintain it unbroken in the future. The Leader of the Liberal party [Sir Herbert Samuel] accepted it, and he too rapidly decided in his own mind that the Government statement was right and that mine was wrong.

That was in November. Only six weeks ago the Under-Secretary of State for Air was put up to say that at that date, in March 1935—that is to say, last March—we had a substantial superiority over Germany, and that in November of this year we should still have superiority.[2] Only six weeks have passed since then, and surely we are entitled to ask what has happened to bring about the extraordinary change in the whole color and configuration of the landscape? We are told that Herr Hitler made a statement to the Foreign Secretary at Berlin in the conversations, which it now seems were most fortunately undertaken—otherwise I suppose we should never have known.[3] We have not always been accustomed to

[2] March 19. See p. 156.
[3] Replying to the debate, later in the day, Sir John Simon said, "We have since been informed that that statement which was made to us was intended to imply that Germany's first-line strength was equivalent to a British front-line strength of some 800 or 850 aircraft. This is not including auxiliary or special reserve units, but it is including the British figures of aircraft overseas."

depend for our information upon statements, however frank and friendly, that may be made by Rulers of other States. All these statements that were made by the Lord President, and later, on behalf of the Government, and under instructions from the Government by the Under-Secretary for Air, are admitted to be untrue. I do not say that they were made in bad faith, but they were utterly wrong. They were the reverse of the truth, and more than the reverse of the truth. [*Laughter.*] Certainly. If the Government statement was that we should be 50 per cent. stronger than Germany at a certain date and we find that they are 50 per cent. stronger than we are, it was the reverse of the truth, and far worse than that. Is there a Member of the Government who will get up now and say that in November next we shall still have a 50 per cent. superiority over Germany? Is there a member of the Government who will still assert that in March last, six weeks ago, we had a substantial superiority, or that we have a superiority today? No, Sir. The whole of these assertions, made in the most sweeping manner and on the highest authority, are now admitted to be entirely wrong. We have had a confession from the Prime Minister today that the then estimates have been found to be below what is now understood to be the truth.

There is a second unpleasant chapter on this subject of which I will merely indicate the title and the contents. The German military machines have all been produced within the last two and a half years. Therefore they are of the latest design. An hon. Gentleman has just placed in my hands a telegram which has arrived and been published in one of the evening newspapers, in which General Goering says, "We have no old machines. Our planes are the most up-to-date in existence." Many of our designs, on the other hand, are seven or eight years old. The average of our machines—these facts are perfectly well known; there is nothing in them that is not known, or I would not say it—is certainly double the age of the designs which have been created in Germany. It cannot be disputed that both in numbers and in quality Germany has already obtained a marked superiority over our home defense Air Force.

But it is the third chapter of this story which is the most grievous. The rate and volume which the output of German military aeroplanes has attained is many times superior to our own. The Under-Secretary told us six weeks ago that the additions that would be made to our first-line air strength, which was then thought sufficient, would be 151. There is reason to believe, as I said on that occasion, that the comparable German output of military machines is between, at least, 100 and 150 per month.

Many people would put it much higher. The German air industry is therefore turning out military machines at perhaps ten times the rate at which ours are turned out, and those machines are being formed into squadrons for which long-trained, ardent personnel are already assembled, and for which an ample number of aerodromes are already prepared. Therefore, at the end of this year, when we were to have had a 50 per cent. superiority over Germany, they will be, at least, between three and four times as strong as we are.[4]

Behind all this rapid peace-time production lies the industry of Germany, fully organized for war manufacture and steadily tending in its character to the condition of war manufacture. This can be drawn upon at any time gradually and to any extent which they choose. Where, then, is this pledge of air parity, and that we would not accept any inferiority to whatever the German air force might be? The Prime Minister said today that the Lord President's declaration stands. It stands only as a declaration. The facts do not support the assertion. It is absolutely certain that we have lost air parity already both in the number of machines and in their quality. It is certain that at the end of this year we shall be far worse off relatively than we are now. Our home defense force will be for a long period ahead a rapidly diminishing fraction of the German air force. It may reasonably be urged that the units of the German Air Force, having been prepared in conditions of secrecy, have not at the present time acquired the efficiency of our squadrons in air tactics and in formation flying. It is very dangerous to underrate German efficiency in any military matter. All my experience has taught me to think that any such supposition would be most imprudent. Anyhow, now that the Germans are openly marshaling and exercising their squadrons and forming them with great rapidity, we may take it that six months of this summer and autumn will amply give them the combined training which they require, having regard to the long careful individual preparations which have been made. Therefore, any superiority which we may at this moment possess in personnel and in formation flying and in air maneuvering is a wasting asset, and will be gone by the end of the autumn, having regard to the enormously increased German air strength and the superiority of their machines.

The Prime Minister in his article in the *News-Letter* used the word "ambush." The word must have sprung from the anxieties of his heart,

---

[4] This forecast was unduly pessimistic in point of time, and in fact the German production after the original bound was slowed down.

for it is an ambush into which, in spite of every warning, we have fallen. I have stated the position in general terms, and I have tried to state it not only moderately but quite frigidly. Here I pause to ask the Committee to consider what these facts mean and what their consequences impose. I confess that words fail me. In the year 1708 Mr. Secretary St. John, by a calculated Ministerial indiscretion, revealed to the House the fact the battle of Almanza had been lost in the previous summer because only 8000 British troops were actually in Spain out of the 29,000 that had been voted by the House of Commons for this service. When a month later this revelation was confirmed by the Government, it is recorded that the House sat in silence for half an hour, no Member caring to speak or wishing to make a comment upon so staggering an announcement. And yet how incomparably small that event was to what we have now to face. That was merely a frustration of policy. Nothing that could happen to Spain in that war could possibly have contained in it any form of danger which was potentially mortal.

But what is our position today? For many months, perhaps for several years, most critical for the peace of Europe, we are inexorably condemned to be in a position of frightful weakness. If Germany were the only Power with which we were concerned, if we stood alone compared with Germany, and if there were no other great countries in Europe who shared our anxieties and dangers and our point of view, and if air warfare were the only kind of warfare by which the destinies of nations was decided, we should then have to recognize that this country, which seemed so safe and strong a few years ago, which bore with unconquerable strength all the strains and shocks of the Great War, which has guarded its homeland and its independence for so many centuries, would lie at the discretion of men now governing a foreign country. There are, however, friendly nations with whom we may concert our measures of air defense, and there are other factors, military and naval, of which in combination we can dispose. Under the grim panoply which Germany has so rapidly assumed there may be all kinds of stresses and weaknesses, economic, political and social, which are not apparent—but upon these we should not rest ourselves.

It seems undoubted that there is an effective policy open to us at the present time by which we may preserve both our safety and our freedom. Never must we despair, never must we give in, but we must face facts and draw true conclusions from them. The policy of detachment or isolation, about which we have heard so much and which in many ways is so attractive, is no longer open. If we were to turn our backs upon Europe, thereby alienating every friend, we should by disinteresting ourselves in their fate invite them to disinterest themselves in ours. Is it then expected that we could go off with a wallet full of German Colonies gathered in the last war and a world-wide collection of territories and trade interests gathered in the past, when the greatness of our country was being built up, while all the time we should in this vital matter of air defense be condemned to protracted, indefinite and agonizing inferiority? Such a plan has only to be stated to be rejected.

There is a wide measure of agreement in the House tonight upon our foreign policy. We are bound to act in concert with France and Italy and other Powers, great and small, who are anxious to preserve peace I would not refuse the co-operation of any Government which plainly conformed to that test as long as it was willing to work under the authority and sanction of the League of Nations. Such a policy does not close the door upon a revision of the Treaties, but it procures a sense of stability, and an adequate gathering together of all reasonable Powers for self-defense, before any inquiry of that character can be entered upon. In this august association for collective security we must build up defense forces of all kinds and combine our action with that of friendly Powers, so that we may be allowed to live in quiet ourselves and retrieve the woeful miscalculations of which we are at present the dupes, and of which, unless we take warning in time, we may some day be the victims.

THE INCREASING TENSION

May 22, 1935

Supply (Defense Policy, considered in Committee)

May 15. Lord Hailsham, in the House of Lords, refuses to entertain the idea of appointing a Minister to direct the policy and method of supply of the three Services. He maintains that effective co-ordination between the three Services is now secured by the Committee of Imperial Defense with the assistance of the Cabinet Secretariat and the Chiefs of Staff Committee.

May 19. General election in Czechoslovakia. Government holds 149 out of 300 seats. Henlein polls 70 per cent. of German votes and obtains 44 seats, thus becoming second largest party in the Chamber.

May 21. Herr Hitler, in a speech delivered in the Reichstag, declares that:
"Germany cannot return to the League of Nations until there is a real equality of status for all members.

"Germany has broken away from those articles of the Treaty of Versailles which involved discrimination against her, but for the revision of other articles she will rely on 'peaceful understandings.' The German Government are ready to accept such limitations of armaments as are accepted by other Powers. They are ready for an air agreement to supplement Locarno.

"The German Government intend not to sign any Treaty which seems to them incapable of fulfillment, but will scrupulously observe every treaty voluntarily concluded, even if it was drawn up before their assumption of power and office. In particular they will hold to and fulfill all obligations arising out of the Treaty of Locarno so long as the other partners are ready to stand by that Treaty The German Government regard the observance of the demilitarized zone as a contribution towards the appeasement of Europe of an unheard-of hardness for a sovereign State. They feel obliged to point out that the continual increase of troops on the other side can in no way be regarded as a complement to these endeavors."

"They propose the gradual abolition and outlawry of weapons and methods of war contrary to the spirit of the Geneva Red Cross Convention. The prohibition of bombing outside the battle zone could be extended to the outlawry of all air bombing.

"The German people wish for peace; it must be possible for the Government to preserve it. Germany neither intends nor wishes to interfere in the internal affairs of Austria, to annex Austria, or to conclude an 'Anschluss.'"

May 22. Mr. Baldwin tells the House:
"First of all, with regard to the figure I gave in November of German aeroplanes, nothing has come to my knowledge since that makes me think that that figure was wrong. I believed at that time

it was right. Where I was wrong was in my estimate of the future. There I was completely wrong. We were completely misled on that subject....

"Subsequent examination in Berlin revealed the fact from those authorized to speak for him that Hitler had at that time from 800 to 850 aircraft In the course of those conversations Herr Hitler made it clear that his goal was parity with France. Now we are basing our estimates on that strength It is always difficult to know what parity is or from what angle it is envisaged We have to make a certain amount of guesswork there, and for our purposes, for the parity of the three nations, we have taken a figure of about 1500 first-line aircraft. That is very much the figure that is given in the League of Nations Annual, and you can take the figure and make a deduction for aircraft in the Far East, and you will get somewhere round about that figure of 1500. And that is the figure to which we intend to proceed with all the speed we can.

"I would repeat here that there is no occasion, in my view, in what we are doing, for panic. But I will say this deliberately, with all the knowledge I have of the situation, that I would not remain for one moment in any Government which took less determined steps than we are taking today. I think it is only due to say it, that there has been a great deal of criticism both in the Press and verbally about the Air Ministry as though they were responsible for possibly an inadequate program, for not having gone ahead faster and for many other things. I only want to repeat that, whatever responsibility there may be—and we are perfectly ready to meet criticism—that responsibility is not that of any single Minister, it is the responsibility of the Government as a whole, and we are all responsible, and we are all to blame."

May 22. Lord Londonderry, Secretary of State for Air, cautions the House of Lords against taking an exaggerated view of Germany's air strength.[1]

[1] See Lord Londonderry's book, *Ourselves and Germany,* p. 73· "Herr Hitler's information [to Sir John Simon] on the subject of German air strength came as a rude shock to the British public, and gave meaning to the repeated advice tendered by myself as Air Minister as to the danger constituted by our depleted armaments and by our endeavor to give an example of disarmament to the rest of the world. The uncertainty of the situation, accentuated by a Press which had long viewed with alarm the apparent complacency of the Government in view of the increasing menace of Continental report, had its effect on the Prime Minister and his nearest colleagues, and my task was transformed from seeking to warn the Government of our weakness in air defense into the very necessary attempt to allay the growing anxiety of those chiefly responsible for the security of the realm, who appeared to imagine that a German air force of trained pilots and up-to-date machines had developed in two years far superior to our own."

THE INCREASING TENSION

THE Lord President was very wise when he declined to form, or to ask the Committee to form, a decisive opinion upon the extremely important speech delivered yesterday by Herr Hitler.[1] It would be a pity, however, if at the very outset there arose a feeling that some new and extremely hopeful situation had been created. I did not find ground for such a feeling. The attitude which was disclosed by the Head of the German Government towards collective security, or pooled security—an excellent phrase which I believe is current on the Front Opposition Bench—was far from encouraging. The attitude towards non-interference in other countries, which had special relation to Danubian problems, was also far from encouraging. The reference made to the demilitarized zone, and to the inconceivable difficulty of Germany observing the sanctity of that zone in view of the French defensive preparations behind their own frontier, was also, I thought, more likely to excite than to allay concern.

I welcomed very much the language which Herr Hitler used against the indiscriminate bombing of civilian populations It gave me pleasure to read those words, and I am sure that that was the feeling of everyone who read them Certainly we must take them as a means of pressing this point forward. At the same time I am bound to remind the Committee that the German air force, which has been so newly created, contains a larger proportion of long-distance bombing machines as compared with other types than any other air force in the world

Lastly, there was the question of the abolition of the submarine. There again we shall all be agreed. No power in the world would be more glad to see the submarine abolished than what is still the first of the naval Powers of the world. But there is not much chance of universal

[1] See p. 180.

agreement being reached upon that subject. It is not likely to be a step which we shall see taken in the near future. There are countries, very differently circumstanced from us, which regard the submarine as a most convenient way in which a Power which cannot afford a battle fleet, and definitely accepts a minor rôle in naval matters, can obtain a very high measure of defensive security without undue expenditure of men or money. Therefore, while I think the statement which the Head of the German State has made is satisfactory so far as it goes, it would be a mistake if the Committee imagined that that reform for which we have pressed so long and so ardently—namely, the abolition of submarines—is likely to come into force in the near future. On the contrary, the new fact with which we are confronted is the construction, contrary to the Treaty, of a certain number of German submarines, which have been prepared under conditions which made their apparition surprising to other countries. Therefore, although I hope that later study may alter my view, it does not seem to me that the position has changed.

But all must welcome the tone of Herr Hitler, his friendly references to this country, and the several important points which he brought forward and which form a good basis upon which conversations could be opened and negotiations, perhaps, be founded. We should welcome that all the more because we are entering a period of ever-increasing anxiety. Germany has armed, and is arming, upon a scale which is vast, and which is indefinite. The figure of 550,000 men is quoted for the German Army, but that means 550,000 men in barracks. That is the permanent number, through which will be constantly flowing the enormous annual quotas of recruits which German manhood supplies each year. Each year German manhood actually supplies double the number that are available permanently. The 550,000 is the body retained with the colors, which will rapidly gather behind it enormous reserves—reserves which in a few years' time will enable that army, which we speak of as an army of 550,000, to mobilize at 2,000,000 or 3,000,000 men. In the meantime, before these reserves have been, so to speak, secreted by the active units, there are the extra formations of the Brownshirts and other organizations in Germany, amounting to very large numbers, which are available to reinforce the men who are now being gathered together under conscription throughout all the barracks of the Reich.

Then there is the question of the German Navy. It is to be 35 per cent. of our Navy. I presume that that means 35 per cent. of the tonnage; I do not know any other way in which a percentage of that kind could be calculated. All I can say is that 35 per cent. of the tonnage of our Navy, if represented by a brand-new fleet, would far exceed 35 per cent. in value. You cannot compare old ships with new. All the *Queen Elizabeths,* the *Royal Sovereigns,* and later on the *Renown* and the *Repulse*—twelve out of fifteen of our battleships—were constructed in the days when I was at the Admiralty more than twenty years ago. These old ships are perfectly capable of doing their duty until newer vessels are built, but then the difference between them and the products of modern science and naval knowledge is such that to confront the two types, old and new, would simply be sending your sailors to a horrible struggle under most injurious and damaging conditions.

If the Germans are going to build 35 per cent. of our tonnage in new construction it is perfectly clear that we must include in our annual program a superior construction of new ships, ship for ship in each type. I will not say what the percentage of superiority should be, but we must at least do that. Otherwise, although we might work out a fairly imposing preponderance in tonnage, when it came to conflict it would be found that we had woefully deceived ourselves and had involved the State in great misfortune. It seems to me that for this purpose we must recover our freedom of design. Not only must we recover our general freedom, because we are limited in all directions, but we must recover particularly our freedom of design.

Looking back upon the Treaty of London, I am very glad to think that the Conservative party gave a united vote against it. In those days the Lord President was wiser than he is now; he used frequently to take my advice. We recorded our vote against it. What a disastrous instrument it has been, fettering the unique naval knowledge which we possess and forcing us to spend our scant money on building wrong or undesirable types of ships; and condemning us to send out to deep waters and sink vessels like the *Tiger,* in itself capable of dealing with the new smaller German battleship, and vessels like the four *Iron Dukes,* which would have been invaluable, if war broke out, for convoying fleets of merchant ships to and from Australia and New Zealand in the teeth of hostile cruisers. I hope, therefore, that we shall have, some time or other, a clear statement from the Admiralty that new construction by Germany will be met by superior naval construction here. Clearly, for that purpose we shall endeavor to recover our freedom to build and our freedom of design at the earliest possible moment.

I said we were entering a period of serious anxieties. It is a period also of increasing tension. I will give the House two causes which, it seems to me, cannot possibly be overlooked. The first is this· German unemployment has been very largely cured by German preparations for war. Several millions of people, who when Herr Hitler was elected looked to him to provide them with work, have had work found for them; and that work has consisted in the preparation of armaments, or the construction of military roads, or the removal of military factories to remote parts of Germany, and generally in all these processes. The great wheels of German industry have been set working, and they are turning out in endless succession every kind of weapon of war. To reverse or stop that would undoubtedly produce a convulsion in the internal domestic life of Germany and one most likely to cause embarrassment and reproach to the régime.

It seems to me, therefore, that words cannot form a foundation for our action unless they are accompanied by deeds; and the likelihood of deeds being done in Germany at the present time which will remove the present danger seems to me remote when you consider what a dire effect it would have upon the immediate economic, industrial and labor situation within that country Suppose that the supply of raw material, and the payments across the exchange become more difficult for Germany, and that for any reason at a time in the not distant future it is found that this great national armament industry in Germany cannot be kept going at its present rate. It is clear that we shall then be in the presence of what I will call a peak of production beyond which a decline may be expected. All I can say is that, should that peak be reached, it will be a period big with fate for Europe and a period in which the greatest vigilance and care must be exercised This is the first reason which leads me to believe that the tension will not diminish and will increase.

But there is another reason, and this second reason I will describe as the suddenness of a possibly decisive attack. That is what is going to increase the strain upon all countries. Before the War only navies were ready. The ships of the Royal Navy can go to war in a few hours. They have only to raise steam, fit the war-heads on torpedoes, bring up the shells and put to sea, and they can fight. They have everything on board— and that applies to a great part of the Fleet. That was the same with the German Fleet before the War. When I was at the Admiralty we were instructed by the Committee of Imperial Defence to have the Fleet prepared at any time, night or day or at any season of the year, for attack without warning or without declaration of war. We did our best to live up to that extraordinarily strict injunction. We were prepared to defend ourselves against any attack.

That imposed a great strain, but it was a strain confined to a very few people. The two persons in charge of the Admiralty, the sailors and the politicians and the principal staffs concerned with the movement of the ships themselves, were all aware of the condition of strain. But the ordinary crews of the ships were not conscious of anything exceptional. They lived their lives in the ordinary way without taking any care of the day-to-day disposition of the ships. But still it was a great strain. And in those days armies could not fall upon each other without a moment's notice. A long and important time-plan of mobilization, more than a fortnight, intervened, and consequently nations could live and go about their ordinary work in a peaceful manner without this haunting and demoralizing fear of a sudden attack, of a bolt from the blue leveled at their heart which might possibly mean destruction. But what is the condition now? That has gone. The motorization and mechanization of large parts of these armies enables plans to be made by which hundreds, even thousands, of motor vehicles may be started in the night from different parts a hundred miles behind a frontier, and in the dawn may be found in possession of important parts of a defensive line.

Imagine what a strain that throws upon the French people. I cannot but wonder at their calmness and composure in the face of those dangers which gather about them. They have a defensive line which they have built from the Alps to the Luxemburg frontier, behind which they shield themselves. What is happening under the new conditions being introduced—not by Germany alone certainly, but by modern scientific development—is that an ever-larger proportion of the French Army is forced to man these ramparts, and they are bound to consider every daily movement they make from the point of view of possibly being attacked. Probably there is no danger. We all hope there is not. But the state of tension must affect any great population when such large numbers of persons are compelled to live under those conditions and their families at home know the conditions they are living under, close to the trenches which they may have to occupy at a moment's notice. For these two reasons I think we must look forward with anxiety and with seriousness to a condition of increasing strain.

Lastly, above all, there is the air, which introduces the most hideous factor of all, because aeroplanes can be dispatched on a mission of destruction or of provocation at almost any moment, and no mobilization need be made beforehand and no warning need be given. Therefore I say that on all these grounds we are bound to realize that we are entering upon a dark and dangerous valley through which we have to march for quite a long time unless some blessed relief comes to us through some agreement—for which there is hardly any exertion that we should not make. The Lord President asked me and asked us all not to indulge in panic. I hope we shall not indulge in panic. But I wish to say this: It is very much better sometimes to have a panic feeling beforehand, and then to be quite calm when things happen, than to be extremely calm beforehand and to get in a panic when things happen. Nothing has surprised me more than—I will not say the indifference, but the coolness with which the Committee has treated the extraordinary revelations of the German air strength relatively to our own country. Certainly it involves a profound alteration in the status of our country. For the first time for centuries we are not fully equipped to repel or to retaliate for an invasion. That to an island people is astonishing. Panic indeed! The position is the other way round. We are the incredulous, indifferent children of centuries of security behind the shield of the Royal Navy, not yet able to wake up to the woefully transformed conditions of the modern world.

We are entering upon a period of danger and of difficulty. And how do we stand in this long period of danger? There is no doubt that the Germans are superior to us in the air at the present time, and it is my belief that by the end of this year, unless their rate of construction and development is arrested by some agreement, they will be possibly three, and even four, times our strength.[2] There is nothing to prevent such a result being reached if the Germans simply continue to maintain this great machine which they have set in motion and keep it revolving. They have created whatever it may be—1000, 1500—brand-new aeroplanes in a comparatively short space of time; and the plant that brought that about can produce double and treble that number with great ease during the present year. I can only hope that they will not think it necessary to use it to that extent.

I come to the new statement which my right hon. Friend has made today. The Royal Air Force is to be raised to 1500 first-line strength. By first-line strength I mean, and I imagine the Government mean, aeroplanes formed in squadrons each with another aeroplane behind it, and each squadron with 50 per cent. reserve for pilots, with all the organization and everything that is necessary. To produce a program of that

[2] See footnote, page 175.

kind is the most formidable advance in British defense which has ever been made, and the Committee should not be at all inclined to underrate the magnitude of the effort which the Government have now proposed to us But I cannot help saying what a pity it is that we did not make this proposal two years ago, or even one year ago, because then we should have been in a position during this critical period to make an output similar to that which is being made in other countries. I have given my warnings in the past, and I am certainly not going to repeat them for the purpose of self-glorification on this occasion; least of all would I do it when the Lord President, with his engaging candor and in his usual manly fashion, has said quite openly that, so far as the rapidity of German expansion was concerned, the figures placed before him were wrong and have been misleading. That is so The confession does my right hon. Friend the greatest credit, but the consequences of what happened remain, and it is characteristic of him that he remains to face those consequences with courage. [Cheers.] I am glad that the significance of that is apparent to the Committee.

I could not follow the Lord President in his description of the difficulties of collecting and finding the information from Germany. It has always been difficult, and, indeed, impossible, to ascertain the top limit of what Germany had or of the rate at which she was producing, or what her capacity was, or what use she meant to make of that capacity. The top limit has always been difficult to ascertain, but for the last two years a whole stream of information has been coming to this country from France, Holland, Italy, Belgium and Switzerland—and from Germany herself. Remember a large part of the population there are estranged in their hearts from the Government. A stream of information came which, though it did not show what the top limit would be, showed with indisputable clearness that the German effort in aviation was on an incomparably greater scale than ours. Therefore, it seems to me rather odd that when the Sub-Committee of Imperial Defence, the one presided over for four months by the Prime Minister [Mr. MacDonald], were examining all these matters in the autumn of last year, they did not get hold of some of this most voluminous information which came into this country. I am very glad, by the way, to hear the Foreign Secretary [Sir John Simon] say that it was not the fault of our Intelligence Service. It used to be the best in the world. In the War the foreigners certainly thought it was the best; both our friends and our foes treated it with the highest respect. No, I think really that at some time or other we ought to have a little more explanation about how it was that the facts did not reach the men at the top. We all know perfectly well that Ministers are absolutely incapable of willfully misleading Parliament It would be an abominable crime to do such a thing, but evidently somewhere between the Intelligence Service and the ministerial chief there has been some watering down or whittling down of the facts. At any rate, at its leisure Parliament should press for further light to be thrown upon that matter.

I have been told that the reason for the Government not having acted before was that public opinion was not ripe for rearmament. I hope that we shall never accept such a reason as that. The Government have been in control of overwhelming majorities in both Houses of Parliament. There is no Vote they could not have proposed for the national defense which would not have been accepted and, if the case was made out to the general satisfaction, as it is now, probably without serious opposition of any kind As for the people, nothing that has ever happened in this country could lead Ministers of the Crown to suppose that when a serious case of public danger is put to them they will not respond to any request. Then it is said—and I must give this explanation of the extraordinary fact—that "we were laboring for disarmament," and it would have spoiled the disarmament hopes if any overt steps to raise our Air Force had been taken I do not admire people who are wise after the event. I would rather be impaled on the other horn of the dilemma and be called one of the "I told you so's" One ought to criticize the Government in the House chiefly upon matters which one had already indicated beforehand might become the subject of public misfortune, and I should like to remind the Committee that for the last three years I have endeavored as far as I could to criticize the drift of our foreign policy, the attempt to weaken the French forces, the undue stress which was put upon disarmament, and I ventured to coin the motto that "Redress of the grievances of the vanquished should precede the disarmament of the victors." [3] That, I believe, was the sound policy, but, at any rate, the moment it was clear that Germany was going to rearm herself there were only two courses, one was a collective representation to her that she must not do so, and the other was concerted counter-armament among the other Powers And that is the position which we have reached now, but only after a long delay.

The Foreign Secretary has used the expression that we were going to "the edge of risk" I think it is a very dangerous thing for a Minister to

[3] See pages 31, 32

boast that we are going to the edge of risk. Along the edge of this precipice the ground is often treacherous, and a fierce gust of wind may sweep the unwary walker into the abyss. See what happens when you try to walk along the edge of risk. I was very glad indeed, in view of these facts, that the Lord President, with his usual generosity, would not allow any undue blame to be thrown upon the Air Ministry. It is a new Department It is not perhaps a very strong Department. It has not the traditions or backing of the older Services of the Crown. It was not, before the German air force was set on foot, one of the most important Departments in the country, and it would have been a wrong thing if any undue responsibility had been cast upon it for a state of affairs for which, as my right hon. Friend has boldly said, the Cabinet as a whole must take complete responsibility.

When are we going to discuss these proposals in detail? Obviously we cannot do it tonight, because the Lord President was naturally vague and general in his statement, and, even if he had given the fullest details, it would have been much too soon for the Committee to attempt to make a reasoned examination of them. But we must ask ourselves, Are they adequate, and, also, within what limits are they executable? Those two questions are interdependent, because it is not merely a matter of money If you get into trouble over unemployment insurance or anything like that, money will cure it, but money will not cure these difficulties. You want time as well as money. The question whether a proposal to increase the Air Force in this country is practicable or not practicable within a certain time can only be decided after a very careful study of all the details.

I do not believe that this problem of building up the Air Force which the Government have now announced, or the greater one which they will have to build, will be solved solely by the existing aircraft industry; nor do I believe that it would be right to trust entirely to the individual efforts of those in the industry. In my opinion, national factories for producing particular types of aeroplanes should play a part in the general strengthening of our Air Forces.[4] But we await the Supplementary Estimate. The test of this scheme is the money it will cost in the present year or in the next year. It is not the slightest use merely putting out orders and hoping that you will get delivery. What Parliament will want to be reassured

[4] Such factories were eventually admitted to be necessary and formed part of the new program announced in the Government White Paper on Defense published on March 3, 1936

about is that large sums of money are going to be earned by the contractors during the year for substantial quantities of material and of aeroplanes. You cannot judge the size of this scheme until you see what are the financial votes by which it is to be started and supported.

There is one suggestion that I would make to the Lord President. He might consider whether we could have a discussion in a secret Session upon this subject I recommended that to Mr Lloyd George during the War, and he took that course. It was a great success and redounded to the advantage of His Majesty's Government. I am not suggesting that there are any deadly secrets which could be disclosed or that the Government would be asked to tell anything that they would not in the ordinary course tell us, but it would be of great advantage if we could discuss some of these technical points without our conversation being heard by all Europe. I think that suggestion should be considered by the Government, because many hon Members would like to bring forward points, but will not do so until they can be brought forward without fear that a bad impression might be created in other countries. That is a piece of friendly counsel which I offer to my right hon. Friend. Meanwhile, let me say—and I am sure it is the feeling of the whole House—that in the face of this very great program which has been put before us, a very great and far-reaching program of air expansion, there is no demand which the Government can make upon the House or upon the country in the present circumstances for the securing of national defense which will not be faithfully and cordially supplied.

FALSE SECURITY

May 31, 1935

Supply (Foreign Office Vote, considered in Committee)

1935

May 27. Mr. Baldwin, speaking in the Albert Hall, asserts:

"No Government in this country could live a day that was content to have an Air Force of any inferiority to any within striking distance of our shores."

FALSE SECURITY

I AGREE with Sir Herbert Samuel when he says that it is impossible for us, in the world in which we live, to treat with blank distrust the utterances of the Leader of so vast a State as Germany. To represent everything that has been said by Herr Hitler as only designed for the purposes of political maneuver would be to destroy the very means of contact and of parley between one great nation and another.

I agree with him also in feeling that the Air Locarno, as it has been called, is in itself an eminently desirable objective towards which we should work, and which, if concluded, will be a matter of real substance and importance I welcome, with him, any steps which may be taken to achieve, if possible, air parity at levels lower than those which are now mentioned. But it is not going to be very easy. I welcome also, and perhaps most keenly, what has been said by the German Chancellor stigmatizing the vile crime of indiscriminate bombing of civilian populations Naturally the Government will be encouraged by all sections in the House to pursue these matters with patience and not without hope. But do not let us under-rate the difficulties which attach to them. There may be many more complications in what is called an Air Locarno than would appear at first sight. Still, for what it is worth, the union of great countries putting their names to a document pledging them all to bomb the bomber would be an event which everyone would hail.

Even more difficulties attend the limitation of air armaments. Air armaments are not expressed merely by the air squadrons in existence or the aeroplanes which have been made; they cannot be considered apart from the capacity to manufacture. If, for instance, there were two countries which each had 1000 first-line aeroplanes, but one of which had the power to manufacture at the rate of 100 a month and the other at the rate of 1000 a month, it is perfectly clear that air parity would not exist between those two countries very long.

One would imagine, sitting in this House today, that the dangers were in process of abating. I believe that the exact contrary is the truth—that they are steadily advancing upon us, and that no one can be certain that a time may not be reached, or when it will be reached, when events may have passed altogether out of control. We must look at the facts. Nourish your hopes, but do not overlook realities.

The Secretary of State for Foreign Affairs [Sir John Simon] dropped out a phrase today which really is in keeping with what I call the illusion basis on which much of this discussion has proceeded. It was one of those casual phrases which nevertheless reveal an altogether unsound conception of the facts. He referred to countries with whom you feel it your absolute duty to remain on terms of air equality. Look at that. A "duty to remain on terms of air equality." We have not got equality. Speeches are made in the country by leading Ministers saying that we have decided that we must have air equality, that we cannot accept anything less. We have not got it. We are already decidedly inferior to Germany, and, it must be said, of course to France. All that lies before us for many months is that this inferiority becomes more and more pronounced. In the autumn of this year, in November, when we are supposed to be 50 per cent. stronger, I hazard the melancholy prediction that we shall not be a third, possibly not a quarter, of the German air strength.[1] What is the use of saying "the countries with whom we consider it our absolute duty to remain on terms of air equality"? This is one of the terrible facts which lie before us and which will not be swept away merely by following the very natural inclination which we all have to say that they do not exist.

The German Army, already developed to twenty-one or twenty-two divisions, is working up to thirty-six as fast as it can, a division a month or something like that coming into full mobilizable capacity, tanks and the whole business. There is the Navy, and submarines have been made. Some are actually, I believe, practicing, training their crews in that difficult art. Let me tell the House that submarines can be manufactured very quickly. I remember in November 1914 arranging for Mr. Schwab, of Bethlehem, to make twenty submarines in what was then considered the incredibly short period of six months. Although these vessels had to be shifted from the United States to a Canadian dockyard for reasons of neutrality, it was possible to put sections on the railway-trucks and to

[1] See footnote, page 175

deliver them in time. How do you know what progress has been made
in constructing such sections? The arms production has the first claim
on the entire industry of Germany. The materials required for the production of armaments are the first charge on the German exchange. The
whole of their industry is woven into an immediate readiness for war.
You have a state of preparedness in German industry which was not
attained by our industry until after the late War had gone on probably
for two years.

Besides this, there is tremendous propaganda, beginning with the
schools and going right through every grade of youth to manhood,
enforced by the most vigorous and harsh sanctions at every stage. All
this is taking place. It is a very nice comfortable world that we look out
on here in this country. It has found an apt reflection in this Debate today,
but it has no relation whatever to what is going forward, and going forward steadily. Mark you, in time of peace, in peace politics, in ordinary
matters of domestic affairs and class struggles, things blow over, but in
these great matters of defense, and still more in the field of actual hostilities, the clouds do not roll by. If the necessary measures are not taken,
they turn into thunderbolts and fall on your heads. The whole of this
great process of psychological, moral, material and technical mobilization
of German war power is proceeding ceaselessly and with ever-increasing
momentum.

It is the growth of German armaments which has fascinated and petri-
fied nation after nation throughout Europe. Just look at what has happened in the last few weeks since we were last engaged in a serious
discussion on foreign affairs. We know perfectly well that Poland continues in the German system The Czechoslovakian elections have created
a new Nazi party in Czechoslovakia, which is, I believe, the second party
in the State.[2] That is a very remarkable fact, having regard to the energy
which the German people, when inspired by the Nazi spirit, are able to
exercise. The Austrian tension increases. Many people talk about guaranteeing the independence of Austria, but guaranteeing that Austria will
be kept separate from Germany is a different thing. You may at any time
be faced with the position that the will of the Austrian people will be
turned in the reverse direction from that which our policy has hitherto
proclaimed. There is the Danubian tour of General Goering. He has
been to Yugoslavia, Bulgaria and to Hungary. He has, in Hungary and
Bulgaria, been renewing those old ties of comradeship and confidence

[2] May 19 See page 180.

which existed between them and Germany in the days of the War. In Yugoslavia undoubtedly his presence has exercised a very important influence there as a counter-influence to others that may be brought to bear. Everywhere these countries are being made to look to Germany in a special way, and let me say that I read in the *Times* on the 30th of May a significant telegram from Vienna dealing with this tour of General Goering, which finished up with these words: "In the circumstances the strength and clarity of German policy gains by contrast"—that is, to the Allied policy—"and the waverers among the smaller States are closely watching events."

There is the question of the relations between Germany and Japan. It seems to me that that is a matter which must be in the thoughts of everyone who attempts to make an appreciation of the foreign situation. There are the difficulties of Italy's preoccupation with Abyssinia There are the obvious stresses through which France is passing, not, indeed, in the matter of national defense, but in almost every other aspect of the life of that people. There is our own weakness in the air which is to become worse and worse month after month All this is going forward.

It is easy, then, for Herr Hitler and the German Government to pursue a policy which I have heard described as "power diplomacy." What a transformation has taken place in the last two or three years! Two or three years ago it was considered sentimental, intellectual, liberally minded, to speak words of encouragement and compassion, and even to speak patronizingly of the German people, and to seek opportunities of making gestures to raise them up to more and greater equality with other countries. Now we see them with their grievances unredressed, with all their ambitions unsatisfied, continuing from strength to strength, and the whole world waits from week to week to hear what are the words which will fall from the heads of the German nation. It is a woeful transformation which has taken place.

It would be folly for us to act as if we were swimming in a halcyon sea, as if nothing but balmy breezes and calm weather were to be expected and everything were working in the most agreeable fashion. By all means follow your lines of hope and your paths of peace, but do not close your eyes to the fact that we are entering a corridor of deepening and darkening danger, and that we shall have to move along it for many months and possibly for years to come. While we are in this position, not only have we our own safety to consider, but we have to consider also whether the Parliamentary Governments of Western Europe, of which there are not many that function in the real sense of the word, are going to be able to afford to their subjects the same measure of physical security, to say nothing of national satisfaction, as is being afforded to the people of Germany by the dictatorship which has been established there. It is not only the supreme question of self-preservation that is involved in the realization of these dangers, but also the human and the world cause of the preservation of free Governments and of Western civilization against the ever-advancing forces of authority and despotism

AIR DEFENSE RESEARCH

June 7, 1935

Debate on the Adjournment

1935

June 2. Herr von Ribbentrop, the "German Special Commissioner for Disarmament questions," arrives in London to engage in preliminary conversations with the British Government on the subject of relative naval strengths.

AIR DEFENSE RESEARCH

I wish to draw the attention of the House and of the public to a question connected with air defense This point is limited, and largely technical and scientific in its character. Nevertheless it is important. It is concerned with the methods which can be invented, adopted or discovered to enable the earth to control the air, to enable defense from the ground to exercise control—domination—upon aeroplanes high above its surface

I have not been able to feel at all satisfied that the limits of the usefulness of artillery have been reached. It is quite true that in the Great War, as every Member who took part is aware, an enormous number of shells were fired at aeroplanes without, as far as my recollection serves, any aeroplane ever actually having been visibly brought down from a great height In consequence, anti-aircraft artillery has been generally discredited, but I think it would be well worth while to pursue that study carefully. The range of guns and the character of the projectiles which they fire should be most carefully considered. After all, an aeroplane, though a very formidable engine of war, is also a very fragile structure, and an explosive charge no bigger than a small cigar is sufficient to bring down the most powerful aeroplane if it strikes a spar or the propeller; even a bird has been the cause of fatal accidents. Merely to fire at an aeroplane in the air is like trying to shoot a flying duck with a pea-rifle What must be aimed at is not the hitting of the aeroplane, but the creation of conditions in the air around the aeroplane which are extremely noxious if not destructive to it. For that purpose it is clear that the effect of the shell which is fired should not be momentary.

At present the moment after explosion a shell is useless, but suppose you were able to create conditions—I am not going into details—which make a considerable area very perilous to an aeroplane for an appreciable period of time, say five minutes, and suppose that a number of these shells were fired at the same time, a large space would become deadly to an aeroplane. That is only one line of inquiry, and there must be many more. The kite balloon, for instance, which was being hopefully examined in the last year of the War, is a line which should be pursued, and methods of sound detection of the approach of an aeroplane, and its range and direction, are also worth study. These are some of the more obvious aspects of the field of scientific inquiry, but no doubt there are many others which are not so well known.

My experience—and it is somewhat considerable—is that in these matters when the need is clearly explained by military and political authorities science is always able to provide something. "Seek and ye shall find" has been borne out. We were told that it was impossible to grapple with submarines, but methods were found which enabled us to strangle the submarine below the water, a problem not necessarily harder than that of clawing down marauding aeroplanes. Many things which were attempted in the War we were told were technically impossible, but patience, perseverance, and, above all, the spur of necessity under war conditions made men's brains act with greater vigor, and science responded to the demand. That being so, I venture to set the research side of air defense in a position of primary importance. I agree that there is nothing which can offer any substitute for an equal or superior force, a readiness to retaliate, but if you could discover some new method the whole of our affairs would be greatly simplified.

During last summer a number of letters were written to the *Times* newspaper by Professor Lindemann, Professor of Experimental Philosophy at Oxford University, pointing out not only the possibility of scientific results being obtained in this sphere, but dwelling upon its enormous importance to this and every other country. I had long conversations with him last autumn, and we endeavored to bring the matter to the attention of His Majesty's Government. We made a pilgrimage to Aix-les-Bains, where we thought we had enthused the Lord President of the Council upon the subject. He appeared to be most interested, but when we came back to London more difficulties arose and the matter seemed to hang in the balance. Many letters were written and interchanged, but no progress made. There was an Air Ministry Committee on this subject, with scientists exploring the matter. This Committee was in existence at the time when the Air Ministry advised the Lord President to make the speech which made such a great impression two years ago, in which he said that there was really no defense; and, consequently, an appearance of giving up the problem undoubtedly rested on the Department concerned. Although the Committee was still working, no real hope stimulated its onward progress.

What we thought was so necessary was to remove this Committee from the Air Ministry and put it under the Committee of Imperial Defence, where the heads of the Government, the most powerful politicians in the country, would be able to superintend and supervise its actions, and also make sure that it was supplied with the necessary funds. What is £100,000 a year if you can discover some method which will make us more secure from this sudden and disturbing menace to civilization? It is nothing at all. At this stage we were joined by Sir Austen Chamberlain, and we continued at intervals to address the Government on the subject. In February we had the good fortune to be received by the Prime Minister personally, and we laid our case before him with as much cogency and force as we could command. No difference of principle at all existed between us. The Prime Minister was most sympathetic as I pointed out the peace aspect of this idea. Nothing would do more to lessen some of the terrors and anxieties which overcloud the world than the removal of these surprise attacks on the civilian population. However, the Prime Minister found difficulty with the Departments concerned in regard to the Committee which was already in existence. Everything went on in a very gradual progression, and finally on the 19th of March Sir Austen Chamberlain had a personal interview with the Prime Minister in which he asked for a specific answer, as a result of which the Prime Minister told us that he was, shall I say, hardening his heart to overcome the Department's resistance.

The result was a satisfactory answer to the question, and the setting up of this new Committee under the conditions we had desired. The Prime Minister said:

> We have, therefore decided to appoint also a special sub-committee of the Committee of Imperial Defence, through which the Air Ministry Committee will report to the Committee of Imperial Defence itself. This sub-committee will have the direction and control of the whole inquiry, and the necessary funds to carry out experiments and to make researches approved by this committee will be made available.[1]

That was all we required. But I asked two days ago how often this Committee had met, and the answer I received was that it had met on no fewer than two occasions in the three months since it was set up. I doubt

[1] March 19, 1935.

very much whether that will be accepted by those who have interested themselves in this matter as at all a satisfactory result. Let us look back on this. Really the whole story is another slow-motion picture. Beginning in August, we have got now to the middle of June. If a really scientific Committee had been set to work, and funds provided, twenty important experiments would be under way by now, any one of which might yield results decisive on the whole of our defense problem.

I am raising this matter today with a view to stimulating and spurring on the action of that Committee. I have ventilated this topic and assigned to it the publicity and importance which it certainly requires, but I must in conclusion once more draw the attention of the House to the value that a discovery of this kind would have upon the whole of our affairs. It is not a matter which interests one nation alone. Every single nation in the world has an interest in this. I wonder that the League of Nations at Geneva does not offer an enormous monetary prize to incite inventors of all countries to discover ways of downing the marauding aeroplane.

It is only in the twentieth century that this hateful conception of inducing nations to surrender by terrorizing the helpless civil population and by massacring the women and children has gained acceptance and countenance amongst men. If it continues, one can clearly see that the conquest of the air may mean the subjugation of mankind and the destruction of our civilization. This is not the cause of any one nation. No; every country would feel safer if once it were found that the bombing aeroplane was at the mercy of appliances erected on the earth, and the haunting fears and suspicions which are leading nations nearer and nearer to the brink of another catastrophe would be abated. But this island people more than any other nation would gain by such a discovery.

We have not only to fear attacks upon our civil population and our great cities, in respect of which we are more vulnerable than any other country in the world, but also attacks upon the dockyards and other technical establishments without which our Fleet, still an essential method of defense, might be paralyzed or even destroyed Therefore it is not only from the point of view of a world effort to eliminate one of the worst causes of suspicion and of war, but as a means of restoring to us here in Great Britain the old security of our island, that this matter should receive and command the vigorous thoughts of the greatest men in our country and in our Government, and should be pressed forward by every resource that the science of Britain can apply and the wealth of the country can liberate.

CONSEQUENCES IN FOREIGN POLICY

July 11, 1935

Supply (Foreign Office Vote, considered in Committee)

11.48

1935

June 8. Government reconstruction. Mr. Baldwin becomes Prime Minister; Mr. Ramsay MacDonald, Lord President of the Council; Sir John Simon leaves the Foreign Office and becomes Home Secretary; Sir Samuel Hoare becomes Foreign Secretary; Sir Philip Cunliffe-Lister (now Lord Swinton) succeeds Lord Londonderry as Air Minister.

June 18. Signing of the Anglo-German Naval Agreement

June 25. The British Government offer a strip of British Somaliland to Mussolini if he will relax his demands on Abyssinia.

June 27. Result of the Peace Ballot announced: eleven million people vote for collective security and for upholding the Covenant of the League of Nations.

July 11. The Foreign Secretary, Sir Samuel Hoare, states in the House of Commons
"The more I look at the future prospect, the more I am sure that a system of collective security is essential to peace and stability, and the League of Nations best provides the necessary machinery."

CONSEQUENCES IN FOREIGN POLICY

When we last discussed foreign affairs I thought there was very general agreement. We were agreed, or we seemed to be agreed, on the declaration of comradeship between the three Great Powers that met at Stresa. We were agreed in supporting the resolution of the League of Nations condemning treaty-breaking by Germany in the matter of armaments. We were agreed to work in combination through the League of Nations for those principles of collective security—real collective security—which mean that the contributions to that security shall be adequate to give a sense of relief and assurance to all. I thought we were all agreed on that. I found myself in closer relation to His Majesty's Government on foreign affairs than I had been in the whole of this Parliament. Curiously enough, it seemed to me that the last act of the former Prime Minister [Mr. Ramsay MacDonald]—who is now Lord President—on foreign affairs, in the Stresa negotiations, made him more truly the mouthpiece of British feeling and British interest than ever before. We have now heard a speech from the new Foreign Secretary [Sir Samuel Hoare] which in no way conflicts with the general principles established when we last discussed foreign affairs.

Meanwhile, however, a number of things have happened which do conflict most markedly with those general principles which the Foreign Secretary has recited to us today. The scene is gravely changed. We have condoned, and even praised, the German treaty-breaking in fleet-building. I see that Lord Beatty, speaking somewhere else, said that we ought to be grateful to Germany for not having demanded 50 per cent. On that basis we ought to be still more grateful that they did not demand 100 per cent. We have condoned this unilateral violation of the Treaty, and we have become a party to it without agreement with any of the other countries concerned. We have, however unintentionally, nullified and stultified the

League of Nations' condemnation of treaty-breaking in respect of armaments, in which we were ourselves concerned, in which, indeed, we took a leading part. We have, it seems to me, revealed, again quite unintentionally, a very considerable measure of indifference to the interests of other Powers, particularly Powers in the Baltic, who were encouraged by our example to join with us in the League of Nations in condemning treaty-breaking. In the name of what 'is called practical realism we have seemed to depart very notably from the principle of collective security.

We have seemed to depart from—although I hope we may return again to—the comradeship agreed upon at Stresa, and from the League of Nations' resolution against treaty-breaking, and we have done it in order to make a side deal with Germany which we thought to be in our interest and not contrary to other interests in Europe. We cannot have done this without affecting prejudicially—although, again, I hope only for the time being—the confidence which exists between us and France, which is so vitally necessary for us at all times, but never more vitally necessary than during these years upon which we are now entering, when our air defense will be so woefully inferior to that of Germany. Thus it is not a very good tale which I have had to tell of what has happened since we last had a full-dress Debate on foreign affairs. But it is only one part of the story At the same time that we have been diverging from the League of Nations in one direction for our particular and legitimate national interest, real or supposed, Italy has made it plain that she means to invade and conquer Abyssinia.

What is reported every day about the movement of troops and the declarations of the head of the Italian State leaves us very little room to doubt that as soon as the season of the year is suitable the only hope of the Abyssinians retaining their territory and the lands on which they have lived for so many thousands of years will be in the fighting qualities of their men. I greatly deplore that. Here is this defiance of the League, and it has happened at the very moment when 11,000,000 people in this island have attested their own fidelity to it. In this short space we have made a separate arrangement for ourselves, of a perfectly innocent character, but still separate, and at the same time the League is confronted with this grave embarrassment through the ambitions of Italy in Abyssinia. By the course we have taken we have made it very difficult for us to remonstrate too strongly with Italy without being exposed to the somewhat severe reply that when we think our particular interests are involved we show but little consideration for the decision against treaty-breaking which we have just urged upon the League of Nations. I have thought it right to place before the Committee these two aspects of what has happened since we last discussed these matters.

There is, however, a third aspect. Simultaneously with all I have recited we have nevertheless seemed to allow—I say "seemed to allow" because I do not attribute it to the policy of the Government at all—the impression to be created that we were ourselves coming forward as a sort of bell-wether or fugleman to gather and lead opinion in Europe against Italy's Abyssinian designs. It was even suggested that we would act individually and independently. I am glad to hear from the Foreign Secretary that there is no foundation for that. We must do our duty, but we must do it only in conjunction with other nations and in accordance with obligations which others recognize as well. We are not strong enough—I say it advisedly—to be the lawgiver and the spokesman of the world We will do our part, but we cannot be asked, and we ought not to put ourselves in a position of being supposed, to do more than our part in these matters. I rejoice, indeed, that my right hon. Friend corrected that, but still the fact remains that throughout Italy we have been regarded with great resentment, which has been fed by altogether false and absurd rumors.

As we stand today there is no doubt that a cloud has come over the old friendship between Great Britain and Italy, a cloud which may very easily not pass away, although undoubtedly it is everyone's desire that it should. It is an old friendship, and we must not forget, what is a little-known fact, that at the time Italy entered into the Triple Alliance in the last century she stipulated particularly that in no circumstances should her obligations under the Alliance bring her into armed conflict with Great Britain.

Lastly, not only have we as it seems got into a position in which we are thought to be working against Italy, but we have made this proposal of handing over a portion of British protected territory in the hope of procuring a relinquishment of Italian ambitions. No explanation has been offered by the Foreign Secretary in his excellent speech of the very unfortunate manner in which this project was put forward. The policy of ceding British protected territory and British protected subjects in order to get round some diplomatic difficulty, or to assuage the disputes of foreign countries, or even to pay our own way from year to year in the modern world, is a very dangerous one for this country to open. When we are considering our vast, innumerable possessions and the reduced state of our means of defense, and at the same time the obvious hunger which is exhibited in so many quarters on the continent of Europe, it seems to me that any steps that might tend to direct appetites upon ourselves should be viewed with the utmost caution and scrutinized with the greatest strictness by Parliament.

Still, supposing that in these years so critical for the peace of Europe the Minister for League of Nations Affairs [Mr. Eden] had returned from Italy with an agreement that she would abandon her dubious and alarming venture, I believe that the gain would have outweighed the loss; but what I do not see, and what I hope we shall be told by my right hon. Friend, is how it ever came to be supposed that this particular proposal would attract the Italian Government. Why should Signor Mussolini want to prolong the standstill on the borders of Abyssinia while Abyssinia enjoyed a corridor to the sea through which a transit of arms could take place year after year? However you look at it, it was a forlorn hope. It was an honest, well-meant proposal, but it was a forlorn hope. We have been told that it was an informal, tentative suggestion, and so forth. Why could not that have gone through ordinary diplomatic channels?

I must say one word to the Minister for League of Nations Affairs Some two years ago I ventured to recite to him those words of Dr. Johnson:

> Ye who listen with credulity to the whispers of fancy, and pursue with eagerness the phantoms of hope, who expect that age will perform the promises of youth,...attend to the history of Rasselas, Prince of Abyssinia.[1]

I am afraid my right hon. Friend has been taking my counsel too literally. Everyone has the greatest hopes of his career, and the whole House, irrespective of party, welcome the appearance of this new figure, but we hope he will choose his occasions with rather stricter discrimination and make quite sure before he undertakes these various journeys that he will not be asked to run risks which injure himself, without sufficient hope of a satisfactory result.

To recapitulate. During the last six weeks the League of Nations has been weakened by our action, the principle of collective security has been impaired, German treaty-making has been condoned and even extolled, the Stresa Front has been shaken, if not, indeed, dissolved. Although I cannot believe that any nation in contact with the British Government can doubt our sincere desire for peace, British influence has to some extent been dissipated, and our moral position, or at any rate our logical posi-

[1] Page 108.

tion, has been to some extent obscured. You could not have had a more complete and perfect example of how not to do it than has been presented by the events which have taken place since we last discussed foreign affairs. Frankly, I cannot understand how it was done. Nothing that has been said shows us how or why it was done. It seems to me as if there were four or five different policies at work inside the Cabinet, and that now one and now the other gains the ascendancy according as the incidents of the hour or the events of the day bring these or those considerations to its attention.

That brings me to the new plan of having two equal Foreign Secretaries. I was very glad indeed that the Prime Minister [Mr. Baldwin] said yesterday that this was only a temporary experiment. I cannot feel that it will last long or ever be renewed. At any rate, it is in the nature of poetic justice that the Foreign Secretary [Sir Samuel Hoare] should, on leaving the India Office, have a personal experience of dyarchy in its most direct and homely aspect. What we want in foreign affairs is not, as the Prime Minister suggested, a team, however loyal—and it certainly will be loyal—and however well disciplined it may be. What we need, first of all, is a plain, simple policy which can be declared in Parliament and to the nation and can be generally approved by both. And we need that this policy should be adhered to through all the chops and changes of the situation. Secondly, we need the integral thought of a single man responsible for the conduct of foreign affairs, ranging over the entire field and making every factor and every incident contribute to the general purpose upon which Parliament has agreed.

The Foreign Secretary, whoever he is, whichever he is, must be supreme in his Department, and everyone in that great office ought to look to him, and to him alone. I remember that we had a discussion in the War about unity of command, and that Mr. Lloyd George said, "It is not a question of one general being better than another, but of one general being better than two." There is no reason at all why a strong Cabinet Committee should not sit with the Foreign Secretary every day in these difficult times, or why the Prime Minister should not see him or his officials at any time; but when the topic is so complicated and vast, when it is in such continued flux, it seems to me that confusion will only be made worse confounded by dual allegiances and equal responsibilities.

The Foreign Secretary dwelt upon the advantages which the Naval Agreement confers upon us. Those advantages are very doubtful. Of course, it is quite wrong to pretend that the apparition of Germany as a formidable naval Power, equipped with submarines and all the other apparatus of war, is the result of the Naval Agreement. That would have happened anyhow. The deep purposes of great nations are not, I am afraid, governed by the ebb and flow of political discussions or by temporary agreements which are made. It has for some time been evident that Germany intends to embark upon a gigantic process of rearming by land, sea and air, which will make her the most formidable military Power in the whole world. I am not blaming upon this Agreement these events and the misfortunes which will follow from them, but when the Prime Minister says, as he did the other day, that he hoped this would be a great measure of disarmament, let me tell him that I am afraid it will not. I hazard the prediction that it inaugurates the arrival of Germany as a great naval Power, and that this will inaugurate an outburst of shipbuilding in almost every country in the world the like of which has never been seen.

Let us suppose that some distinguished and powerful person who has played a great part in life dies, and his posts, offices, appointments and possessions are distributed, and then he suddenly comes back from the dead. A great deal of inconvenience would be caused. That is what has happened in the resuscitation of German naval power. The equilibrium— such equilibrium as we have been able to establish—in naval matters is entirely ruptured and deranged, and we shall find in every country, in the present temper of the world, that great new construction, replacing old ships or increasing the total tonnage, will be begun without the slightest delay. And let me say that if the first German program, which has already been announced, and which is really last year's program, the program of 1934, is followed by similar programs in the next few years, the German 35 per cent. limit will have been laid down, if not completed, by 1938 or 1939, and in the same period, if we are not to endanger our naval security, it will be necessary for us to rebuild and lay down in new construction practically half the tonnage of our existing Fleet. I cannot feel that this German Naval Agreement is at all a matter for rejoicing. I remain still under this impression, that the one great fear of Europe is the power and might of the rearmed strength of Germany, and that the one great hope is the gathering together of Powers who are conscious of that fear, but have no aggressive intentions of any kind, in a system of collective security under the League of Nations, in order that this tremendous process of the rearmament of Germany may not be attended by some lamentable breakdown of peace.

THE ANGLO-GERMAN NAVAL AGREEMENT

July 22, 1935

Supply (Navy Estimates, considered in Committee)

THE ANGLO-GERMAN NAVAL
AGREEMENT

I HAVE never felt that there was very much in this offer which the Germans made to co-operate with us in abolishing the submarine I should have thought it was a very safe offer for them to make—for any country to make—when the condition attached to it was that all other countries should agree at the same time, and when it was perfectly well known that there was not the slightest chance of other countries agreeing. The First Lord of the Admiralty [Sir Bolton Eyres-Monsell] says we cannot tell now whether other countries will agree or not. Does he really suppose that at this forthcoming multilateral conference, to which he is looking forward, and which must take place in some form or other before the end of 1936, there is the slightest chance of securing a world agreement on the abolition of the submarine? I should have thought that the French, the Italian, and the Japanese views would all be absolutely adverse to it. If that be so, it seems to me that the Germans have not run any great risk of diminishing their facilities for making war at sea by offering to co-operate with Great Britain in securing this abolition.

Another statement which was made on the subject of submarines was that the Germans were willing to subscribe to the terms of the international agreement which many of the Powers have signed restricting the use of the submarine in such a way as to strip submarine warfare against commerce of inhumanity. I feel very great difficulty in being entirely reassured by that. Lord Beatty said the other day that the battle fleet was now practically secure against submarines if properly protected by its flotillas, etc. I believe that to be correct. Submarines are not needed, then, for attack upon the battle fleet. If they are not needed for that purpose, and the Germans are not going to use them in the only way in which they can be effectively used, against commerce, it seems to me strange that they should dwell with so much reiteration on the importance of having not merely 35 per cent., but 45 per cent , and in the long run in some circumstances up to 100 per cent , of our tonnage in this category. If neither of the spheres of activity for submarines is to be used by them, it seems strange that they should attach so much importance to the possession of this weapon, which they have begun to construct in considerable numbers in flat defiance of the Peace Treaty. If we are to assume, as we must for the purposes of this discussion, the ugly hypothesis of a war in which Britain and Germany would be on opposite sides and the British blockade would be enforced on the coast of Germany as it was in the late War, who in his senses would believe that the Germans, possessed of a great fleet of submarines and watching their women and children being starved by the British blockade, would abstain from the fullest use of that arm? Such a view seems to be the acme of gullibility.

The chief argument which has been put forward in many quarters is that all of a sudden the Government broke away from the course on which they were proceeding in European affairs—namely, Stresa, Geneva, and the collective disapprobation of the breaking of treaties—and made this side arrangement with Germany.

I do not quite see why Germany should have been singled out for such exceptional treatment in this matter. The right hon. Gentleman asked what would have happened if we had refused her suggestion? I do not suggest that it should have been arbitrarily turned down, and that we should have said there was no question of our ever making any agreement with Germany. The proper course would have been to say that this Agreement involves a breach of the Treaty, and that we have joined with other Powers in condemning breaches of the Treaty and unilateral action, and that we must, while noting all the facts, refer this matter to the other nations with whom we have so recently joined in expressing a decided and definite view. I do not believe that if that had been done the position would have been worsened. The position is very bad. Do not let us underrate it. The German Fleet which is to be constructed under this Treaty is to be 35 per cent. of the British Fleet. We have seen the first year's program of its construction. It is already far on the way down; even the battleships are laid down. I do not know how the Admiralty came to be without information that even battleships [of a size], contrary to the Treaty, were being laid down before the end of 1934. I am astounded at such a thing. We always believed before the War that battleships could never be laid down without our knowledge. The Germans were entitled to build 10,000-ton ships according to the Treaty, but they, by a concealment which the Admiralty were utterly unable to penetrate, converted these into 26,000-ton ships. Let us be careful when we see all these extremely awkward incidents occurring

Let me say one word about France. It is true that if we take mere tonnage the First Lord is able to show a satisfactory arrangement for France in the percentage of superiority which she would possess; but what is to be the position of the French Navy if the Germans in the next four years build by four programs a fleet of 35 per cent. of the British Fleet? The entire navy of France, except the latest vessels, will require to be reconstructed. The new German Navy, although somewhat behind the French in the matter of percentages, would undoubtedly be overwhelmingly superior from the point of view of material. Therefore, we cannot feel at all reassured about this position unless we know the programs, and it seems most dangerous to continue month after month, and even year after year (because I gather it may not be till next year we can be told), with the House of Commons not knowing these vital programs on both sides, although they are known to all the Cabinets of the various nations with whom we have had these conversations. Even after hearing the able statement to which we have listened I must say that I regret that we have condoned this flagrant breach of the Treaty. It would have been far better, even though we could not get complete assurances in regard to the ratio of Germany with ourselves, to have carried these matters forward to the League of Nations and endeavored to use this further breach of the Treaty by Germany as a means of gathering forces for a policy of collective security among all the nations of the world.

I do not believe for a moment that this isolated action by Great Britain will be found to work for the cause of peace. The immediate reaction is that every day the German Fleet approaches a tonnage which gives it absolute command of the Baltic, and very soon one of the deterrents of a European war will gradually fade away. So far as the position in the Mediterranean is concerned, it seems to me that we are in for very great difficulties. Certainly a large addition of new shipbuilding must come when the French have to modernize their Fleet to meet German construction, and the Italians follow suit, and we shall have pressure upon us to rebuild from that point of view, or else our position in the Mediterranean will be affected. But worst of all is the effect upon our position at the other end of the world, in China and in the Far East. What a windfall this has been to Japan! Observe what the consequences are. The

First Lord said, "Face the facts." The British Fleet, when this program is completed, will be largely anchored to the North Sea. That means to say the whole position in the Far East has been very gravely altered, to the detriment of the United States and of Great Britain and to the detriment of China.

The evils that have arisen in the Far East have arisen largely since the War; the injury to British interests has come since the War. Since the War we have certainly had a mobility for the British Fleet very much greater than we possessed during the years of the German danger before the War. But that mobility is going to pass away, and the whole advantage of our having a great naval base at Singapore upon which a battle fleet can be based, if necessary, to protect us in the Indian Ocean and to maintain the connection with Australia and New Zealand, for that is the purpose, is greatly affected by the fact that when this German Fleet is built we shall not be able to keep any appreciable portion of the British Fleet so far from home. Those are serious reactions. I do not say that they are reactions from the Naval Agreement, but from the fact that Germany is breaking treaties and re-establishing her naval power.

I regret that we are not dealing with this problem of the resuscitation of German naval power with the Concert of Europe on our side, and in conjunction with many other nations whose fortunes are affected and whose fears are aroused equally with our own by the enormous development of German armaments. What those developments are no one can accurately measure. We have seen that powerful vessels, much more powerful than we expected, can be constructed unknown even to the Admiralty. We have seen what has been done in the air. I believe that if the figures of the expenditure of Germany during the current financial year could be ascertained the House and the country would be staggered and appalled by the enormous expenditure upon war preparations which is being poured out all over that country, converting the whole mighty nation and empire of Germany into an arsenal virtually on the threshold of mobilization.

In the face of that danger I believe we should do well, by every means in our power, to try to knit up again those connections with the other Powers with whom we were associated at Stresa and those with whom we have been working on the League of Nations at Geneva, and to endeavor to secure a common front as far as possible against infractions of treaties. Let me say that, above all, we ought to take the necessary measures in good time. Face the facts—yes. The facts are that we have to rebuild the Fleet with great rapidity. The "escalator clause" should be invoked Not a day should be lost in getting on, as far as we may under present treaties. If we may not build battleships till 1937 it is all the more necessary to bring some of the cruiser construction to the fore in the interval That step must be taken. An hon. Member opposite spoke of a loan. There is a proposal for a very large national loan, a large use of national credit, and I think it satisfactory at this juncture that the pundits of Liberal financial orthodoxy should be of opinion that no serious damage would be done to our financial structure and that no serious violation of the canons of finance would occur if a very large use of the excellent credit we have were put into operation at the present time.[1]

Let the defense of the country be the first charge on that loan. Let the rebuilding of the fleet and the necessary steps in the other forces be a first charge upon the use of British credit; and let the necessary measures be taken without the slightest delay.

[1] Mr. Lloyd George and a number of economists, including Sir Walter Layton and Sir Basil Blackett, had recently advocated the expenditure of a thousand million pounds of borrowed money as part of their "New Deal" proposals.

THE ITALIAN COMPLICATION

October 24, 1935

Debate on the Adjournment

.

August 24. The British Cabinet resolves that Britain shall uphold its obligations under its treaties and under the Covenant of the League.

September 10. The French Government ask the British Foreign Office to what extent they might be assured in the future of the immediate and effective application by Great Britain of all the sanctions provided by Article 15 of the Covenant in the event of a violation of the Covenant of the League of Nations and a resort to force in Europe.

September 11. Sir Samuel Hoare addresses the League Assembly:

"I will begin by reaffirming the support of the League by the Government that I represent and the interest of the British people in collective security....

"The attitude of His Majesty's Government has been one of unwavering fidelity to the League and all that it stands for.

"The ideas enshrined in the Covenant, and in particular the aspiration to establish the rule of law in international affairs ... have become a part of our national conscience.

"It is to the principles of the League and not to any particular manifestation that the British nation has demonstrated its adherence. Any other view is at once an underestimate of our good faith and an imputation upon our sincerity. In conformity with its precise and explicit obligations the League stands, and my country stands with it, for the collective maintenance of the Covenant in its entirety, and particularly for steady and collective resistance to all acts of unprovoked aggression.

"There, then, is the British attitude towards the Covenant. I cannot believe that it will be changed so long as the League remains an effective body and the main bridge between the United Kingdom and the Continent remains intact."

September 12. Battle cruisers *Hood* and *Renown,* accompanied by the Second Cruiser Squadron and six ships of the Sixth Destroyer Flotilla, arrive at Gibraltar, making a total of six capital ships on the Mediterranean station.

September 26. The Foreign Secretary, Sir Samuel Hoare, replying to French inquiry, emphasizes the fact that Great Britain stands for the collective maintenance of the Covenant and particularly a steady and collective resistance to all acts of unprovoked aggression and not merely to the one now under consideration. He further points out that this declaration, while technically binding only on the present Government, has the overwhelming support and approval of the British people and is practically certain to be endorsed by any future Government.

October 4. Italy starts war against Abyssinia.

October 8. Mr. Lansbury resigns the leadership of the Labour party owing to disagreement with policy of sanctions.

October 10. By 50 votes to 2 the League Assembly decides to take collective measures against Italy. A Committee of Five is appointed to make further efforts for a peaceful solution.

October 14. Speaking in Glasgow, Mr. Chamberlain rebukes Mr. Amery:

"I know there are some people who would tell us that these issues do not really concern us, that as we are happily surrounded by the sea we can rest safely and comfortably in this little island of ours and let the rest of the world go down to chaos and ruin. Mr. Amery, for instance, told a Birmingham audience the other day that he was not prepared to send a single Birmingham lad to his death for Abyssinia. I think it would be difficult to cram into a few words a more mischievous distortion of the realities of the situation than was comprised in that one sentence of Mr. Amery's....

"The choice before us is whether we shall make a last effort at Geneva for peace and security, or whether by a cowardly surrender we shall break a promise we have made, and hold ourselves up to the shame of our children and their children's children."

THE ITALIAN COMPLICATION

WHEN WE separated in August the House was concerned about the scale and rapidity of German rearmament. What has happened in the interval? The process has continued remorselessly. The incredible figure of more than £800,000,000 sterling is being spent in the currency of the present year on direct and indirect military preparations by Germany. The whole of Germany is an armed camp. Any Member of the House who has traveled there can add his corroboration of that statement. The industries of Germany are mobilized for war to an extent to which ours were not mobilized even a year after the Great War had begun. The whole population is being trained from childhood up to war. A mighty army is coming into being. Many submarines are already exercising in the Baltic. Great cannon, tanks, machine-guns and poison gas are fast accumulating. The Germans are even able to be great exporters of munitions as well as to supply their own enormous magazines The German air force is developing at a great speed, and in spite of ruthless sacrifice of life. We have no speedy prospect of equaling the German air force or of overtaking Germany in the air, whatever we may do in the near future.

We had a speech yesterday—it was a very welcome episode—from Mr. Lloyd George. He gave us some advice. But I must remind the House that he was very slow to recognize these tremendous developments in Germany. When I pointed out two or three years ago what was then beginning, he derided the idea; and he was not the only one. But neither he nor His Majesty's Government will, I imagine, disagree today with the statement that Germany is already well on her way to become, and must become, incomparably the most heavily armed nation in the world and the nation most completely ready for war. *There* is the dominant factor; *there* is the factor which dwarfs all others, and affects the movements of politics and diplomacy in every country throughout Europe; and it is a melancholy reflection in the last hours of this Parliament that we have been the helpless, perhaps even the supine, spectators of this vast transformation, to the acute distress of Europe and to our own grievous disadvantage.

I do not, of course, suggest that German rearmament is directed against us. It may well be that we are the last people the Germans would wish to attack. Certainly it would be in their interest to have our goodwill while they decided their deep differences with other countries. There is even a theory that the Germans are rearming only out of national self-respect and that they do not mean to hurt anyone at all. Whatever you believe, whatever you think, I venture to submit that we cannot have any anxieties comparable to the anxiety caused by German rearmament. The House will pardon me if I continue to press that anxiety upon it. I bear no grudge; I have no prejudice against the German people. I have many German friends, and I have a lively admiration for their splendid qualities of intellect and valor and for their achievements in science and art. The re-entry into the European circle of a Germany at peace within itself, with a heart devoid of hate, would be the most precious benefit for which we could strive, and a supreme advantage which alone would liberate Europe from its peril and its fear, and I believe that the British and French democracies would go a long way in extending the hand of friendship to realize such a hope.

But that is not the position which exists today. We cannot afford to see Nazidom in its present phase of cruelty and intolerance, with all its hatreds and all its gleaming weapons, paramount in Europe. In the shadow of German rearmament other dangers have taken shape on the Continent. We have, for instance, this war between Italy and Abyssinia, of which the newspapers are so full and which has occupied a good deal of our attention during this Debate. It is a very small matter compared with the dangers I have just described. I do not believe that Signor Mussolini would have embarked upon his Abyssinian venture but for the profound preoccupation of France with German rearmament, and, I must add, but for the real or supposed military and naval weakness of Great Britain. It was the fear of a rearmed Germany that led France to settle her differences with Italy at the beginning of this year, and very likely when these matters were being settled what is called a "free hand in Abyssinia" was thrown in. We may regret it, but we must first see and consider the forces operating upon France before we presume to utter reproaches. At that time, in January of this year, neither France nor Italy knew the length to which Great Britain was prepared to go in support of the League of Nations. They knew our views, but they did not know with what vigor we should press them The whole world has been astonished at the energy and vehemence displayed by His Majesty's Government, and I think we have been astonished ourselves.

I am very glad that Mr. Lloyd George recognized yesterday the difficult position of France. He told us, and I have every reason to believe he is correct, that the French agreement with Italy achieved in January of this year was worth eighteen divisions, that it meant a relief of eighteen divisions to the French Army by releasing all those additional troops for the defense of France in manning the long range of fortifications which, with their far smaller population, the French have found it necessary to erect against the terrors of a potential third Teutonic invasion. All these years we have urged France to make friends with Italy. It is a very grievous thing for them to be forced to choose between the League of Nations and Great Britain on the one hand, and their newly contracted arrangement with Italy on the other. Let us see what it means to France. The shadow of not merely two, but even of three years' compulsory military service falls once again upon the homes of France.

We all know that the French are pacific. They are quite as pacific as we are. They want to be left alone, as we do, and, I would add, as the people of Soviet Russia also wish to be left alone. But the French seem much nearer to the danger than we are. There is no strip of salt water to guard their land and their liberties We must remember that they are the only other great European country that has not reverted to despotism or dictatorship in one form or another.

In all the circumstances I submit that the efforts that France has made to give effect to the Covenant of the League of Nations, and the decision to which France has come to aid the British Fleet in certain remote contingencies, deserve the warmest recognition from all parties in the House.

It is upon this basis of German rearmament and French apprehension that the Italian-Abyssinian war and the dispute between Italy and the League of Nations can alone be properly considered. We are all agreed that we should walk soberly and warily and discreetly and peacefully, and even humbly, through this dangerous world. We are all agreed as to the peaceful demeanor to adopt and the abstention from violent speech which we should observe. Then there is a division. Some people say, "Put your trust in the League of Nations." Others say, "Put your trust in British rearmament." I say we want both. I put my trust in both. We have to run risks for both, and we have got to make exertions for both. I see no antagonism between the two. Neither is there any antagonism between those who would defend the Covenant of the League of Nations with their lives and those who would defend the British Empire. I believe these two ideas are at present only practical counterparts of one another.

It is quite certain that the British Empire will never fight a war contrary to the Covenant of the League of Nations. Any attempt to embark upon a war of aggrandizement or pride or ambition would break the British Empire into fragments, and any Government that was even suspected of such a motive would be chased from power long before its machinations could become effective. Therefore, if ever the British Empire is called upon to defend itself, its cause and the cause of the League of Nations will be one. Where, then, is the difference? The fortunes of the British Empire and its glory are inseparably interwoven with the fortunes of the world. We rise or we fall together. Indeed, if we survive today it is because even in bygone times our ancestors so managed that in the main the special interests of Britain conformed to the general interests of the world. Read history and find there anything which can contradict what I have said. I therefore make no secret of the fact that I regard the British Navy and its sister Services and all that is implied in the Covenant of the League of Nations as combined insurances for our peace and safety, and I am sure we need them both, and we need, besides, all our wit and wisdom, and all our patience and common sense, if we are to escape ourselves and to help the modern world out of the dangers which encompass us.

What is the great new fact about the League of Nations? What is the change that has taken place since we separated last August? It is this. The League of Nations is alive. It is alive and in action. It is fighting for its life. Probably it is fighting for all our lives. But it is fighting No one can ever pretend that without the United States the League of Nations could be a supreme authority, but the question has been for a long time whether it was not dead and a sham. People were despairing of the League of Nations. They pointed, and the Member for Sparkbrook [Mr. Amery] still points, with accusing and wounding finger, to its powerlessness in the Far East and to its indifference in the Chaco war.

When we separated in August the League of Nations was becoming a byword. Look at what has happened since. Here are fifty sovereign States solemnly sitting down together to devise and concert hostile economic action against a Great Power, prohibiting the export of arms to Italy, encouraging such export to Italy's enemy, taking concerted measures to destroy Italian credit and financial strength in every quarter of the globe, laying an embargo on many kinds of exports to Italy, and even attempting a complete boycott of Italian imports into each country. When we are told that there are leakages and loopholes, that difficulties will arise and disputes will break out between the boycotters, and so forth, that may all be true, but these are, to anyone who views things in their due proportion, only the exceptions which are proving a most impressive rule Such a system of pains and penalties has never been proclaimed against a single State, as far as I am aware, in the whole history of the world. If we could get away a little farther from the scene and take a more general view than is possible to us living through events from day to day, I am sure we should see that we are already in the presence of a memorable event.

Still more remarkable is the Italian acceptance of these sanctions. When we separated in August, when these matters were viewed in an academic light, the story was that economic sanctions meant war, and certainly the original attitude of Italy was that any attempt to apply sanctions would be treated as an unfriendly act and an affront. But what has happened? All this has proved to be untrue. Signor Mussolini—I think it is a sign of his commanding mind; to me it seems one of the strongest things he has done—has submitted to these invidious sanctions and still preserved his contact with the League of Nations. Instead of saying, "Italy will meet them with war," he says, "Italy will meet them with discipline, with frugality and with sacrifice." That is a great saying in the difficulties in which he stands. So I say that we are not only in the presence of an assertion of the public law of Europe, but of its recognition by the State affected and by the historic figure at the head of that State. That is also a truly remarkable fact, and one that is full of hope.[1]

---

[1] It was not apparent at this time that Signor Mussolini was accommodating himself to these sanctions because he had satisfied himself that none would be applied that could materially affect the progress of the war. Subsequently Signor Mussolini indicated that if further sanctions were imposed they might precipitate a European war. No further sanctions were imposed.

What does the House suppose has been the underlying cause of the transformation in the activity and force of the League of Nations which we have seen operative in the short time that we have been absent from this House? Sir Herbert Samuel seems to be entirely unconscious of it. He seems to suppose that it is simply the moral force of public opinion and the many good arguments used by the Liberal party and by Liberal writers which have produced this transformation. One is quite sorry to undeceive him. One would like him to have nursed his delusion for a little longer. But the truth is so apparent that it cannot be concealed. The reason why the League of Nations is now a reality and is now gripping all men's minds and inspiring loyalties in we know not what other countries which have hitherto regarded it as an academic proposition is that there has been behind it, as there was behind so many causes vital to human progress and freedom, the Royal Navy.

How did this arise? Let us see exactly in what context it arose. As I understand it, when the Government determined to take a strong line upon the League of Nations Council, it was certain that it would bring us into antagonism with Italy in the Mediterranean. We have ancient and valuable naval and military establishments in the Mediterranean. We have a fleet, a vital part of our own main fleet, in the Mediterranean. No doubt all these have been allowed to fall into a very easy peace-time state, and the Government would have been greatly to blame if they had pursued the course on which they had decided at Geneva without at the same time making our defenses safe in the Mediterranean. So the great machine was set in motion, and after an interval of a few weeks the impressive effect of superior sea power became manifest. That power has not been transferred to the League of Nations. Nevertheless it lies in a certain sense behind it, and it has invested every decision and every debate at Geneva with a gravity and a significance which it never otherwise could have possessed.

Sir Herbert Samuel was interrupted in his speech on Tuesday and asked a question which, apparently, disconcerted him. He was asked whether he would use force in support of the Covenant of the League of Nations. I did not think very much of the answer that he gave on the spur of the moment. I suppose many of us will be asked that question in the country. I can only state the answer that I am going to give. If I am asked, "How far will you go in support of the Covenant of the League of Nations?" I shall say we ought to go the whole way with the whole lot. But what would have happened if this trouble had arisen not now but three or four years hence, as other troubles may arise three or four years hence? Consider our position if today there was a German fleet a third as large as our own and, being entirely new, equal to two-thirds in modern quality, and if at the same time the two Italian 35,000-ton Dreadnoughts which are advanced in building were actually in commission. Could England have dared to speak her mind upon the Council of the League of Nations as she has done? Certainly she could not have done it without the deepest anxiety lest most grievous reprisals should be made against her establishments in the Mediterranean, upon Egypt, upon Palestine, upon the Suez Canal, upon the route which joins us with our possessions in the East. If there is one practical moral to be drawn from our present experience, it is that we must, without delay, and apart from any obligations that may arise in the North Sea, provide for the secure and lasting command of the Mediterranean.

I share the feeling common throughout the country of sympathy for the primitive, feudal people of Abyssinia who are fighting for their hearths and homes and for the ancient freedom of their mountains against a scientific invader. The native independence of Abyssinia cannot be made a matter for compromise or barter. But no one, least of all the Liberal party, can justify the conditions that prevail in that country. The Abyssinian Government themselves do not pretend to do so. Whether they have the power to correct them is another matter, but they cannot justify them. No one can keep up the pretense that Abyssinia is a fit, worthy and equal member of a league of civilized nations. The wisdom of the British policy was shown in our opposing her admission to the League, and the unwisdom of Continental countries, who now bitterly regret what they did, was shown in their consenting to it. It was a mistake. Steps must certainly be taken to make sure that the oppression by the dominant race in Abyssinia of the tribes which they have recently conquered is not perpetuated as the result of League of Nations action. Even in their own home and center, now that they have appealed to the League of Nations, now that the searchlights of the world are beating their glare upon the history and conditions of this region, the Abyssinians must be made to put their house in order. It is of the utmost importance to the House and country to realize that the League of Nations cannot take one-sided action in a matter of this kind, and only look at the faults of one side without considering its responsibility for putting right abuses and great evils on the part of the other party which has appealed to its jurisdiction.

It was said yesterday that the economic sanctions will not really embarrass the Italian Dictator, and he knows they will not embarrass him or else he would never have bowed to them. That all depends upon the length of time they are maintained. We live in such a febrile and sensational age that even a month or two is enough to make people not merely change their views, but forget the views and feelings they entertained before. I agree with the Chancellor of the Exchequer [Mr. Neville Chamberlain] that this matter will be one involving a long strain which will require a cool and phlegmatic temperament. The limitations of the action which can be taken by the League of Nations are defined and well known, and no one has suggested that we could do more than we have done, or that we should take isolated action. As far as we are concerned, one of the causes and circumstances which make the strain painful to us is the prolongation of the spectacle we shall have to witness in Abyssinia —the painful spectacle of the desperate resistance of these people barely armed against all the resources of science. [Hon. Members: "Hear, hear!"] Certainly. But still do not let us suppose that the measures which are being taken are not most formidable. We must not only look a month or two ahead. Where will the Italian Dictator be at this time next year? He may be far into Abyssinia with an army of a quarter of a million men, wasting rapidly by guerilla warfare and disease, and all the time Italy, under the boycott and censure of practically the whole world, will be bleeding at every pore, her gold reserve melting away, her prices rising, her credit gone. Do not let us undervalue the extreme importance of the long, slow pressures which are being applied, and do not let us underestimate the dangers which they necessarily cause by increasing the tension which prevails throughout all Europe.

We have moved on and we are not going to move back. The League of Nations has passed from shadow into substance, from theory into practice, from rhetoric into reality. We see a structure always majestic, but hitherto shadowy, which is now being clothed with life and power, and endowed with coherent thought and concerted action. We begin to feel the beatings of a pulse which may, we hope and we pray, some day —and the sooner for our efforts—restore a greater measure of health and strength to the whole world. We can see these difficulties and dangers for ourselves, but if we confront them with a steady eye, I believe the House and the country will reach the conclusion that the case for perseverance holds the field.

THE PROCESS OF REARMING

March 10, 1936

Debate on a motion for approval of the Government's defense policy

1935

October 28   Publication of the Government's General Election manifesto.
"The League of Nations will remain as heretofore the key-stone of British foreign policy The prevention of war and the establishment of peace in the world must always be the most vital interest of the British people, and the League is the instrument which has been framed and to which we look for the attainment of these objects. We shall therefore continue to do all in our power to uphold the Covenant and to maintain and increase the efficiency of the League In the present unhappy dispute between Italy and Abyssinia there will be no wavering in the policy we have hitherto pursued "

November 9.   Sir Samuel Hoare, speaking at the Guildhall
"The British people are determined to keep their word to Europe and the world They are determined to join in any honorable attempts that will bring the Abyssinian war to an end   Soberly and steadfastly we intend to carry out our obligations and strive for peace wherever peace is threatened This is our policy It is simple and clear It has not changed since my speech at Geneva, nor will it change after the election "

November 14.   General Election. Government returned with majority of 247.

December 6   Sir Samuel Hoare visits M Laval in Paris

December 9.   The French Press publish various versions of the Hoare-Laval plan
The Cabinet approve the Hoare-Laval plan to partition Abyssinia between Italy and the Emperor

December 10.   Mr Baldwin tells the House of Commons:
"I have seldom spoken with greater regret, for my lips are not yet unsealed Were these troubles over I would make a case, and I guarantee that not a man would go into the Lobby against us."

December 13   Publication of full text of the Hoare-Laval proposals.

December 18   Sir Samuel Hoare resigns.

December 19   Mr. Baldwin tells the House of Commons
"We were not aware until it had been accomplished that an agreement had been come to It was not until breakfast time on Monday morning [December 16] that I received a letter from Sir Samuel Hoare urging that the Cabinet might endorse what he had done. Almost immediately afterwards, and before we had

had time to study the documents, the leakage took place. We were summoned to consider whether we would endorse the action of our colleague or whether we would repudiate it. We had to decide quickly. There was no time for discussion owing to the leakage that had taken place. We had to decide quickly because we knew that a storm of questions would be upon us and that the matter would be raised in this House. We none of us liked the proposals; we thought they went too far. ..

"I am telling the House exactly how we all felt, and, having, as I said, felt that these proposals went too far, I was not at all surprised at the expression of feeling in that direction I was not expecting that deeper feeling that was manifested in many parts of the country on what I may call the grounds of conscience and of honor. The moment I am confronted with that I know that something has happened that has appealed to the deepest feelings of our countrymen, that some note has been struck that brings back from them a response from the depths I examined again all that I had done, and I felt that with that feeling, that was perfectly obvious, there could not be the support in this country behind those proposals even as terms of negotiation It is perfectly obvious now that the proposals are absolutely and completely dead. This Government is certainly going to make no attempt to resurrect them. If there arose a storm when I knew I was in the right I would let it break on me, and I would either survive it or break. If I felt after examination of myself that there was in that storm something which showed me that I had done something that was not wise or right, then I would bow to it."

December 20. Mr Chamberlain, speaking at Birmingham:
"We must, therefore, go back to the policy of sanctions, and in due course I trust that the League of Nations will show, as I believe they will show, that they are prepared to make themselves ready to resist any attack that may be made on any one of their members."

December 23. Mr Eden becomes Foreign Secretary. The post of Minister for League of Nations Affairs is abolished.

1936

February 27. Mr. Baldwin announces that he has decided to appoint a Minister to co-ordinate defense.

March 3. Publication of White Paper on the rearmament program, outlining erection of "shadow factories" for aircraft production

March 7. Hitler reoccupies the Rhineland, denounces the Treaties of Versailles and Locarno, but states that the reoccupation is purely symbolic. The German Ambassador in London, Herr von Hoesch, hands Mr. Eden a memorandum containing proposals for a twenty-five years non-aggression pact between Germany, France and Belgium, and possibly Holland, with Great Britain and Italy as guarantors, a Western air pact, and the return of Germany to the League of Nations

March 9.   The Foreign Secretary [Mr Eden] tells the House of Commons that the British Government still considers the Locarno Treaty to be binding, and that, should there take place in the near future any attack on France or Belgium which would constitute a violation of the Treaty, they would consider themselves in honor bound to go to the assistance of the country attacked.

THE PROCESS OF REARMING

I LISTENED TO the most full and painstaking statement which the Home Secretary [Sir John Simon] made to us upon the machinery of the Committees of Defence which are now in existence and upon the reform which it is now intended to work in them. Certainly no one could accuse him of not wishing to meet faithfully all the questions which were asked or all the arguments which were adduced; but there was one very simple question which he overlooked in regard to this reform in our system of defense co-ordination. Why has it been delayed until now? I remember a Debate which took place in July last, eight months ago, in this House, and I remember a memorial of 140 Members to the Prime Minister asking for something of this very kind. Is there an argument now which was not well known then? Why have these very important eight months been lost in this matter?

It would seem, on the face of it, rather odd to invite the co-ordinator after the co-ordination is, according to the Government White Paper, already perfect and complete; to appoint the man who is to concert the plan after it has already been made and embodied in the detailed Estimates for the current year. The usual process, if I may model myself on the somewhat simple types of exposition in which my right hon. and learned Friend [Sir John Simon] excels, is to put the horse before the cart, the idea being, I presume, although I do not wish to take anything for granted, that as the horse moves forward he, as it were, drags the cart behind him. That, of course, would be the usual and normal procedure, but no doubt there may be very good reasons for having adopted the contrary one in this case.

I cannot feel that the Debate, so far as it has proceeded, has done full justice to the anxiety which the House feels about the condition of our national defenses The Prime Minister yesterday and the Home Secretary today were concerned to offer two explanations of that condition. Both these explanations are familiar, and neither is without validity. The first is that we tried to set an example in disarmament. We continued to disarm while others were rearming, and consequently we very soon fell very far behind. The second is the ten-years rule about which the Home Secretary has given the House a great deal of valuable information this afternoon. Now, I think there was a great deal to be said for the ten-years rule in 1919 and in 1924. As a matter of fact, the time has passed— the ten years have expired without the world being disturbed by a major war. As a means of giving a rough-and-ready guide to Departments the ten-years rule in those days was valuable, but, of course, it had to be revised each year. Every year you had to see whether it was ten, nine or eight years, or whether you had to abandon the principle altogether. There is nothing, I think, that anyone who supported that principle in those years after the War has any reason to regret.

After all, Germany was completely disarmed. France was heavily armed and our friend. Italy was our friend. The British battle fleet ten years ago was not as old as it is now; it was in its prime. In those days such a provision was entirely justified. No one will found a criticism upon this Government, or upon any Government from either side of the House, because during the years of assured security, armaments were continually reduced, as they should be, and as they always have been during the progress of a long peace. But that hardly meets the point on which criticism arises. As the Prime Minister said, speaking of 1933, a great change came over the situation, and today the Home Secretary mentioned 1932 as the year when this ten-years rule was abandoned.

The cause of that change was that Germany began to rearm, secretly at first, but soon more openly, to create armed forces of various kinds, particularly in the air, and these forces became very soon increasingly formidable in their character. It was somewhere in that period 1932-33 that the Government scented the first signs of danger and abandoned the ten-years rule. But they ought to have done a great deal more than that. Then was the moment when the change took place, and I think I may say that there were some of us in this House who gave full warnings on every occasion on which we had an opportunity to do so of the gravity of the change which was coming over the scene. The pages of the Official Report are dark with the warnings which we gave, and I cannot believe that the very admirable Intelligence Service of this country, which in the

Great War was considered to be the best in the world, did not give its warnings through other channels.

The gravamen of the criticism which lies against the Government is that they did not realize effectively, or at any rate that they did not act in accordance with, the marked deterioration in world affairs which occurred in 1932 and 1933. They continued to adhere to a policy which was adapted to one set of circumstances after an entirely different set of circumstances had supervened. They persisted in spite of all that we could say to the contrary. I suppose they resented the warnings which were given, although the warnings which I gave to the House were sober warnings, specific warnings and friendly warnings Let us take the year 1933. In 1933 there was plenty of time to put our house in order The bulk of the German preparations have been made since then. Everyone knows that in three years enormous results can be achieved. If three years ago the preliminary steps had been taken to repair our deficiencies we should not feel the anxiety—the unspoken anxiety—which underlies the Debate this afternoon.

Let us survey the scene. The scale on which foreign rearmament is proceeding is prodigious. Some time ago I made a statement that Germany had spent, directly or indirectly, on armaments in the year 1935 upwards of £800,000,000 sterling. These figures startled people—at least, they startled those people who are capable of taking in anything I made that statement on good authority, and I have had the assistance of a financial authority who has worked out for me a long argument, much too long to quote in debate, showing how money has been secretly found for these purposes in the German finances. Broadly speaking, since the arrival of Herr Hitler in power three years ago the Germans have spent about £1,500,000,000 sterling upon warlike preparations directly or indirectly. The money has been raised by internal borrowing, and the revenues of Germany are already mortgaged two or three, or possibly four, years ahead. These figures are stupendous. Nothing like them has ever been seen in time of peace. Supposing they are exaggerated and that the figure which they spent in 1935 is only £600,000,000, we should still be confronted with facts which are unprecedented, unparalleled and immeasurable in their consequences. It must also be remembered that in all probability money goes further in Germany than here. In face of these figures it surely seems unreasonable to blame His Majesty's Government for the modest sum for which they are asking in the Estimates of the year and for the additional expenditure that will be required under the White Paper.

The fact that Germany is spending at this enormous rate upon armaments warns us not only of the magnitude of the danger, but possibly of its imminence Expenditure on armaments means wages. The weekly livelihood for a very large proportion of the German people has now become dependent upon military preparations. Several millions of people in Germany who were unemployed have found employment in munitions manufacture or in the armed forces. On the other hand, the whole is supported by borrowed money on a large scale, and the financial situation has become such that this cannot go on indefinitely.

It cannot go on, but how can it stop? A terrible dilemma lies ahead of the most peacefully minded Government in Germany. If they go on, there is bankruptcy; if they stop, there is tremendous unemployment. There is no chance of Germany finding additional substitute employment by trading with tropical colonies, or by the peaceful conquest of our markets or those of other nations, which would in the immediate future in the slightest degree compensate for the curtailment of the vast munitions program on which the whole of Germany is now engaged. The German Government will have to choose at no distant date between an internal and an external catastrophe. Can we doubt what course the man at the head of Germany would be likely to choose?

It is easy to say this cannot go on, but what will happen when it stops? It is that which invests the situation with the most alarming urgency, with a kind of doom-like inevitableness which causes the most melancholy and alarming reflections. Germany, we are told, is not yet ready for war. Some say she is only half ready. Yet we see already that she is the only nation in Europe unafraid of war. If what we have seen in the last few days is the mood of a partially armed Germany, imagine what the tone will be when these colossal preparations are approaching their zenith, and when at the same time the limits of internal borrowing are already in sight.

Wars do not always wait until all the combatants are ready. Sometimes they come before any are ready, sometimes when one nation thinks itself less unready than another, or when one nation thinks it is likely to become, not stronger, but weaker as time passes. I fear, indeed, that there may be a culminating point in the history of Europe—the armaments history of Europe. I cannot tell when it will be reached. It will certainly be reached in the lifetime of the present Parliament Let us never accept the theory of inevitable war· neither let us blind our eyes to the remorseless march of events.

I was glad to hear the Prime Minister devote so much of his speech yesterday to the problem of supply. There are two ways of preparing for the supply side of national defense. First, there is the accumulation of reserves of munitions of all kinds, which under modern conditions must be enormous, and the storing of them at great expense in magazines. That method was the only one which was known and practiced up to the Great War. There is a second method, the modern method, which is quite different. The whole industry of a country is prepared in time of peace for an alternative form of manufacture. Even the smallest workshops play their part in making components. Assembly centers are provided where the components can be fitted together. Thus the whole industry of the country is ready to turn over from peace to war conditions on the pressing of a button.

If we had only begun to act three years ago when the danger first made itself apparent, we should possess a reserve power today which could spring at any moment into full preparatory activity. Very little disturbance three years ago would have produced enormous reserves at the present time. I am well aware that something has been done. What is immediately needed is to bring it out into the open, to support it with ample money and staff, and to press it forward with the utmost vigor. Let me make myself clear. This does not mean any immediate increase in the deliveries. It does not mean immediately more ships, more munitions, more aeroplanes, but it does mean that you have an industry which, if the need ever arises, will not fail you, and will not interpose between you and your safety two horrible years of hiatus such as some of us in positions of responsibility went through in the Great War. What a thing to see the roads of this country covered with the volunteer youth of the nation drilling for a year with nothing but broomsticks and wooden muskets, and what a much more terrible thing to see those who were in the fighting line, in the trenches, under a continuous bombardment with batteries behind them that were limited to firing one round per battery per day!

Your industry must be ready to sustain you. This work should have been begun in vigor three years ago, it should have been in progress two years ago, it should have been completed one year ago. All I urge is— do it now. Here in a nutshell is the history of munitions production: first year, very little; second year, not much, but something; third year, almost all you want; fourth year, more than you need. We are only at the beginning of the second year, whereas Germany is already, in many respects, at the end of the third. Therefore, my recommendation to the Prime Minister is to create as soon as possible a skeleton Ministry of Munitions, with a Munitions Council of ten or a dozen selected businessmen who would serve as before in an honorary capacity. I am sure this should be set on foot at the earliest moment, and unless it is we shall not get even the restricted deliveries which we are hoping to get under the present scheme.

I must utter this warning which is borne in upon me. Contractors are usually glad to book orders from the Government, however large those orders may be, because they know that when they are found to be behind-hand in their deliveries the Government cannot punish them, since it has become dependent on them, and all it can do is to come along and help them out. It was a cruel mortification to Lord Kitchener, in the first year of the War, when he found that so many of the promises made by the contractors—not the regular War Office contractors, but the outside contractors—in the excitement of the early months were completely falsified by events, and that deliveries bore no relation to what had been counted upon or what the troops in the field counted upon.

There is a sentence in the White Paper which shows how very urgent this matter is. It is on page 10, paragraph 3, dealing with the Territorial Army:

> For the present, owing to the demands upon the capacity of industrial output which must necessarily be made, in the first instance, by the Regular Army, it is not possible simultaneously to recondition the Territorial Army.

Just think of that! Why? These two forces put together are only a quarter of a million men, and we are told that our vast, flexible, buoyant, rich, fertile, adaptable British industry is incapable of conducting the equipment of these two comparatively small forces simultaneously! I refuse to believe such a thing. What is it they are needing? It is not weapons, but the equipment, which is to be delayed. I suppose wagons, and appliances of various kinds, field-cookers, and all the different appliances which the Territorials require. These are the things which, we are told, cannot be made by industry in Britain. Do you want anything other than this tell-tale sentence to prove that industry has not been organized?

Let me apply this consideration for a moment to aeroplanes. Eight months ago, when the present Secretary of State for Air [Lord Swinton] took office, the aeroplane industry was roused to a most urgent exertion Very large orders of all kinds were placed with the existing firms, which were already building to their utmost capacity. What the results have been no one can tell. That this great volume of production is going forward in the existing factories is undoubted, but we cannot tell how far the deliveries will correspond. That has been done, and very rightly done, by the energetic Minister who occupies that post; but we have not, I believe, attempted in any concrete physical manner to organize the manufacture of components by firms not normally accustomed to produce aviation parts, nor have we provided the suitable assembly plants necessary in times of emergency.

Here is the great disadvantage at which we stand compared with the German air industry. I am not mentioning this for the first time. I told the House eighteen months ago of the extraordinary development of this method which was proceeding in Germany. There is not the slightest reason why it should not be set on foot here. It might have corrected to some extent the boom in aircraft shares. It would, anyhow, have given a reserve, if trouble comes, without which, although you may have a force at the beginning of the war, you will not have the power to keep that force in continuous activity, and it will come to an end after a few months. There is no doubt that this method of the widely distributed manufacture of components ought to be as much a part of the life of an industrial country in this present unhappy modern age as the practice of archery on the village green was in medieval England. It is the simplest and most primary method by which the freedom of a country can be assured, and it is the very heart of modern national defense.

The air power of any country cannot be measured by the number of aeroplanes, nor by any of the particular definitions which are given. It must be measured by the number of aeroplanes which can be placed in the air simultaneously and maintained in action month after month. It is dependent not only on the number of organized squadrons, but upon the expansive power of the industrial plant. A mere comparison of the number of machines possessed by the different countries, or the number of pilots trained, or even the number of squadrons formed, is no true guide. The organization of the aeroplane industry is not merely the production or the accumulation of so many thousands of aeroplanes by a given date. It must also ensure the continuous flow of supplies from the date of the outbreak; and the supreme advantage which Germany has seized at the present time resides in this fact. They do not need to have any considerable reserve. They can feed the fighting squadrons direct from the factories and testing grounds, just as, in the last year of the War, when Mr. Lloyd George's great national shell factories and gun plants came into operation, we were able to feed the field armies direct from the factories without the need to accumulate supplies short of the actual fighting zone.

In these circumstances it is, I am sorry to say, not likely that we shall be able to overtake Germany and achieve air parity, as was promised, unless and until Germany herself decides to slow down or arrest her air expansion. Clearly a saturation point will be reached when those who are guiding Germany decide that they have given to air development all that portion of their resources which they can spare, having regard to all other needs. If, when that point is reached, we continue to develop our force, ultimately we shall achieve air parity, but that day will be fixed by decisions which will be taken in Germany and not by decisions which will be taken here, whatever we do

Let us see what we are doing. It is a general impression that we are overhauling Germany now; that we started late, it is true, but are making up for lost time, and that every month our relative position will improve. That is a delusion. It is contrary to the truth this year, and probably for many months next year. I am not saying anything which is not known in every country in the world. These matters are thoroughly understood. Germany will be outstripping us more and more even if our new programs are accepted, and we shall be worse off at the end of this year than we are now, in spite of all our exertions. The explanation of this unpleasant fact lies in the past. Take the simple test of money. I am assuming that the Government are doing all they can. I am absolutely certain that the Chancellor of the Exchequer is putting no financial restriction on any money that can be usefully spent in achieving our security. But let us look at the position. We spent in the financial year which is now closing £29,000,000 on the air, under the original and supplementary Estimates. In about the same period— the dates do not quite tally—the French voted nearly £70,000,000 and spent, I expect, at least £60,000,000.[1] The Germans spent certainly far more, though I cannot hazard a figure; but both France and Germany

[1] This last estimate was, unhappily, not true.

spent on their air development at least twice what we were able to spend last year, and, as I have said, money goes farther in those countries than here.

I have no doubt His Majesty's Government would gladly spend more money than was asked for, but it is no use to clamor for larger programs. The Government could easily double their paper programs and get a cheap cheer from uninstructed persons, but they would be doing nothing except deceiving the public. Before I press the Government for any larger programs of aeroplanes I should like to feel sure that the present programs are being executed, and I very much doubt whether, with the existing methods, they will be.

Will there be time to put our defenses in order? We live in contact with the unknown, but we are not defenseless now Will there be time to make these necessary efforts, or will the awful words "too late" be recorded? I will never despair that we can make ourselves secure. The Royal Navy, especially after the toning up which it has received, is unsurpassed in the world, and is still the main bulwark of our security; and even at this eleventh hour, if the right measures are taken and if the right spirit prevails in the British nation and the British Empire, we may surround ourselves with other bulwarks equally sure, which will protect us against whatever storms may blow.

THE VIOLATION OF THE RHINELAND

March 26, 1936

Third Reading of the Consolidated Fund Bill

1936

March 12 Franco-Soviet Pact ratified by the French Senate.

March 13. Mr. Baldwin appoints the Attorney-General [Sir Thomas Inskip] Minister for the Co-ordination of Defense.

March 14 The Council of the League of Nations meets in London and invites Germany to send a delegate.

March 18. Herr von Ribbentrop arrives in London to attend League Council meeting

March 20. Publication of a White Paper containing the results of the League Council deliberations Germany is invited to submit her case against the Franco-Soviet Pact to the Hague Court and to undertake not to increase her troops in the Rhineland pending further negotiations If Germany refuses these proposals the British and Italian Governments undertake to carry out the steps entailed by their obligations under the Treaty of Locarno and to hold Staff conversations with France and Belgium.

THE VIOLATION OF THE RHINELAND

IT IS OFTEN usual to say what a good Debate we have had, but in this case there has not been much debate. The remarkable fact which emerges today is that upon one of the most delicate and one of the most grievous topics that could possibly be discussed there is an overwhelming agreement. For that we owe a good deal to the speech of the Secretary of State for Foreign Affairs [Mr. Eden]. It was a speech which required courage of soul. We were with him when he said that he would not be the Foreign Secretary to break the word of Britain. Ministers of the Crown have great problems to settle; often those problems do not admit a satisfactory solution either way; often Ministers make mistakes. But as long as they are prepared to back their policy with faith and with conviction they may rely, if not on the approval of the House, at any rate upon its sympathy and respect. In this case my right hon. Friend has carried the House with him at a most critical moment, and on a most decisive utterance. I only wish that guidance had been given to the country earlier. Three weeks have passed without those notes which he struck with such resonant clarity. It is a pity that more active measures have not been taken to place the realities of which he spoke before our public.

There is an extraordinary volume of German propaganda in this country, of misstatements made on the highest authority—which everyone knows could be easily disproved—but which obtain currency, and which, because they are not contradicted, are accepted as part of the regular facts on which the public rely. Ministers and Members who are in agreement with the policy of the Government must exert themselves to explain these matters to an anxious, but loyal and courageous public. I feel very much relieved and even exhilarated by the speech to which we have listened, because of two considerations which lay heavy on my mind What is, after all, the first great fact with which we are confronted? It is this: an enormous triumph has been gained by the Nazi régime. The German Chancellor, perhaps advised against the course he took by his military experts, nevertheless decided on ordering the violation of the Rhineland and the destruction of the Locarno Treaty. He has succeeded—it is no good blinding ourselves to it—his troops are there, and who is to say that they will be removed? He has accomplished this end, and although the world has been alarmed and shocked, and many protests have been made, the event has occurred.

And what an event! Under the brazen surface of the totalitarian State there stir and seethe all the emotions of a great, cultured, educated and once free community. The Protestant, the Catholic, the Jew, the Monarchist, the Communist, the Liberal—all these forces are there, held in suspense, held in a certain grip and vice, but they are there. Let us suppose that any one of us were a German and living in Germany, and perhaps entirely discontented with many things that he saw around him, but thinking that here is the Fuhrer, the great Leader of the country, who has raised it so high—and I admire him for that—able to bring home once again a great trophy. One year it is the Saar, another month the right to have conscription, another month to gain from Britain the right to build submarines, another month the Rhineland. What will it be next? Austria, Memel, other territories and disturbed areas, are already in view. If we were Germans, and discontented with the present régime, nevertheless on patriotic grounds there is many a man who would say, "While the Government is bringing home these trophies I cannot indulge my personal, sectional or party feeling against it." This country is in the presence of facts which, apart from the technical consequences of the military occupation of the Rhineland, constitute an immense blow at the League of Nations and the principle of the reign of law, and an immense gain in prestige to the Nazi Government.

There is another reason why I feel that the Foreign Secretary was bound to make the speech he did. We had something to do with the events which made the conditions under which the Germans acted. From the highest and most benevolent motives—and I do not dissociate myself from the general course which the Government took—we have pressed upon France a policy of sanctions against Italy that is estranging these two countries. When I was invited to give my opinion on the matter last August,[1] I said that we must do our duty under the Covenant of the League, but that we should not press France unduly, and that we should not go beyond the point where we could carry France. I think we went much farther than that in sanctions. As I tried to point out to the House, the friendship between France and Italy was vital to the defense and security of every home in France; and France, out of regard for Britain and out of loyalty to the principles of the League of Nations, went very far—not so far as some enthusiasts would have wished her to go, not so far as those who did not understand how fast she was moving expected her to move; but very far she did move, and considerable injury was inevitable in the relations of France and Italy. That produced a situation in which, it seems to me, all the elements were present which led to the recent outrage upon international law and upon the Treaties which regulate the peace of Europe.

When we, think of the great power and influence which this country exercises we cannot look back with much pleasure on our foreign policy in the last five years. They certainly have been disastrous years. God forbid that I should lay on the Government of my own country the charge of responsibility for the evils which have come upon the world in that period! I would not do such a thing, but certainly in that period we have seen the most depressing and alarming change in the outlook of mankind which has ever taken place in so short a period. Five years ago all felt safe; five years ago all were looking forward to peace, to a period in which mankind would rejoice in the treasures which science can spread to all classes if conditions of peace and justice prevail. Five years ago to talk of war would have been regarded not only as a folly and a crime, but almost as a sign of lunacy. Look at the difference in our position now! We find ourselves compelled once again to face the hateful problems and ordeals which those of us who worked and toiled in the last struggle hoped were gone forever.

Some responsibility rests upon our own conduct of affairs. I do not think it is easy to set out over those years the various acts of policy and the utterances of successive British Foreign Secretaries and connect them into one harmonious theme. We have sometimes bewildered the Continent, and we have erred also in trying to gain sympathy and transient applause by putting forward platitudes and hopes which no one really felt could be realized. In this period we have undoubtedly disturbed

[1] Mr. Churchill, Sir Herbert Samuel, Mr. Lloyd George and Mr. Lansbury had been asked to visit Sir Samuel Hoare at the Foreign Office.

Europe—from the highest motives. Nothing was more honorable than the disarmament which Britain practiced on herself, nothing was more idealistic than the counsels which we gave to others differently situated. Even upon this question of sanctions we have taken the lead. A very great responsibility rests upon us in that matter.

In this island—where we are still blessed by being surrounded by a strip of salt water, in spite of the alterations which later developments have caused—we ought to be careful that in our interventions in the foreign sphere we understand fully the consequences they may bring to those who live upon the Continent and the feelings which they may create there, in contrast with the sentiments which they arouse in us. I trust that 'the Government will not seek to win the easy applause of public opinion, but will confront the nation steadily and robustly with the realities of the situation, knowing the comprehension which the nation will give in return to those who deal with it faithfully.

The violation of the Rhineland is serious from the point of view of the menace to which it exposes Holland, Belgium and France. It is also serious because when the Rhineland is fortified—and I listened with apprehension to what the Secretary of State said about the Germans declining even to refrain from entrenching themselves during the period of negotiations; I listened with sorrow to that—when there is there a line of fortifications, as I suppose there will be in a very short time, it will produce reactions on the European situation. It will be a barrier across Germany's front door, which will leave her free to sally out eastward and southward by the other doors.

What is the real problem, the real peril? It is not reoccupation of the Rhineland, but this enormous process of the rearmament of Germany. There is the peril. Mr. Lansbury says that in the Election I seemed to be haunted by this thought. I confess that I have been occupied with this idea of the great wheels revolving and the great hammers descending day and night in Germany, making the whole industry of that country an arsenal, welding the whole of its population into one disciplined war machine. There is the problem that lies before you. There is what is bringing war nearer. This Rhineland episode is but a step, a stage, an incident in this process. There is fear in every country, all round. Even here, in this island, with some protection from distance, there is fear, deep fear. What is the fear and what is the question which arises from that fear? It is, "How are we going to stop this war which seems to be moving towards us in so many ways?"

There are, of course, two practical foreign policies for our country The first is an alliance between Great Britain and France, the two surviving liberal democracies of the West, who, strongly armed, rich, powerful, with the sea at their disposal, with great air forces and great armies, would stand with their backs to the ocean and allow the explosion which may come in Europe to blast its way eastward or southward. That is a practical foreign policy, but I hope we shall not resign ourselves to that without an earnest effort to persevere in the other policy—namely, the establishment of real collective security under the League of Nations and of the reign of law and respect for international law throughout Europe. We should endeavor now with great resolution to establish effective collective security. All the nations and States that are alarmed at the growth of German armaments ought to combine for mutual aid in pacts of mutual assistance approved by the League of Nations and in accordance with the Covenant of the League.

We hear talk of the encirclement of Germany. The last speaker quite justly said that war encirclement would be intolerable, but peaceful, defensive encirclement may be inevitable before the alarms of the nations are allayed. We would impose no arrangement on Germany that we would not submit to ourselves. It is not a case of the encirclement of Germany, but of the encirclement of the potential aggressor. If *we* are the aggressors, let us be encircled and brought to reason by the pressure of other countries. If France is the aggressor, let her be restrained in the same way; and if it be Germany, let Germany accept the measures meted out to her by countries who submit themselves to the law which they are prepared to take a share in enforcing The first thing we ought to do is to make these pacts of mutual aid and assistance. Mr. Lloyd George, who is not here now, spoke words of warning about military conventions But you cannot have effective arrangements for mutual aid in contingencies of peril unless you have conventions. That is the first thing.

In the second place, once the Powers are woven into this strong confederacy for defense and peace, they should give Germany an absolute guarantee of the inviolability of German soil and a promise that if anyone offends her all will turn against that one, and if she strikes at anyone all will stand by and defend that victim. I am looking for peace. I am looking for a way to stop war, but you will not stop it by pious sentiments and appeals. You will only stop it by making practical arrangements. When you have these two conditions established firmly, when you have linked up the forces at the disposal of the League for defense, and when you have offered that guarantee to Germany, then is the first moment when you should address Germany collectively, not only upon the minor question of the Rhine, but upon the supreme question of German rearmament in relation to other countries Further, at the moment you must invite Germany to state her grievances, to lay them on the council board and have it out. But do not let us be a rabble flying before forces we dare not resist. Let us negotiate from strength and not from weakness; from unity and not from division and isolation; let us seek to do justice because we have power.

The whole history of the world is summed up in the fact that when nations are strong they are not always just, and when they wish to be just they are often no longer strong. I desire to see the collective forces of the world invested with overwhelming power. If you are going to depend on a slight margin, one way or the other, you will have war. But if you get five or ten to one on one side, all bound rigorously by the Covenant and the conventions which they own, then you may have an opportunity of a settlement which will heal the wounds of the world. Let us have this blessed union of power and of justice· "Agree with thine adversary quickly, whiles thou art in the way with him " Let us free the world from the reproach of a castrophe carrying with it calamity and tribulation beyond the tongue of man to tell.

THE FORTIFICATION OF THE RHINELAND

April 6, 1936

Supply (international situation considered on going into Committee)

‐

THE FORTIFICATION OF THE
RHINELAND

I WAS abroad when the Hoare-Laval crisis occurred, but I certainly sustained the impression, at a distance from this country, that something very serious had happened to the Government, and also that the Prime Minister had been affected, and had been affected in those qualities which have commended, and still characteristically commend, him to the British public. At any rate, one felt that there was a great deal that was not easy to understand about his first speech, about his lips being sealed, about the subsequent change of policy, and about the circumstances which led to the Foreign Secretary leaving the Government. It was a very obscure and difficult situation, and when I returned to this country I was conscious of a different atmosphere in the House of Commons from that which had existed when we all met so triumphantly after the General Election.

One incident has certainly filled me with surprise. Some few weeks ago Sir Austen Chamberlain made a most serious speech of criticism, and even of censure, addressed to the Prime Minister in his own presence. It astonished me that the Prime Minister did not rise at once and say whatever occurred to him to say. After all, this is a forum of debate, and an indictment preferred by a Member of high responsibility, especially a Member who has long been the buttress, and on one occasion at least the savior, of the Prime Minister's Government, ought not to be left unanswered. There ought to be the cut-and-thrust of debate and I am surprised that the right hon. Gentleman, if not at that moment, at any rate at the earliest opportunity, did not take up the points of argument which were addressed to him. If issues of this kind are pushed aside and ignored, and an attempt is made to carry the business of Parliament forward with the influence of the Whips, of the Central Office and of an indulgent Press—if that is to become the process, there is bound to be a weakening in the ties which unite the House to the Government and which preserve the vitality of our Parliamentary institutions.

The Government ask for a Vote of Confidence. They do not ask it because they have done exceptionally well. They will no doubt get the Vote of Confidence, but I hope they will not make the mistake of thinking that it is a testimonial, or a bouquet, or that it arises from long-pent-up spontaneous feelings of enthusiasm which can no longer be held in check.

There are many matters that are in order in this Debate. It is very difficult to judge what is happening in the military sphere in Ethiopia, but it looks as if the Ethiopian people were being heavily defeated, and there are some authorities who doubt whether their resistance can even be prolonged until the rains come. If that should be so—I cannot attempt to prophesy—then quite soon all those Abyssinians who have not been destroyed by poison gas will be subjugated and their native land annexed by Italy. If that happens it will be certainly a melancholy chapter in the recent records of the British people. The aggressor will be triumphant. He will be rewarded with gains far beyond the Hoare-Laval proposals. The League of Nations—fifty nations led by one, as Signor Mussolini said, in a phrase of formidable significance—will have been unable to do anything of the slightest use to the Abyssinians. Indeed, all we have done for them, as far as I can remember, is to put an embargo on their obtaining arms before they were attacked. Otherwise we have done nothing for them at all—except, of course, the speeches which have been made.

There is a heavy score on the other side of the account. We have incurred the antagonism of Italy in the Mediterranean. That, I expect, will mean in future years a greatly increased charge for our military, naval and air forces in protecting all the important establishments we have in that area. We shall, in fact, only maintain the independence of Egypt in the future and keep open the road to India by an increasingly serious strain upon our resources. We have in this matter fallen between two stools. We have managed to secure the disadvantages of all the courses without the advantages of any. We have pressed France into a course of action which did not go far enough to help the Abyssinians, but went far enough to sever her from Italy, with the result that the occasion was given to Herr Hitler to tear up treaties and reoccupy the Rhineland. Incidentally, it is for these results that we have paid £6,000,000 or £7,000,000 sterling, as the Supplementary Navy Estimates show, and have inflicted a very considerable strain upon the personnel of our Fleet.

The responsibility, not for the events of the world, but for the conduct of our interventions in this matter, must rest in a direct manner upon the Government, nor can you exclude the Prime Minister from his share. There is an old constitutional doctrine that the King can do no wrong, and if the King does what is thought to be wrong it is his bad advisers who are blamed; but to apply that doctrine to the controversial head of a political Government would be an altogether undue extension of the principle. Both the last and the present House of Commons have followed very docilely and faithfully the course recommended to them in regard to our interventions, and the degree of our interventions, in the Italo-Abyssinian sphere, and here is where we have been led. Now, Sir, I say it was a very grievous thing to lead these fifty nations up the blind alley of fatuity and frustration. It was a grievous thing also to encourage, however indirectly, a primitive population to a desperate resistance and then, in the event, to leave them to their fate. We cannot undo the past, but we are bound to pass it in review in order to draw from it such lessons as may be applicable to the future, and surely the conclusion from this story is that we should not intervene in these matters unless we are in earnest and prepared to carry our intervention to all necessary lengths.

When the former Foreign Secretary [Sir Samuel Hoare] made his famous speech at Geneva in September,[1] and when my right hon. Friend who was Minister for League of Nations Affairs [Mr. Eden] at that time was busy arranging sanctions at Geneva, as it was his duty to do, in accordance with the policy of the Government at that time, we seemed to take a leading position in the world. But all the glamour and fame of those days has to be paid for now, when, apart from material losses, we are likely to look extremely foolish. That price has now to be paid because the Government have been conducting their intervention without either sufficient resolution to carry it through or sufficient strength of character to confront those who would have been their critics if they had refused to go in so deeply. If we had merely done our duty as a member of the League of Nations without aspiring to take so prominent a position, without aspiring to take the lead with all its prizes, with all its penalties, with all its honor, and with all the reverse of honor which sometimes follows in case of misfortune, we should have fulfilled our obligations

[1] September 11, 1935.

under the Covenant, and we should be in a far less questionable and dangerous position than we are today.

There is one particular evil consequence I must mention that has arisen out of this policy which we have pursued. The former Foreign Secretary as part of his speech at Geneva made a declaration about raw materials which, though carefully guarded, did in fact bring up the whole colonial question. Now, where do we stand upon this question of the return of the mandated colonies to Germany? We ought to know. We ought to know not only where we stand at this moment, but what are the convictions and principles by which the Government will be guided in dealing with this matter in the future. The statements of Ministers are somewhat conflicting. The Colonial Secretary made what seemed to me and many of my friends who sit on these benches a very satisfactory statement, especially in the context in which it was uttered. But then the Under-Secretary of State for Foreign Affairs is reported in the public Press as having said that on this matter he had an open mind; and the former Minister without Portfolio [Lord Eustace Percy] concluded a speech the other night, fresh as he must be from the very center of Ministerial thought, by saying, in effect, that we must alter our conceptions about the British Empire and prepare ourselves to make considerable sacrifices.

What does all that mean? What is the conviction of His Majesty's Government? Have they an open mind upon the future? Are they waiting to see who pushes the hardest? Are they wondering which is likely to be the line of least resistance? I ask the Chancellor of the Exchequer [Mr. Neville Chamberlain], who, I understand, is to reply, and who has a heavy burden nowadays with the Budget and all the rest on his shoulders—I appeal to him to give us a plain answer tonight. Does he or does he not accept the view put forward the other day by Sir Austen Chamberlain that there should be no question of handing over even mandated territories to Germany while race-persecution is rife in that country? I ask him also whether it is not a fact that we could not in any case hand over these territories to Germany, but only to the League of Nations, which alone could decide upon their future destiny? The Government must have a view, and they ought to declare it to us. We do not want to have another muddle about these colonies similar to that into which we have been led about Abyssinia. We do not want to excite all sorts of hopes, and in this case arouse all kinds of appetites, and then, when it comes to the issue, refuse point-blank to do anything effective.

The gravity of the general situation is in no way diminished by the fact that it has become less exciting than it was two or three weeks ago. When you are drifting down the stream of Niagara, it may easily happen that from time to time you run into a reach of quite smooth water, or that a bend in the river or a change in the wind may make the roar of the falls seem far more distant; but your hazard and your preoccupation are in no way affected thereby. In this northern problem also dictatorship has gained an immense triumph. Herr Hitler has torn up Treaties and has garrisoned the Rhineland. His troops are there, and there they are going to stay. All this means that the Nazi régime has gained a new prestige in Germany and in all the neighboring countries But more than that. Germany is now fortifying the Rhine zone, or is about to fortify it. No doubt it will take some time. We are told that in the first instance only field entrenchments will be erected, but those who know to what perfection the Germans can carry field entrenchments like the Hindenburg Line, with all the masses of concrete and the underground chambers there included—those who remember that will realize that field entrenchments differ only in degree from permanent fortifications, and work steadily up from the first cutting of the sods to their final and perfect form.

I do not doubt that the whole of the German frontier opposite to France is to be fortified as strongly and as speedily as possible. Three, four or six months will certainly see a barrier of enormous strength. What will be the diplomatic and strategic consequences of that? I am not dealing with the technical aspect, but with the diplomatic reactions. The creation of a line of forts opposite to the French frontier will enable the German troops to be economized on that line, and will enable the main forces to swing round through Belgium and Holland. That is for us a danger of the most serious kind. Suppose we broke with France. Suppose these efforts to divide the last surviving free democracies of the Western world were successful and they were sundered, and suppose that France, isolated, could do no more than defend her own frontier behind Belgium and Holland by prolonging her fortress line, those small countries might very speedily pass under German domination, and the large colonial empires which they possess would no doubt be transferred at the same time. These are matters that ought not to escape our attention.

I thought that the Prime Minister's remark which he made some years ago about our frontier being the Rhine [2] was liable at the time to be misunderstood; but if he meant that it was a mortal danger to Britain to have the Low Countries in the fortified grip of the strongest military power upon the Continent, and now, in these days, to have all the German aviation bases established there, he was only repeating the lesson taught in four centuries of history. That danger will be brought definitely and sensibly nearer from the moment that this new line of German fortifications is completed. But then, look East. There the consequences of the Rhineland fortification may be more immediate. That is to us a less direct danger, but is a more imminent danger The moment those fortifications are completed, and in proportion as they are completed, the whole aspect of Middle Europe is changed. The Baltic States, Poland, and Czechoslovakia, with which must be associated Yugoslavia, Rumania, Austria and some other countries, are all affected very decisively the moment that this great work of construction has been completed.

Some of those nations, but not all, are now balancing in deep perplexity what course they should take. Should they continue in their association with the League of Nations and with what is called collective security and the reign of law? Or should they make the best terms they can with the one resolute, warlike Power which is stirring in Europe at the present time? That is the question they have to ask themselves If nothing satisfactory has been achieved by the negotiations and conferences which no doubt will occupy a large part of this year, we may see many powerful nations, with armies and air forces, associated with the German Nazi system, and the other nations who are opposed to that system isolated and practically helpless. It is idle to say that these are not matters which the House of Commons should view with vigilance and attention It is idle to pretend that these are only matters affecting the obscurities, the politics and the hatreds of Central Europe.

This brings me to the Staff conversations which are to begin tomorrow or the day after in London. The Foreign Secretary made a manly speech the other day. He took his political life in his hands, and Parliament sustained him very decidedly. It is extremely important that there should be a responsible Foreign Secretary and not a headless committee. I trust that the result of that Debate will give my right hon. Friend the necessary power to produce some coherent theme which the country can understand, and which Parliament can faithfully pursue. Almost any honorable policy would be better in times like these, and safer, than a

[2] July 30, 1934. See p. 128.

succession of attempts, however well-meant, to find the line of least resistance and to avoid saying things which might offend this or that well-meaning section of British public opinion Let us beware, henceforth, of being mealy-mouthed in these matters which affect our lives and our future.

Staff conversations are now to begin. I do not expect that those generals will have very much to tell each other which they do not know already unofficially. It is certainly unusual to elevate Staff conversations into a prime feature of policy or diplomacy, and it would hardly be possible to choose a more awkward counter for the Government to use as a means of conveying to France and Belgium the assurance that Great Britain stands by her obligations; but the very awkwardness of the counter and its unusual use for this purpose positively emphasizes its healthy significance. It surely means, and it is taken to mean, and meant to mean, that Great Britain has linked herself with France and Belgium in the event of an unprovoked invasion of their soil, and that Great Britain will not go back upon her word, even if that involves war. That is what is meant. Let us face that, if we are agreed upon it. The importance of this act is in no way diminished because, as a matter of fact, Germany is not in the slightest degree likely to invade France or Belgium in the next few months. No doubt the Government hope by this act to steady opinion in all the Central European countries which I have mentioned, which are in great apprehension, and to rally them to the earnest support of the League of Nations.

We ought, therefore, to support the Government and to defend them in the country, even if some of us do not think that this would be actually the best method to adopt. But I must point out that any steadying effect which this act of Great Britain may produce will be more than wiped out by the development and completion of the German fortress barrier, because that will be a decisive closing of the door upon the influence of the Western democracies on the fate of Central Europe. Therefore, I hold that the time is coming for a final and lasting friendly settlement with Germany. The time available is short. What should be our next step? I hope we shall not repeat the Abyssinian theme; I hope we shall not claim an undue prominence, more than we are ready to make good. I should regret to see this issue drawn as if it were one between Great Britain and Germany; I should regret to see the discussions conducted any further as if they were conversations or correspondence between the

Foreign Secretary and Herr von Ribbentrop or any other German representative. We have not yet the needful solidarity of conviction, nor have we adequate defenses, to take a line of undue prominence or to seek to dominate this matter.

We must do our part, but not more than our part, and that is why I agree with the Leader of the Opposition in the view which he has expressed, and which I gather was not at all unwelcome to the Foreign Secretary, that these supreme issues should not be settled by any single Power, but by all those Powers, or all who matter, at Geneva, and within the circle and under the authority of the League of Nations. We ought therefore to intimate to Germany that the points raised in Herr Hitler's interesting and important Note [3] involve the whole of Europe, and that, without prejudice to our specific obligations under Locarno, it would be far better that they should be discussed at Geneva, and that our answers should be made as far as possible from Geneva and with the broadest possible backing of the Powers associated under the Covenant of the League.

It does not follow, because the League of Nations has been ineffective and impotent in protecting Abyssinia, that it will not have a real power to deal with the perils which have arisen in Northern Europe. Here you have strong nations banded together by solemn treaties, armed most powerfully, whose vital interests are affected; here you have nations small in numbers who, individually, may be helpless, but who, organized and united under the authority of the League, may exert a very great power indeed. Thus the League of Nations, in dealing with these matters for all the interested countries, ought not to lack champions. That is why I agree with what has been proposed. There is safety in numbers, and I believe also that there may be peace in numbers.

The Leader of the Opposition twitted me the other night with having become a recent convert to these ideas of collective security, and I ask the indulgence of the House to do what otherwise I should be loth—to read in vindication of myself a very few words which I used two and a half years ago, on the 7th of November, 1933 I was urging Mr. Ramsay MacDonald's Government to desist from endeavoring to persuade France to disarm, and I was urging him to begin the rearmament of Great Britain, in view of all the news that was reaching us about German preparations. This is what I said:

[3] March 7, 1936. See p. 237.

I believe that we shall find our greatest safety in co-operating with the other Powers of Europe, not taking a leading part, but coming in with all the neutral States and the smaller States of Europe which will gather together anxiously in the near future at Geneva We shall make a great mistake to separate ourselves entirely from them at this juncture. Whatever way we turn there is risk But the least risk and the greatest help will be found in re-creating the Concert of Europe through the League of Nations, not for the purpose of fiercely quarreling and haggling about the details of disarmament but in an attempt to address Germany collectively, so that there may be some redress of the grievances of the German nation and that that may be effected before this peril of [German] rearmament reaches a point which may endanger the peace of the world.[4]

That was the counsel which I offered to the House nearly three years ago, when all was so easy; it is still the counsel which I renew tonight, when all has become so hard.

[4] See p 82.

GERMAN ARMS EXPENDITURE

April 23, 1936

Budget proposals (considered in Committee of Ways and Means)

1936

April 8. Publication of British questionnaire addressed to the German Government

April 15. Conversations begin in London between General Staffs of Britain, France and Belgium, to make provisional arrangements for military co-operation in the event of unprovoked aggression by Germany against France or Belgium.

April 18. Mr Baldwin, speaking at the Worcester Guildhall, says.

"I wish to make it clear beyond all doubt that the policy that the Foreign Secretary is taking in this matter [of sanctions] is not his own policy but the considered policy of the whole Government, and I would add that it is a policy which I am convinced is supported by an overwhelming majority of the British people."

April 20 Mr. Eden, speaking at League Council meeting in Geneva, insists that existing sanctions must be maintained.

GERMAN ARMS EXPENDITURE

WE heard a great deal of talk, before Parliament met, about a £300,000,000 loan to put our defenses in order, and, above all, to give us air parity with neighboring countries. In the Defense Debate I pointed out that, owing to the restrictions which were imposed upon us by past neglect on the part of His Majesty's Government—neglect to take heed of the warnings which were so plainly given by Members in many parts of the House—the Government, however urgent their need, however sincere their desire, would not be able to spend any very large sum this year, because the contractors would not be able to earn it. I remember very well that when I said I doubted whether they could spend more than £50,000,000 over and above the current Estimates, I saw a look of incredulity on the faces of many Members of the House. But at the present time it is not £50,000,000 that they can spend; it is only £20,000,000 that can be spent on the air and on the other two branches together in addition to the Estimates. When the Chancellor announced that the Supplementary Estimate would not in his opinion exceed £20,000,000, he proclaimed the failure and the inadequacy of our defense effort this year. One is told that you cannot spend more under peace conditions, however great the need may be, without disturbing the economic and social life of the country; and I noticed that the Minister for the Co-ordination of Defence [Sir Thomas Inskip], a few days after he had taken up his office, made a very important pronouncement. He explained that he was working under peace conditions. I was much concerned at that statement, and thought it premature for my right hon. and learned Friend to commit himself so early to such a limitation upon his powers.

Surely, the question whether we should continue working under peace conditions depends upon whether working under those conditions will give us the necessary deliveries of our munitions—upon whether the gun plants and the shell plants and, above all, the aeroplane factories can fulfill the need in time. If they can do so, then peace conditions are no doubt very convenient; but if not, then we must substitute other conditions—not necessarily war conditions, but conditions which would impinge upon the ordinary daily life and business of this country. There are many other conditions apart from war conditions—preparatory conditions, precautionary conditions, emergency conditions—and these must be established in this country if any real progress is to be made, and if Parliament and the nation are not to find themselves deluded in the future by mere paper programs and promises which in the result will be found to be utterly unfulfilled. I think my right hon. and learned Friend would have done far better to wait until he had ascertained the actual facts about our defense industries before committing himself to such a very serious contraction of his functions and facilities, and I hope he will not consider himself finally bound by what he has said.

When the Supplementary Estimates are laid before us we shall have to examine the programs; how they are being executed and how far they are falling short either of what was planned or of what we need. We must endeavor to establish accountability for any neglects in the past. We have to look back upon a record of many squandered weeks and months. If the appointment of the Minister for the Co-ordination of Defence had been made last year, when Parliament asked for it, he would have had a great advantage today in the work that he has to do. If a separate Ministry of Supply or Munitions had been set up a year ago, it would have been working now. Nothing is being done even now. I read in a paper today that no meeting had yet taken place between the Government and the trade unions in regard to questions of apprenticeship and dilution and transference, without settling which you cannot possibly expand your munitions production. You cannot do anything without a working arrangement with the trade unions, and here we are on this day of April 1936, and it is said that no meeting has yet taken place upon that matter.[1] Nothing effective has been done about profiteering. I regard it as impossible to carry out this process of putting our affairs in good order and our defenses in a state of security without the co-operation of the trade

[1] The first meeting between the Government and the trade unions was ultimately arranged two years later, in April 1938; but so far no agreement has been reached.

unions. You will not get the effective co-operation of the working people so long as they think there are a lot of greedy fingers having a rake-off. We are still drifting and dawdling as the precious months flow out.

Meanwhile what is happening abroad? The Chancellor of the Exchequer [Mr. Chamberlain] used a most grievous expression when he said we could already feel the heat of the flames upon our faces. That is a formidable expression to be used in opening the Budget by a Minister who is characteristically restrained in his language. I have for a long time past made what I consider grave and startling statements about Germany's expenditure on warlike preparations. I obtained my information originally from a source which I cannot divulge. I have, however, attempted to check it from every possible quarter, and I have been assisted by very able people, in good faith. A private Member has not the resources that are open to the Government, but I give the results for what they are worth.

From the end of March 1933 to the end of June 1935 the official publications of the German Government show an increase in the public debt to a minimum figure of over seven milliards of reichsmarks, to which must be added the yield from increased taxation in that period, which has been used for Government expenditures, and which amounts to five milliards. Therefore, the minimum expenditure for two and a half years above the preceding Budget expenditure is twelve milliards, or £1,000,000,000 at the official rate of exchange. That is all that is acknowledged, but there are two other lines of approach which suggest that that figure is far below the actual fact. A veto prevails in Germany on all expansion of private plant for purely economic purposes. The capital expenditure of Germany other than for residential buildings may therefore be regarded as almost exclusively devoted to warlike preparations, in which, of course, I include the preparation of those great military roads where four columns of troops can march abreast, which may play a greater part in a future war than the fortifications that are being built.

Again, taking the figures from German official sources, the expenditure on capital account, deducting the expenditure on residential buildings, has been as follows: in 1933, nearly five milliards of marks; in 1934, nearly eight milliards; and in 1935, nearly eleven milliards—a total of twenty-four milliards, or roughly £2,000,000,000. I am taking the rate of exchange at twelve marks to the pound, and I am making no allowance for the fact that armament production is much cheaper in Germany than it is here. [An hon. Member: "Why?"] Wages are much lower. Look at those figures—five, eight and eleven for the three years. They give you exactly the kind of progression which a properly developing munitions industry would make.

There is a second line of approach to these figures. There is a marked increase in the German national income. Again I take this from official German figures. The increase in the national income has not gone into consumption. Wages have remained unchanged and the cost of living, if anything, has risen. Therefore, the increase in the national income has gone into constructional work, the bulk of which is represented directly or indirectly by armaments. Look at the increase in the figures of the German national income—in 1933, 1,200,000,000 reichsmarks; in 1934, 7,000,000,000; and in 1935, 11,500,000,000—practically the same progression as I showed in the previous calculation. That is exactly what you would expect from an industry getting on its feet, opening out and finally coming into full blast. These figures make a total, since Herr Hitler came into power, of nearly 20,000,000,000 reichsmarks. The year 1935 shows, on this calculation as well as on the previous one, the same figure of over 11,000,000,000 marks, which is considerably over the £800,000,000 which I have for some months past been bruiting about the country.

There are other means by which this progress can be checked. There is the number of persons employed in the armament and cognate industries and in military forces. There has also been an elaborate investigation into the number of stamps which have been affixed to the three-months' bills which are used for effecting this extraordinary process of internal inflation, but that is too complicated to trouble the Committee with now. They will see from what I have said that there is very considerable justification for the startling statement that I have advanced, and to which I most strictly adhere, that £800,000,000 was spent on warlike preparations in 1935 alone Do the Government contradict these figures? Unless they are to contradict them specifically and can show reasons why they are wrong I think my statement might be allowed to stand, and might be taken into the general currency of thought on this topic.

The Chancellor of the Exchequer used an argument about how expenditure would rise to a peak, then fall a little and then remain level, but at a much greater height than at the present time. That is not the future as I foresee it. I cannot believe that, after armaments in all countries have reached a towering height, they will settle down and continue at a hideous level far above the present level, which is already crushing, and that that will be for many years a normal feature of the world's routine.

Whatever happens, I do not believe that will. Europe is approaching a climax. I believe that climax will be reached in the lifetime of the present Parliament. Either there will be a melting of hearts and a joining of hands between great nations which will set out upon realizing the glorious age of prosperity and freedom which is now within the grasp of the millions of toiling people, or there will be an explosion and a catastrophe the course of which no imagination can measure, and beyond which no human eye can see. I believe also that a strongly armed Britain, resolutely and valiantly led, seeking peace but ready to run risks for peace, may conceivably turn the scale between the blessing and the cursing of mankind.

A MINISTRY OF MUNITIONS SUPPLY

May 21, 1936

Supply (Treasury and subordinate Departments considered in Committee)

1936

May 6 Sir Austen Chamberlain demands the lifting of sanctions.

A MINISTRY OF MUNITIONS SUPPLY

THE Minister for the Co-ordination of Defence at the outset of his speech opined that what he called "the closed season" as affecting himself was over, and that he was now liable to be shot at. I should like to reassure him that, so far as I know, he is certainly not to blame for anything that has gone wrong in the present situation No responsibility for the position in which we stand rests upon his shoulders, whatever may be the responsibilities which he is contracting towards the future. He has succeeded to a lamentable inheritance. The delays which have taken place in putting our defenses in order have been intolerable. Three years ago the plainest warnings and the fullest accounts were given of what was happening elsewhere. The Leader of the Liberal party asked why the Minister for the Co-ordination of Defence was not appointed before the defense scheme was settled. A very obvious question. I have asked it myself, but where is the answer? There is no answer. It was not until February of this year that the White Paper defining the office of that Minister was given to Parliament, and even after that there were three weeks' delay in selecting the man to fill the office. No explanation has ever been forthcoming of all this wasted time in the fulfillment of what is now represented as a necessary, though I admit a subsidiary, step. That is where we are today. While no one is going to try to fix responsibility upon the new Minister or harass him in his difficult task, he must not expect that, because having been appointed to this office, he must necessarily study these matters and acquire knowledge of them, the criticism and investigation of the House of Commons into defense matters will be suspended during that period in this most critical time.

First I will deal with the character and scope of the new office which has been created. I do not think such a plan could have been made by anyone who comprehended the problem.

There are the Service Departments—the Admiralty, the War Office and the Air Ministry—and there is also a fourth Department now represented by the Supply Board, which is virtually a Ministry of Munitions in embryo. These four Departments are all concerned with defense, and it is incongruous and a serious fault in organization that a Minister who has to concert the combined action of all four Departments should be also the head of the Supply Branch—or of the Ministry of Munitions into which it may broaden. The work of the Minister of Supply, or Minister of Munitions, or the head of the Supply Branch—by whatever name you like to call him—is so exacting that, in my judgment, it now requires, and has long required, the attention of an important Minister. It touches immediately the most delicate and formidable Parliamentary issues—profits and profiteering on the one hand; dilution, apprenticeship, training and transference upon the other. All those matters fall in that scope, and nothing could be more unreasonable than to link the functions of head of the Supply Board or a Minister of Munitions with the function of co-ordinating strategic thought, with the choice of the major instrumentalities of war, or the final advice to the Cabinet upon priority. They are two entirely different functions. One is the hustling, bustling, day-to-day job, with frequent contact with the House of Commons; the other requires broad directives achieved in a somewhat rarefied atmosphere and under conditions necessarily, in most cases, of secrecy. No single man could do those two jobs. I do not believe there is bred the kind of man, however good he may be for either of them, who would be capable of undertaking both of them at the same time.

Let me mention by way of illustration a few of the questions which we want to feel assured that the high co-ordinator has passed through his brain and reached conviction upon. Many of them are in the minds of the Committee. Upon some of them, he has told us, he is already engaged. There is the question of the air bomb versus the battleship, the question of the Fleet Air Arm, the obtrusion of treaty requirements upon the common-sense development of the Royal Navy, the question whether we should promise any foreign country to send an expeditionary force to the continent of Europe on the outbreak of war and, if so, how we are to create that expeditionary force, or whether, on the other hand, our aid in the first instance should only be by the air, by sea and by the world influence which the British nation and Empire is able to exert.

There is the question of how we should retain our command in the Mediterranean in view of the new diplomatic conditions which will prevail there in future years, how far it should be by the Navy and how far by the Air Force, or by what combination of the two.

There is the question of the military value of Russia, a tremendous question upon which my right hon. Friend has the responsibility of being the adviser to His Majesty's Government—a matter, I may say, not to be dealt with by the War Office, or the Admiralty, or the Air Ministry, but obviously by a combination of the three, together with a political officer who has comprehension of the political and economic issues involved. There is a very important new question which seems to be swimming into our ken. Are we in danger in this island of invasion from the air? I do not mean invasion by hostile aeroplanes which cast bombs, or thermite bombs, though in all conscience that is bad enough, but whether it is not possible now, or whether it may not be possible soon, to land from the air substantial forces which, in a country where none or very few are armed or trained, might seize important points and rule important districts for a long time.

I have only mentioned these as typical questions on which the Minister for the Co-ordination of Defence will have to bear the responsibility of advising the head of the Government and the Cabinet. But how absurd to combine all this intense obligation of thought with the responsibility of providing enough cobalt, or chromium, or nickel, or a hundred and one other commodities. Equally vital is the question whether our oil supplies are adequate, or whether the supply of precision tools is equal to the demand, and how soon it can be made equal, and by what emergency method! Another question is whether the trade unions will agree to the necessary processes of dilution, apprenticeship and transference, and how negotiations should be undertaken, and whether any good plan can be devised which will, to use an American term—a term which I think we must get into our minds—"take the profit out of war," and thus cleanse the life-defense of the nation from the taint of sordid personal gain.

Another question is how we are to get the delivery of the goods. That is a practical question. What are the right processes to use in the factories; how are you going to make the thousands of cannon, the millions of shells, of air bombs, of trench-mortar bombs and all other kinds of projectiles in the proportions which your own schemes need and which every other country is arranging to provide on a far larger scale? How are you going to provide for the overseas supplies for 45,000,000 people whose shipping has been greatly reduced since the late war? What about gas masks, and the defense of the civil population from aerial attack by chemical means? It would be easy to extend the list of questions Have I not shown to the Committee the two vast sets of functions which exist in different spheres? Fancy trying to combine those two sets of functions in a single individual! No one who has any practical experience or is willing to learn from the experience of the past would ever have suggested it. I am quite sure that if my right hon Friend had understood the conditions of his office he would either have asked for less responsibility or for more power. Probably he would have been well advised to ask for both, for the appointment which has been given to him and the burden which has been cast upon him do not conform to any principle of rational organization, and in my opinion they are not a fair load to lay on any man.

I now turn to the main issue: what is our own position in the matter of defense? We do not hesitate to give the law to nations, and to arraign delinquent peoples at our bar. How stands our own defense? Before and during the General Election the Prime Minister freely exposed its deficiencies. Oddly enough, he dwelt particularly on the deficiencies in the Navy, which appears to be the only Service which this year, and probably next year, is not unequal to its immediate responsibilities. But then, towards the end of the election, he was at pains to say, "I give you my word there will be no great armaments." Frankly, I do not understand that statement in the circumstances in which we are or in the context of our thought and discussions. Is not doubling or trebling the Air Force a great armament? Is not trying to have an Air Force—trying vainly, I admit—equal to that of Germany or France a great armament? What is the point of saying we are not to have great armaments? There is only one explanation, and that is that these great armaments will exist only on paper, and that it is not in our power for a very long time to obtain the deliveries which would turn them into realities. There followed the White Paper setting forth in extremely vague terms the plan for a very large rearmament. As a paper plan, I have nothing to say against it. That was three months ago.

Let me draw attention to the rapid passage of time. Three months—passed in a flash. All the time all over the world events are moving. Three months and— Hullo, another Defense Debate! Three months ago I ventured to say that it was no use asking the Government for a larger program because, except perhaps in the building of destroyers for the

Navy where work could be placed out in smaller yards, they would not be able to execute the programs which they had already declared and on which they were engaged. The limited sums of money which the Departments are able to spend are an unfailing tell-tale of the truth that they are not able to carry out this process of rearmament which they desire and which they have the utmost need to execute. I defy anyone to rise from the Treasury Bench and say that the programs to which they have set their hands are going to be carried out punctually to the dates which have been assigned to them.

Three months have passed since I urged upon the Government the formation of a Ministry of Munitions or Supply. We are now told that that may be necessary in the future, but it is a dividing line, so said my right hon. Friend, between the Government and me—or it is one of the dividing lines—that I advocate the creation of a Ministry of Munitions and that they do not think it is time to undertake it. It ought to have been created a year ago. No doubt it will be created six months or a year hence. What has been gained by the past delay? What will be gained by the further delay? Have things got any better since this time last year? Have the Government any assurance that they will get better by this time next year? Everything has become worse as every month has passed. Show me a single quarter in the world where there is the slightest improvement. Show me a single great new fact which should give us reassurance.

The rearmament of Germany is proceeding upon a colossal scale, and at desperate break-neck speed. All Europe is arming and preparing the whole of industry for war. At the other end of the world Japan is fiercely arming and is in a state of the highest martial exaltation. All the old, evil factors which were apparent a year ago, all the old perils, are now presented in an aggravated form. The only new factor, the only great new prime factor, is the grave antagonism which has grown up between us and Italy. Can anyone deny that everything is worse, from the point of peace and safety, than it was this time last year? Three months ago there were many complaints in the Defense Debate about the vagueness of the White Paper. Why did the Committee suppose that it was vague? I imagine it was vague because the Government had not the slightest idea of how and when it could be executed. But in this matter time is the supreme condition. You may draw up a program to be executed in three years. You may feel sure and tell Parliament that it will make us reasonably safe. So it might, if it could be executed in that time and if nothing else happened abroad before that time. But will anyone on the Treasury Bench say that punctuality can be achieved? Already we hear that the three years may be four or five years, and so forth. What does that mean? Of course it means that the program is already hopelessly in arrears, that deliveries are not coming to hand, that what the Government themselves think necessary for the safety of the country to be accomplished in no more than three years can only be accomplished in five. Therefore we shall not be provided with the safety which we need, because everything turns on time, and because, to use Burke's famous phrase, "Every single set of circumstances involves every other set." Where will others be then, if you are late? What, for instance, will be the strength of the German Army or the German Air Force in 1938 or 1939?

Let it be observed that it is not simply a question of spreading what ought to be done in three years over five; it is much worse than that. I have endeavored to explain very respectfully to the Committee that the first and second years of a munitions program are comparatively unproductive. Everything that has fallen from my right hon. Friend this afternoon would confirm that. In these somber fields in the first year you have to sow, and in the second year you harrow; the third year is your harvest. In the first year you make your machine tools and designs. In the second year you make your plants and you lay them out. You marshal and secure your labor, skilled and unskilled. In the third year come deliveries. No doubt all those processes overlap and you get, over three years, a yield rising very sharply in the latter period; but, broadly speaking, the effective result comes only in the third year. Now, if you dawdle a three years' program over five years, it means that your results do not come to hand on a large scale until the fourth or fifth year, and you have to pass, and we shall all have to pass, through a very long valley of unprotected preparation. It is in this period, these three or four years which lie between us and the proper placing of our country in a state of domestic security, that I fear the affairs of Europe may reach their climax.

What, I ask again, is the object in delaying the formation of a Ministry of Munitions? Last week, when I was passing the Hotel Metropole and saw all the vans gathered there to carry away the furniture, in order that the hotel shall be a temporary Government office while some rehousing scheme of the various Departments goes on, I said to myself, "Late as it is, here is the moment. Here is the place." [1] It is a very difficult task for a

---

[1] The Ministry of Munitions was housed in the Hotel Metropole in the Great War.

private Member to make constructive proposals. I do not content myself
with criticisms and with recriminations about the past, although the day
for those may come, but I venture, appealing to the indulgence of the
Committee for anyone who, from a private station, makes a considerable
constructive proposal in some detail, to offer most respectfully to the
Government the following course of action:

Let them choose a Minister. They have competent ones upon that
bench—they are not always given a chance, but there are very able men.
Let them appoint a Minister of Munitions Naturally, you would not
want to use, at this moment, all the powers which rested with the Minister
of Munitions in time of war. It is only darkening counsel to pretend that
the issue is whether you shall go on as you are or go to the full wartime
extreme of Governmental control. There are many intermediate stages
between those conditions. Only a portion of the powers of the old Minister
of Munitions need be brought into play at the outset. More can be added
by Parliament as they are needed, as they can be used and as the dangers
grow.

Then, I would suggest, this Minister should form a council of a dozen
of the best live, active, youngish business-men and manufacturers in the
country. I am told that the new generation of British business-men is as
good in ability, in force and in organizing power as, or better than, the
one that carried us through the period of the Great War. Give them a
chance; let them get their teeth into this job. Do not put it all on a
Minister who has so many other duties and so many distractions. Let each
of those be given a sphere, and a section of work to plan and supervise—
but also with collective responsibility as a member of the Munitions
Council—for the general work of the Department. Let them be supported
by competent civil servants; many of those are already in the Supply
Board, and no better could you find than the admirable Sir Arthur
Robinson who has been mentioned, and who is struggling so hard at the
Supply Board. You must have the civil servants and the business-men if
you are to have good administration.

Let the Government transfer to this Ministry, by installments, as soon
as it is ready to undertake the task, the whole business of supply and
design for the Air Force and for the Army, and such portions of Naval
supply as are not concerned in the construction of warships and certain
special Naval stores. These, and certain ancillaries, I would leave to the
Admiralty because, to a very large extent, they have already their own
great plants in existence and in operation, because they have the Royal

Corps of Naval Constructors, and because expansion for defense purposes does not strain the Navy in the same degree as it does the other two Services. The Navy is already upon a European or a world scale, but, so far as the Army and the Air Force are concerned, the whole of the staffs employed, not only in production but, I repeat, in design, ought to be handed over. I admit it sounds a hard thing for these military Departments to be asked to hand over design, but that was the lesson which, in the War, we learned only very late, and in a very hard school.

The relation of the Ministry of Munitions to the fighting Services is the relation of a shopkeeper to his customers. There the maxim, I am told, is, "The customer is always right." The customers prescribe the requirements and the shopkeeper supplies them. Although the maxim that the customer is always right should apply to all good business, it does not prevent the shopkeeper pointing out how best the convenience of the fighting Services can be suited, or even drawing attention to some attractive article of which the customer might never have heard. These are the relations which should exist between a competent Ministry of Munitions or Supply and the fighting Departments.

Before the Government brush aside this proposal let us again turn our gaze abroad. Take Germany, for instance. I choose Germany because of the excellent arrangements which they have made. There they have organized the whole industry of the nation for war, and a very large part of it is actually working on a war basis. All their designs have been conceived for mass production. Sometimes not quite the best article has been chosen, because the second best would lend itself more readily to mass production. Simplicity has been the aim of the immense process which is taking place in Germany; above all, the power to make complicated munitions upon a great scale by unskilled labor, and, in war-time, by female labor. Since the Nazi régime began, three years ago, 4,000,000 more persons are employed in Germany, practically all upon munitions or in the fighting forces. These are additional to all those who were so employed before, and they were very numerous The public have simply no idea, nor will the speech of the Minister give them any idea, of the efficiency of German war production, of its enormous scale, or with what marvelous smoothness it can be made to pour out an almost limitless flow of the most horrible weapons of human destruction which have ever been placed in the unworthy hands of man.

For the present, of course, we are bound to rely upon existing types and patterns. These cannot be relinquished until new forms of production are ready to take their place, but those new forms must be prepared for an emergency. But even the process of working on the supply of existing patterns cannot be extended to meet our needs, or even go half-way to meet them, under the present system, or under the direction of the Service Departments. I heard the other day the following remark: "You would surely not deprive the Secretary of State for War of the responsibility for his own munitions supply?" That is exactly what I would do. Curiously enough, those words sounded like an echo from the past. They were the very words which I heard Lord Kitchener use in the early months of 1915. "I could never give up," he said, "responsibility for the ammunition of the Army." But he had to. He had to be made to, and unless he had been made to and been willing to give it up—and afterwards he was thankful—his soldiers could never have been supplied with all that they needed. This is one of the lessons which we all had to learn with blood and tears. Have we really got to learn them all over again now?

In quiet times in a long peace you may, without serious disadvantage, leave your munitions supply to the Service Departments. They have their list of normal Government contractors and their Government factories. Their requirements are small and regular. You can get along in that way. But from the moment you begin to expand upon a great scale the question of supply ceases to be a Service question. It becomes a vast trade and industrial question, and the people who must direct that business can only be the people who know all about modern scientific manufacture and who are accustomed, from lifelong experience, to the organization and conduct of great productive plants. You cannot possibly leave this immense business in the hands of ordinary permanent officials of the Service Departments You will neither get the best designs nor will you get the swiftest methods and the required deliveries. I cannot understand why the Government think it a virtue to dally and hesitate here. Have we not suffered grievously by what has already happened? Why should paralysis be paraded as phlegmatic composure, and wavering between half a dozen policies be acclaimed as sobriety and wisdom? Three years of procrastination, which have perverted to its aid all the loyalties of this country, have wrought us an injury which we can now see, and of which only the future knows the measure.

Already, in the last Parliament, we had confessions of failure and of miscalculations about the air. My right hon. and learned Friend has this afternoon revealed to us the terrible hiatus which must intervene before machine tools and gauges can be supplied Suppose, three years ago, when the Government were first warned, and when what was taking place abroad became widely known, they had said, "We will, at any rate, begin to put our industries into a state of preparation. No one could say that is provocative."—Ordering battleships and so forth might have disturbed your disarmament policy, but to make the simple provision of getting these indirect, but very vital, implements could not have been called provocative.—"We will make the lay-outs of the factories. We will see about the precision tools. We will have everything ready, so that, if our well-meant example of disarming should not be followed by other countries, and if we pursue it to the last moment and then find ourselves in a difficult position, we shall, at any rate, have got ready underneath the means of repairing the risk that we have run. We can begin at once to rearm." If only two years ago the measures which have now been taken had been put into operation we should be getting very considerable supplies. You would have your future in your own hands. You would be the masters of the events and not, perhaps, their victim. Even a year ago, when there was no dispute about the danger, when it was common ground among all parties and when the Prime Minister admitted that mistakes had been made—even then there was just time to do a lot. Then "Why stand we in jeopardy every hour?" Why still, now at the eleventh hour, are we unable to decide on measures equal to the emergency? Is there no grip, no driving force, no mental energy, no power of decision or design? We are told that we must not interfere with the normal course of trade, that we must not alarm the easygoing voter and the public. How thin and paltry these arguments will sound if we are caught a year or two hence, fat, opulent, free-spoken—and defenseless. I do not ask that war conditions should be established in order to execute these programs. All I ask is that these programs to which the Government have attached their confidence shall be punctually executed, whatever may be the disturbance of our daily life.

MACHINE TOOLS

May 29, 1936

Debate on the Adjournment

MACHINE TOOLS

I AM SURE everyone will feel that the right hon. Gentleman who fills the office of Minister for Co-ordination of Defence is extraordinarily capable of co-ordinating the Parliamentary defense of the Government and its policy against whatever criticism may be directed upon it from any quarter of the House.

Allow me to say that the impression which my right hon. Friend has given that all is being done, that everything is for the best in the best of all possible worlds and that nothing could be done better, does not tally with the information which I have been able to acquire by keeping in touch with the movement of affairs in the country. I say that all your programs are in arrear without exception. I say that two years ago there was time to make a move. No move was made My right hon Friend has announced plans for great factories to produce aeroplane frames or engines. Admirable. Two years ago it was seen, and full warning was given in this House, that the Germans were making gigantic air preparations. Surely it cannot be counted as a virtue to the Government that it is only now taking measures which were obviously necessary if we were to keep that parity which we were so often promised and which we have now fatally lost.

It is a very well-known phenomenon in Parliamentary debate that if a Minister makes some new statement about a great factory or something like that everybody is well pleased, but you have to see these things in their proportion and in their sequence. Such an announcement only shows how regrettable it is that the action was not taken at an earlier stage. My right hon. Friend said the other day that you must not cry over spilt milk, and he said it today in other words, when he spoke of recriminating about the past, and so forth. The use of recriminating about the past is to enforce effective action at the present. It is no use recriminating about the past simply for the purpose of censuring and punishing neglect and culpability, though that, indeed, may at times become the duty of Parliament. But there is great necessity for recriminating about the actions of the past and the neglects of the past when one is not satisfied that all is being done at the present time. That is the justification for it.

Take the question of machine tools. That was the most formidable statement that my right hon. Friend made. These machine tools, I presume, are needed for the additional program—the ammunition, the guns, and all the innumerable detailed appliances for placing our Army and our defenses in a condition of security. Surely this ought to have been foreseen a year ago. What is this argument that it was necessary to wait for the General Election before Ministers could do their duty and place their country in a state of security? There is no justification in that, and I am astonished that my right hon. Friend should use that argument.

It has been said that before the General Election there was no mandate to do it, but there is no mandate so imperative on Ministers of the Crown as that they should guard the safety of the country. Throughout the last Parliament there was never a moment when the Prime Minister—either the present Prime Minister or the previous Prime Minister—could not have asked both Houses of Parliament to support him in any measures necessary to maintain the security of the country. Nothing relieves Ministers from that prime duty. It is the first object for which Governments are called into being.

But even since the Election eight months have gone by. If these machine tool orders which my right hon. Friend tells us he is putting out this week, or is conferring about putting out this week, had been given eight months ago—if they had been given when the Prime Minister spoke at the beginning of the Election of all the dangers that were attaching to our defenses —the position would have been entirely different now; for it takes eight months to make these tools. That is an extraordinary omission. I stand aghast at it. We are assured that all is going on in a perfect manner; we were given the same assurance a year ago. Every suggestion that any difficulty or danger would arise was brushed aside, and with just the same Parliamentary arts, and the consciousness of a good safe majority. But now it appears that great errors were being committed then. These factories, which should have been laid down then, have only just been conceived. We know now that these machine tools which we are about to order should have been ordered then, but were overlooked.

That is the kind of thing that has happened, and my right hon. Friend now exhibits it to the whole world. As we see by the telegrams from different countries, it produced a shock, because while everyone knows that the industry of Britain is vast and flexible, if it has not these particular appliances it cannot manifest itself. A hideous hiatus of eight months must elapse before it can manifest itself, and after that it takes another eight months to make a gun. So that an enormous vista of anxiety lies before us, what I may call this valley of the shadow that we are going to move through for a long time—month after month of deep anxiety, when efforts will be made increasingly every month, every week, when anxiety will grow in the nation, when my right hon. Friend will be exerting himself night and day, I have no doubt. God speed him in it! But, all the same, he will be paying the penalty. It is not his fault, but he will be paying the penalty of these previous neglects. As Macaulay said:

> There is a *crassa ignorantia* and a *crassa negligentia* on which the law animadverts in magistrates and surgeons, even when actual malice and corruption are not imputed.

That is the sentence that may, indeed, be applied to whoever was the official or the Department to blame for not looking ahead and seeing that this comparatively petty expenditure upon machine tools, and the machinery for making them, was put in order at a time when you could see Europe darkening round you, when you could see every nation arming, and you were appealing to the nation for a mandate to rearm. These recurrences from the past justify one in continuing to press and to exert a vigilant scrutiny upon the Government, and upon a system and a habit of mind which have already brought the State into danger, which system and habit of mind are largely prevalent and regnant today, and may well, if not arrested and galvanized into action in time, bring us to a catastrophe fatal to our race and fame.

FALLING FARTHER BEHIND

July 20, 1936

Supply (salary of the Minister for the Co-ordination of Defence considered in Committee)

1936

June 3. Haile Selassie arrives in London.

June 5. Sir Samuel Hoare rejoins the Government as First Lord of the Admiralty

June 10. The Chancellor of the Exchequer [Mr. Neville Chamberlain], addressing the 1900 Club, describes the idea of continuing the policy of sanctions as "midsummer madness."

June 18. The Foreign Secretary [Mr. Eden] says in the House.
"Whatever view we take of the course of action which the League should follow, there is one fact upon which we must, of course, be agreed We have to admit that the purpose for which the sanctions were imposed has not been realized."

June 26. Lord Londonderry, speaking at Newcastle-upon-Tyne, says·
"I was one of the Defense Ministers, and I can say on my own behalf—and I have no doubt my late colleagues will endorse all I say—that I continually kept the Government informed of our deficiencies and of our weakness and also of the increasing armaments of other countries. It was surprising, therefore, when Mr Baldwin announced to the House of Commons that he had been misled in relation to German rearmament. Mr. Baldwin never was misled."

July 1 Mr. Eden at Geneva proposes the abandonment of sanctions.

July 2. Mr. Baldwin, speaking at a dinner of the City of London Conservative Association, intimates that he has no intention of retiring.

July 11. Agreement reached between Germany and Austria restoring normal relations Germany unconditionally recognizes the political independence of Austria and acquiesces in the suppression of the National Socialist Party. Germany will abandon propaganda in Austria for an "Anschluss."

July 15. Sanctions raised

July 20 Sir Thomas Inskip says in the House of Commons:
"The speed of machines in production today for regular use in the Air Force would, five years ago, have made them serious competitors for the Schneider Cup. These are not specimens, not what I would call protoplanes, that are being produced, but they are machines in regular, orderly production for the regular everyday use of the Air Force."
Mr Churchill: "Are they being delivered now?"
"Yes Some have been delivered. They are in orderly delivery, and

they will be delivered in ever-increasing volume. The equipment of the expanded Air Force must be the equipment most suitable for the emergency which it is designed to meet, and I am in a position to say, happily, that the equipment of the expanded Air Force will be a new product Suppose the expansion had taken place earlier My right hon. Friend, the Member for Epping, quite naturally, is fond of telling the Government that they ought to have begun this program two or three years ago. That may be so He may be right See what the consequences would have been Our Air Force today would have been equipped with machines which would have been out of date for any emergency that they would have to meet in the future .

The fact remains, and it is an answer to those who are apt to be wise after the event, that, at any rate, we have secured this happy advantage that we shall now be equipped with machines that will be adequate for the pilots who fly them."

FALLING FARTHER BEHIND

I AM not going to follow the Minister for the Co-ordination of Defence, except on one point, into the account which he gave of the progress of Air expansion, but I must say that the picture which he drew of streams of new machines of the very latest quality pouring out of the factories to the squadrons of the Royal Air Force is one which is based on a larger measure of anticipation than of reality. I am sure that some of the statements which he made will be received, not only with interest, but with surprise, in the ranks of the Royal Air Force. I could draw a very different picture, but I am not going to do so, because, frankly, I do not feel that here today, in open debate in this Chamber, I should like the case which I feel capable of stating to be stated; nor do I think it would be right for the Government to give all the information that they have at their disposal.

There is, however, one point to which I must refer. My right hon. Friend used an extraordinary argument. He said that, if we had begun to expand our Air Force three years ago, or words to that effect, we should be worse off than we are now—we should be cumbered with a mass of inferior machines. This is an altogether new defense for the miscalculation which the Government have admitted in respect of the relative strength of the British and German air forces In fact, I do not know why, on this basis, the Prime Minister ever needed at all to stand in the most handsome way in a white sheet, because apparently this was not an oversight; it was not an accident. this was some deep design, a truly Machiavellian stroke of policy, which enabled us to pretend that a miscalculation had been made while all the time we were holding back in order to steal a march on other countries by the production of great numbers of machines of the latest type. That is a most remarkable defense. If it be true, I think Lord Londonderry has been rather hardly treated,

and I trust that, now the Government are able to avow clearly the methods
they have been pursuing in the matter, some steps will be taken to
re-establish the most cordial and happy relations between that former Air
Minister and all his old colleagues who were combining with him in this
innocent and, for us, so highly beneficial fraud.

Alas, I fear there is not much truth in this suggestion. If our aircraft
factories had been set to work three years ago, albeit on the old type of
machines, that would not have prevented the substitution of the new
type for the old at the same date which is now operative. On the contrary, the effect would have been exactly the reverse. If the factories had
been thrown into activity, if apprentices had been engaged, if plant and
staff had been extended and developed, they would have been all the
more capable of taking the new types, the transference would have been
made with far better facilities and the deliveries would have flowed out
in far greater volume at an earlier date. I was a little sorry that my right
hon. Friend should have suggested that the young pilots who are now
joining the new Air Force would have had little cause to thank me if my
advice on this matter had been accepted, as they would have been condemned to fly in inferior machines. I have, and have had for many years,
a good many friends in the Air Force, and I am sure they do not think so
badly of me as that As a matter of fact, if you had a large stock of new
machines, albeit of old pattern, you would find it a very great facility at
this moment, and you would not have to draw away reserve machines
from squadrons in order to assist in the business of training your rapidly
expanding force. I really think the Minister lapsed into an argument there
which was not quite worthy of him, and still less worthy of the gravity of
the subject we are debating this afternoon.

But I have no quarrel with my right hon. Friend. Indeed, he has my
sincere sympathy. It is not with his speech that I am going to deal so
much as with the position in which he finds himself He has an office so
absurdly constructed that the very conditions of his commission reveal a
confusion of mind and a lack of comprehension in those who have defined
it He has allowed himself to become the innocent victim of responsibilities so strangely, so inharmoniously, so perversely grouped, endowed with
powers so cribbed and restricted, that no one, not even Napoleon himself,
would be able to discharge them with satisfaction. My right hon. Friend
has three separate tasks. The first is the co-ordination of high strategic
thought on all our affairs by land, sea and air, with which, apparently,
is combined also the enormous question of the food supply of this island

in time of war. That is his first task. His second is to secure the punctual execution of the existing very large program—another terrific task; and his third task is to plan and organize British industry and British labor so that if need be they could spring quickly into wartime conditions. Was there ever such an impossible jumble cast upon a single man—and a man, as has been pointed out in this Debate, who is without a staff under his control, without what I should call a composite brain? Other Ministers with great Departments have composite brains. Even anyone leading a party must have a brain larger than his own, must have numbers of people through whom he can operate. The Government have created a labyrinthine tangle of committees, with an able and unfortunate Minister flitting about between them, and they call it the Co-ordination of National Defence.

That is why I ask that the function of co-ordinating high strategic thought between the Services, and of deciding the main priorities in all classes of munitions production, should be separated from all functions connected with the problem of material supply and of the detailed preparation of factories in case we had to turn over from peace to war. I asked that many months ago, and I ask it now. I have not the slightest doubt that it is going to be done. The new appointment of an Admiral to the Army Council as Director-General of Munitions Production, and the regrouping under him of certain important Supply Departments, is, of course, a tentative and in some ways necessary preliminary step to that end. I have no doubt whatever that, after further prolonged, costly, vexatious, purposeless, and insensate delays, a Minister of Supply will be appointed, and that then there will be another equally injurious set of delays in clothing him with adequate powers.

The supplies that I have in mind are rifles and ammunition, cannon of all kinds, except the largest; shells, bombs, projectiles of all kinds, explosives, propellents, except for the Navy; machine-guns which concern the Air Force as well as the Army, trench mortars, medical stores, gas masks, tanks; mechanical transport of all kinds and equipment of every description. This is an enormous sphere How can the right hon. Gentleman proceed with the complicated and responsible task that he has accepted? It is always possible for a Minister to tell a good tale, but one has to consider the proportion of such statements to the general events and facts of the world around us. Last autumn I made a statement about Germany spending at the rate of the equivalent of £800,000,000 directly and indirectly upon warlike purposes, including strategic roads. I have often repeated the statement, and it has often been challenged. I gave a very full account of the methods of calculation that I had employed Now the Chancellor of the Exchequer at Question Time has given an answer, with the full knowledge of the Government, which in no way contradicts what I said, and anyone who reads the answer carefully will see that it is a complete acceptance of what I have said.[1] I think, therefore, the Committee may take it that £800,000,000 was the equivalent of German expenditure in 1935, and, as that rate is continuing, perhaps it may be £900,000,000 in the current year.

Now, there are the figures by which we can judge the scale of our own efforts In January there was some talk of spending £300,000,000, apart from normal upkeep. Of course, it was absurd to suggest that any such sum could be spent this year. The Government were quite right not to tie themselves to spending any particular figure. I remember that I warned the House that I doubted if they could spend more than £50,000,000 additional to the regular Estimates. Now Supplementary Estimates have been presented of £30,000,000, but that does not do justice to the Government's effort. There is a good deal of abnormal expenditure in the ordinary Services this year, and it is fairer to compare with 1934, and therefore I take it that there is an increase of £75,000,000 towards making up deficiencies and towards expansion, above the 1934 expenditure.

When the Opposition complain of the size of these Estimates we must ask them to compare them with the German expenditure I make full allowance for the fact that we do not need to keep a great Continental army in this country. That makes the comparison between the two countries not at all exact. Nevertheless, it is of value to compare them for the purpose of seeing the scale on which the events are proceeding. If you want to compare them, you should first deduct from the £800,000,000 at least £300,000,000 for the upkeep in 1936 of the German forces. That leaves £500,000,000 for extraordinary expenditure and expansion—for

---

[1] Mr. Churchill had asked the Chancellor of the Exchequer "Whether he is aware that the expenditure by Germany upon purposes directly and indirectly concerned with military preparations, including strategic roads, may well have amounted to the equivalent of £800,000,000 during the calendar year 1935, and whether this rate of expenditure seems to be continuing in the current calendar year "

Mr Chamberlain· "The Government have no official figures, but from such information as they have I see no reason to think that the figure mentioned in my right hon Friend's question is necessarily excessive as applied to either years, although, as he himself would agree, there are elements of conjecture."

something very serious which may happen quite soon This £500,000,000 compares with our £75,000,000. That gives us the scale.

My anxieties are not at all diminished by anything I have heard today. On the contrary, I feel that they are deepened and aggravated Everyone is going away on holiday, and when we come back we shall all be looking forward to the Coronation, but do not forget that all the time those remorseless hammers of which General Goering spoke are descending night and day in Germany, and that the most warlike and, in many ways, the most efficient people in Europe are becoming welded into a tremendous fighting machine equipped with the fearful agencies of modern science. That is a spectacle which I will not say is one that has never before existed, because it would be meaningless; it would fall utterly short of the facts. All I will say is that it is a machine upon which £800,000,000 or £900,000,000 are being spent for the second year in succession.

We are going away on our holidays. Jaded Ministers, anxious but impotent Members of Parliament, a public whose opinion is more bewildered and more expressionless than anything I can recall in my life —all will seek the illusion of rest and peace. We are told, "Trust the National Government. Have confidence in the Prime Minister [Mr. Baldwin], with the Lord President of the Council [Mr. MacDonald] at his side. Do not worry. Do not get alarmed. A great deal is being done. No one could do more." And the influence of the Conservative party machine is being used through a thousand channels to spread this soporific upon Parliament and the nation. But, I am bound to ask, has not confidence been shaken by various things that have happened, and are still happening?

I have already referred to the melancholy story of the miscalculations about German air power. Let me come to one or two more recent instances. When we met in January we asked for more destroyers, and the demand was voiced from all quarters of the House—more destroyers We were assured that there was no need for more destroyers. All the highest authorities were convinced that more destroyers would be a superfluity. The requisite number had been provided, and the highest expert opinions were available to justify that view. Now, after six months in which no new naval facts have come to light, we are to have more destroyers. The "escalator clause" has been used and a new flotilla is asked for in these Estimates, and I believe that further destroyer construction is in contemplation. It ought to give the House more confidence in its own opinion than in the opinion of these very high authorities, who in January will say one thing, and in July will present an equally cast-iron, hide-bound conclusion, backed by the same solid consensus of expert authority.

Take another instance—the question of food supply. When the House became very anxious a few months ago about our existing granaries being only about half full, and some hon. Members had the audacity to suggest that perhaps it might be just as well to fill them right up and keep them almost filled instead of half empty, the Minister for the Co-ordination of Defence came forward with a plan. It was the kind of plan which is always popular, always acceptable, and always most effective in allaying agitation and staving off Parliamentary questions. His plan was to have an inquiry. There would be an inquiry over which he himself would preside. Of course, once that has been announced, obviously all other questions whenever they are raised can be answered most effectively by saying, "Hush! The inquiry is still proceeding; the case is *sub judice*. We must not interrupt these most searching toils and studies which are being undertaken. We must wait with patience until the whole matter can be presented." That inquiry is still proceeding.

But what happened the week before last? At the beginning of the week Lord Hailsham in another place unfolded an argument obviously based on the fullest official information, the effect of which was to deprecate even the filling up of our existing granaries at the ports on the ground that they might become targets of an air attack. He also at the same time deprecated building small granaries in different parts of the country on the ground of the expense and inconvenience that might arise, and on Monday of that week he assured us that we had three months' supply of the essential foodstuffs in the country. So much for the view of one of the highest officials in the Government. But at the end of the same week, on Saturday, the First Lord of the Admiralty [Sir Samuel Hoare] made a speech at Southampton in which he declared that if our sea-borne supplies were interrupted, we should all be dead of starvation in six weeks. Here you have two Ministers, both in the most powerful situations, abso-lutely at variance upon the actual facts; you have your granaries still only partly filled, and you have the Minister for Co-ordination of Defence still inquiring into the general question. I beg his pardon. I took down the actual words. I must not say that the question is being inquired into, but is "being examined with a view to action." The first task of the Minister for Co-ordination of Defence is to co-ordinate the contradictory utterances of his high colleagues, both of whom have already prejudged the result of his inquiry in opposite directions.

I have one more point to offer to the Committee. Have we satisfied ourselves, as former Parliaments would have done, as to where we stand and what is being done? I have scrupulously refrained in this Debate from saying anything which is not obviously known to foreign countries. I have always tried to make that my rule. But I and many others have a number of questions to ask which we do not wish to ask in public. They are questions to which full answers could not be given in public. We have statements to make which we should like to have answered, but not here before all the world. The times have waxed too dangerous for that. What then have we to do—apart from going away on our holidays?

There is the question of a secret Session. I urged a secret Session on Mr. Asquith and on Mr. Lloyd George during the War. Mr. Asquith declined it for reasons which were the same as are given now. But Mr Lloyd George, when Prime Minister, had a secret Session, and I believe I am right in saying that none of the evils which were forecast took place, and the Government emerged from it with a sensibly enhanced advantage. We were told that Members would leak, and that the Press would invent even if it did not hear. I believe that in dangerous times, once public danger is made known, we should be found not less worthy of the handling of confidential matters than were the rugged generations which built up this island's greatness. Nothing would give me greater pleasure than to be absolutely stultified in a secret Session by the Government, and proved to be an alarmist. I would endure with patience the roar of exultation that would go up when I was proved wrong, because it would lift a load off my heart and off the hearts of many Members. What does it matter who gets exposed or discomfited? If the country is safe, who cares for individual politicians, in or out of office?

I dare say that the Government will not agree to a secret Session. If that be so, I make this request on behalf of myself and a number of my hon. Friends who are supporters of the Government—will the Prime Minister, with any of his colleagues concerned, receive a small deputation composed of Members who have served many years in this House, if possible representing all parties—I do not know what view other parties may take—and allow a case which can no longer with safety be made in public to be submitted to him under the following condition of secrecy—

that nothing said by the Government not already known to members of the deputation shall be made known or used in any way? [2]

I have tried to show that the efforts that the Government are making, albeit great efforts, are only a small fraction of what is going on elsewhere. As far as this year is concerned, and I fear also as far as next year is concerned, we shall not overtake them, but only fall farther behind. This does not apply to the Navy, but to the other two Services. In these circumstances we have a right to say that conditions of emergency have supervened. The Secretary of State for War [Mr. Duff-Cooper] has told us that conditions are worse than in 1914. How, then, can it be argued that conditions of emergency have not supervened? I do not ask that war conditions should be established for the production of munitions; it would not be necessary or helpful. All I ask is that the intermediate stage between ordinary peace-time and actual war should be recognized, that a state of emergency preparation should be proclaimed, and that the whole spirit and atmosphere of our rearmament should be raised to a higher pitch; that we should lay aside a good deal of the comfort and smoothness of our ordinary life, that we should not hesitate to make an inroad into our industry, and that we should make the most strenuous efforts in our power to execute the programs that the Government have in mind at such pace as would make them relevant to the ever-growing dangers that gather round us.

[2] This latter request was acceded to, and a deputation led by Lord Salisbury, the late Sir Austen Chamberlain, and Mr. Churchill was received by the Prime Minister on July 28 and 29, 1936.

PART III
GERMANY ARMED

COLLECTIVE SECURITY

November 5, 1936

Debate on the Address

1936

September 5 First meeting of the Spanish Non-Intervention Committee

October 22 Lord Nuffield after a dispute with Lord Swinton withdraws from the Air Ministry "shadow" scheme, alleging that the manufacture of aero-engines by component parts in separate factories is an unsound method of organization

October 28. Government publish a White Paper on production of aero-engines.

October 31. Publication of report of the Royal Commission on the private manufacture of armaments.

November 5 Publication of report of Committee appointed to consider the vulnerability of capital ships to air attack. The report states that, though it is plain that capital ships cannot be constructed so as to be indestructible by bombing from the air, to cease to build them would lead to grave risk of disaster

COLLECTIVE SECURITY

THE MOST important thing, it seems to me, in regard to British policy is for us to have a plan and to stick to it. The repeated chops and changes, hot fits and cold fits, with which even the last melancholy twelve months have acquainted us have sensibly diminished our influence and augmented the dangers which menace us and others. No one can look out upon the surface of the world without profound anxiety, not only because of the causes of unrest, but because of the amount of unfavorable regards which are turned in our direction from many countries. No one can do that without feeling that at every stage events have darkened and turned against us. You can hardly think of anything that has happened in the last year that has not made our position one of greater anxiety. One has to note every week some occurrence which seems to tell against our view and against our influence in the world.

That is why I plead for a plan, and I think there is a plan which is open to us. It is the same plan that nearly all the Members who were elected talked about at the General Election and gained votes for urging —namely, the plan of standing by the Covenant of the League of Nations and trying to gather together, under the authority of the Covenant, the largest possible number of well-armed, peace-seeking Powers in order to overawe, and if necessary to restrain, a potential aggressor, whoever he may be. Why, Sir, a very great number of people, of our people, have given their faith to this conception of the reign of law in Europe, and if possible in the world; but when we speak of the reign of law we must mean a reign of law supported by adequate and, if possible, by overwhelming force. The days of saving money on armaments have gone by. They may well return in happier conditions, but in this grim year 1936, and still more in its ominous successor, our aim, our task, is not to reduce armaments. It is something even more intense, even more vital—namely, to prevent war, if war can be staved off. Horrible war, blasting in its devastation the prosperity of the world, can only be prevented by the marshaling of preponderant forces, sustained by world opinion, as a deterrent to any aggressor who breaks the peace.

While I welcome the speech of the Foreign Secretary [Mr. Eden], I think we ought to play, not only because it is our duty, but also because it is for our safety, a manly and a resolute part in this. I believe we should run more risks by standing out of what is called collective security than by coming in and trying to make a reality of what has hitherto proved only a sham. I do not see what we lose by making a new and vehement effort, and I interpret the speech of the Foreign Secretary in that sense—that he intends to make a new and resolute effort. If we succeed, then we shall have borne our part in preventing a renewal of Armageddon If our exertions are not supported in proportionate measure by others, if we are not backed by a very large number of countries, great and small, then, of course, collective security will be shown to be a fraud, and the League of Nations nothing but an idle dream.

Even if that happens, I do not see how our affairs will be worsened from the bad position in which they now stand. There will still remain the two great Parliamentary democracies of the Western world, the two great nations whose thought and action have shaped its destiny and cleared the path of progress. These two great nations, Great Britain and the French Republic, will still, if everything else fail, remain possessed of considerable means of common defense. Together they will be very dangerous to attack. Together they will be very hard to destroy. It seems highly probable, therefore, that even if we fail in re-establishing a decent, tolerable life for the whole European family, which is our first endeavor, we shall nevertheless be so much considered that the fury of an aggressor will not fall upon us, or, if it should, we shall be able to survive and ride out the storm as we have ridden out others in the past. There is no greater mistake than to suppose that platitudes, smooth words, timid policies, offer today a path to safety. Only by a firm adherence to righteous principles sustained by all the necessary "instrumentalities," to use a famous American expression, can the dangers which close in so steadily upon us and upon the peace of Europe be warded off and overcome. That they can be overcome must be our hope and our faith.

It will be said, of course, that these words lead in one direction. "What you really mean," it will be said, "is the gathering together under the ægis of the League of Nations of what amounts to a grand defensive alliance against Germany." Germany, we are assured, is a most peace-loving country. It is true they are scraping together a few weapons, but that, we are told, is only because of the terror in which they dwell of a Russian Bolshevik invasion. Night and day the fear, we are told, of the aggression of Soviet Russia rests upon Germany. If that be their trouble it can easily be healed. Let them come into the system of collective security, and if Russia is the aggressor and the invader, then all Europe will give to Germany guarantees that they will not go down unaided They have only to ask for guarantees for the defense of the soil of Germany and they will find them forthcoming in the fullest measure from many nations, both powerful and small alike.

What, then, is this talk about encirclement? It is all nonsense. There is nothing that we ask for ourselves under collective security that we will not willingly concede, nay, earnestly proffer, to Germany. Let her join the club, and make her great contribution and share its amenities and im-munities. Let me make it clear that those who are devoted and sincere supporters of the Covenant of the League of Nations do not confine their position to an armed and combined defense of the *status quo*. We con-template machinery for the redress of legitimate grievances between nations, and we must contemplate that if a grievance is shown to be justified it shall be corrected even against the wishes of nations who would be unwilling to make the sacrifice. Four years ago—I do not know whether the House can go back so far, for nowadays memories are so short—I ventured to submit to the House the doctrine that the redress of the grievances of the vanquished should precede the disarmament of the victors.[1] Those days are gone. We have fooled them all away.

Now under infinitely harder circumstances the same issue presents itself in a somewhat different form. One desires to see among the nations who were the victors a certain association of strength in order that they may reach a position where they can discuss on even terms the redress of grievances. It is said that there must not be a front against any nation, against Germany. All I can say is that unless there is a front against poten-tial aggression there will be no settlement. All the nations of Europe will just be driven helter-skelter across the diplomatic chessboard until the limits of retreat are exhausted, and then out of desperation, perhaps in some most unlikely quarter, the explosion of war will take place, prob-ably under conditions not very favorable to those who have been engaged

[1] See pp. 31, 32.

in this long retreat. I believe that the next twelve months may be our last chance of averting a European conflict and of preventing that conflict from darkening into a world war.

I rejoice that the Foreign Secretary has this afternoon told us in unmistakable terms that he will make one more effort at Geneva to establish the reign of law backed by adequate force. Because these efforts have failed in the past, as he says himself, there is no reason why they should fail in the end. That is why I say that we must have a plan and a theme. We must have a cause, and all necessary subordinations of pique, prejudice or pride must be made to that general theme. If this policy is openly proclaimed and frankly avowed, the people in this island will not be the last to understand it or the least willing in measures to sustain it. We shall be no longer drifting about hither and thither. Today, as the evils of the time unfold and one sinister event after another crops up, every section of public opinion represented in the nation, or in the Cabinet, has its day, has its expedient. Something happens here to favor the Nazi régime, and those who are its opponents then raise their voices. Something happens on the other side, and another set of gentlemen find their ideas apparently receiving some confirmation from the course of events. To be governed in your foreign policy by the ups and downs of events in times like these is the way to ruin. Without a theme boldly proclaimed on which the great majority of the nation is united, which commands the assent of many classes and parties—without that there will be no means of finding our way through these extraordinary dangers.

Look back on the past twelve months and see the varieties of policy to which not only the Government but this House has given vehement expression. It is not only for ourselves that it is a serious peril. It baffles friends; it fans the wrath of foes. It makes the remaining authority and influence of Britain a positive embarrassment to Europe instead of being the main anchor, as it should be, of honesty, courage and stability. With a plan, with a theme and with a cause to which we adhere, even though circumstances run counter to it for a time, you will bring other people to conform to your movement. You have no chance of doing it while you are drifting this way and that.

With such a plan minor difficulties cease to count. We could with combined strength speak with a united voice; and these little minor daily affairs and distractions could no longer disturb us. The principles would be proclaimed of submission to international law, of resolve to enforce international law, of determination to secure the means to enforce it, and of appealing to others similarly minded to join hands with us. Such a policy may well inspire the conscience of the British Empire, and may yet command the action of the world. That is why I am most grateful to the Foreign Secretary. He has acted in the only way in which he could possibly act in proclaiming his intention not to cast aside the Covenant of the League, not to lose heart at this critical moment, but to make a renewed effort adequate to the seriousness of the time in order to establish, in defiance of past experience, in spite of disappointments, the principle of collective security against aggression, without which we cannot see how a future conflict is to be prevented.

There are some practical points, however, to which I would refer because they are difficult points, and it is no use talking about a subject if you avoid the difficult points. Take this question of collective security. The phrase has come to be derided now. People point to what happened in Abyssinia, and elsewhere, and then they say, "Will it not commit us to an enormous extension of our liabilities and dangers?" I hold that the doctrine of collective security must mean that no one is in until enough are in. It seems to me good sense. If other Powers and small Powers are not going to do their part, they must take their fate. Some of the small countries have vast colonial possessions, empires almost. If there is to be a stampede among them to join the martial dictators, the Western democracies can do nothing to save them, still less to save their possessions.

So when I suggest we ought to pledge our faith to collective security I mean that in these troublesome times the nations adhering to the Covenant should have by far the greater force and make all preparations to make that force effective The idea that Great Britain should multiply her risks indefinitely without receiving in return accessions of combined strength which will be capable of holding an aggressor to parley, or, if all fails, of forming a solid defensive front—that is certainly not a policy of sense or reason We have not yet got this security Let us labor to get it, and do not let us despair too early or repent too soon. I cannot see how the practice of this policy during the present year and in the future can deprive us in the slightest degree of any security we enjoy at the present moment. On the contrary, it may invest the action of Britain with a unity and a harmony which will go far to add to our strength abroad and facilitate our task of putting our defenses in order at home.

What ought to be our policy towards Italy? At any rate, we can see what it ought not to be It ought not to be a policy of nagging Very serious antagonism existed between Great Britain, doing her part as a member of the League of Nations, and Italy over the conquest of Abyssinia. In that antagonism we have not prevailed. We have been humiliated, but we have not been dishonored. However we may have been guided, we are not regarded either as knaves or cowards. Friends of mine tell me that the Italian Dictator has repeatedly said that he both understands and respects the British point of view. He has also made public a statement of certain submissions which Italy will make to the League of Nations about the character of Italian rule in Abyssinia. I do not know whether those have been departed from or not, or whether they still apply. It seems to me that any statements of that kind are of value and importance.

The relations between Great Britain and Italy in the Mediterranean have always been those of special amity. For more than 200 years we have held naval command of the Mediterranean. I cannot conceive that the time has come when we should abandon it. Therefore, we could never enter into any convention which limited the naval or air forces we might find it necessary to place in the Mediterranean, and, as a matter of fact, the making of such a limitation is physically impossible. Nothing can possibly prevent the stronger navy from placing in a few days any force it may desire and which it can spare from home waters in the Mediterranean. I gathered from the Foreign Secretary's statement that he had no idea of making any convention limiting our right to defend our interests in the Mediterranean as we may think fit. But surely the corollary is that the naval Powers in the Mediterranean should reciprocally bind themselves not to molest each other's sea communications. The molestation of communications is, of course, as great an onslaught upon a country as an invasion across her land frontier would be. It seems to me that if it were possible to have relations with all the Mediterranean Powers which gave a greater feeling of the freedom and security of the Mediterranean, a feeling that it was, as it were, an area which was not to be disturbed by the storms of war, there would be another great and essential step forward to the securing of world peace, and also, it might well be to the reinforced action of the League of Nations.

To sum up, let me say, with the freedom which a private Member enjoys, that we ought to aim at a pact assuring the peace and freedom of the Mediterranean and encouraging neighborly and helpful relations between the great Mediterranean Powers. Secondly, we must await with patience, however strained, developments which are taking place in Russia in the hope that she may play a part in preserving the general peace.

Above all, we must use our full strength and influence to rebuild the League of Nations, to make it capable of holding a potential aggressor in restraint by armed power, and thereafter to labor faithfully for the mitigation of just and real grievances which, if unremedied, are likely to provoke a renewal of the quarrels, the crimes and the miseries of mankind.

THE LOCUST YEARS

November 12, 1936

Debate on the Address

1936

November 10. Sir Thomas Inskip tells the House of Commons:

"At this moment, while some supplies are already adequate or are being produced in satisfactory quantities, there are others of which the production has not yet begun, and others again in which the production, although it has begun, will not come into what I may call the full tide of construction until the early or middle months of next year Often we have had to face the fact that designs have not yet been settled. The years have passed in the atmosphere of the ten-years rule and the Disarmament Conference, and design and trial have not been going on Whatever I or anybody else could do, the utmost expedition which is being devoted to the completion of design and the testing of these machines will not permit us to organize supply on the basis of any design which has not yet been thoroughly tested and proved. This is particularly a matter in which you cannot recover the years that the locusts have eaten.

"We have to settle designs, we have to test them, we have to run the machines on the ground and in the air, and until a design has been settled, although the utmost of expedition is being used, it is impossible in these cases to go into production. I share entirely the anxiety which is being felt by many as the result of what I have now broadly stated without going into detail The Amendment on the Paper in the name of Mr Churchill and others no doubt represents their sincere anxiety. All I would say is that they are largely pushing at an open door."

THE LOCUST YEARS

I HAVE, with some friends, put an Amendment on the Paper [1] It is the same as the Amendment which I submitted two years ago, and I have put it in exactly the same terms because I thought it would be a good thing to remind the House of what has happened in these two years.[2] Our Amendment in November 1934 was the culmination of a long series of efforts by private Members and by the Conservative party in the country to warn His Majesty's Government of the dangers to Europe and to this country which were coming upon us through the vast process of German rearmament then already in full swing. The speech which I made on that occasion was much censured as being alarmist by leading Conservative newspapers, and I remember that Mr. Lloyd George congratulated the Prime Minister, who was then Lord President, on having so satisfactorily demolished my extravagant fears.

What would have been said, I wonder, if I could two years ago have forecast to the House the actual course of events? Suppose we had then been told that Germany would spend for two years £800,000,000 a year upon warlike preparations; that her industries would be organized for war, as the industries of no country have ever been; that by breaking all Treaty engagements she would create a gigantic air force and an army based on universal compulsory service, which by the present time, in 1936, amounts to upwards of thirty-nine divisions of highly equipped troops, including mechanized divisions of almost unmeasured strength, and that behind all this there lay millions of armed and trained men, for whom the formations and equipment are rapidly being prepared to form another

---

[1] The Amendment stood in the names of Mr. Churchill, Sir Robert Horne, Mr. Amery, Captain F. E. Guest, Colonel Gretton, and Lord Winterton.

[2] See p. 141.

eighty divisions in addition to those already perfected Suppose we had then known that by now two years of compulsory military service would be the rule, with a preliminary year of training in labor camps; that the Rhineland would be occupied by powerful forces and fortified with great skill, and that Germany would be building with our approval, signified by treaty, a large submarine fleet.

Suppose we had also been able to foresee the degeneration of the foreign situation, our quarrel with Italy, the Italo-German association, the Belgian declaration about neutrality—which, if the worst interpretation of it proves to be true, so greatly affects the security of this country—and the disarray of the smaller Powers of Central Europe. Suppose all that had been forecast—why, no one would have believed in the truth of such a nightmare tale. Yet just two years have gone by and we see it all in broad daylight. Where shall we be this time two years? I hesitate now to predict.

Let me say, however, that I will not accept the mood of panic or of despair. There is another side—a side which deserves our study, and can be studied without derogating in any way from the urgency which ought to animate our military preparations. The British Navy is, and will continue to be, incomparably the strongest in Europe. The French Army will certainly be, for a good many months to come, at least equal in numbers and superior in maturity to the German Army. The British and French air forces together are a very different proposition from either of those forces considered separately While no one can prophesy, it seems to me that the Western democracies, provided they are knit closely together, would be tolerably safe for a considerable number of months ahead. No one can say to a month or two, or even a quarter or two, how long this period of comparative equipoise will last. But it seems certain that during the year 1937 the German Army will become more numerous than the French Army, and very much more efficient than it is now.[3] It seems certain that the German air force will continue to improve upon the long lead which it already has over us, particularly in respect of long-distance bombing machines The year 1937 will certainly be marked by a great increase in the adverse factors which only intense efforts on our part can, to any effective extent, countervail.

The efforts at rearmament which France and Britain are making will

[3] This forecast was unduly pessimistic in point of time. As far as can be judged, the German Army will not exceed the French Army in strength till the end of 1938, and even then the French Army will still be more matured

not by themselves be sufficient. It will be necessary for the Western democracies, even at some extension of their risks, to gather round them all the elements of collective security or of combined defensive strength against aggression—if you prefer, as I do myself, to call it so—which can be assembled on the basis of the Covenant of the League of Nations. Thus I hope we may succeed in again achieving a position of superior force, and then will be the time, not to repeat the folly which we committed when we were all-powerful and supreme, but to invite Germany to make common cause with us in assuaging the griefs of Europe and opening a new door to peace and disarmament

I now turn more directly to the issues of this Debate. Let us examine our own position. No one can refuse his sympathy to the Minister for the Co-ordination of Defence. From time to time my right hon Friend lets fall phrases or facts which show that he realizes, more than anyone else on that bench it seems to me, the danger in which we stand. One such phrase came from his lips the other night He spoke of "the years that the locust hath eaten." Let us see which are these "years that the locust hath eaten," even if we do not pry too closely in search of the locusts who have eaten these precious years. For this purpose we must look into the past. From the year 1932, certainly from the beginning of 1933, when Herr Hitler came into power, it was general public knowledge in this country that serious rearmament had begun in Germany. There was a change in the situation. Three years ago, at the Conservative Conference at Birmingham, that vigorous and faithful servant of this country, Lord Lloyd, moved the following resolution:

> That this Conference desires to record its grave anxiety in regard to the inadequacy of the provisions made for Imperial Defence

That was three years ago, and I see, from the *Times* report of that occasion, that I said:

> During the last four or five years the world had grown gravely darker. ... We have steadily disarmed, partly with a sincere desire to give a lead to other countries, and partly through the severe financial pressure of the time. But a change must now be made. We must not continue longer on a course in which we alone are growing weaker while every other nation is growing stronger.

The resolution was passed unanimously, with only a rider informing the Chancellor of the Exchequer that all necessary burdens of taxation would be cheerfully borne. There were no locusts there, at any rate.

I am very glad to see the Prime Minister [Mr. Baldwin] restored to his vigor, and to learn that he has been recuperated by his rest and also, as we hear, rejuvenated. It has been my fortune to have ups and downs in my political relations with him, the downs on the whole predominating perhaps, but at any rate we have always preserved agreeable personal relations, which, so far as I am concerned, are greatly valued. I am sure he would not wish in his conduct of public affairs that there should be any shrinking from putting the real issues of criticism which arise, and I shall certainly proceed in that sense My right hon. Friend has had all the power for a good many years, and therefore there rests upon him inevitably the main responsibility for everything that has been done, or not done, and also the responsibility for what is to be done or not done now. So far as the air is concerned, this responsibility was assumed by him in a very direct personal manner even before he became Prime Minister. I must recall the words which he used in the Debate on 8th March, 1934, nearly three years ago. In answer to an appeal which I made to him, both publicly and privately, he said:

> Any Government of this country—a National Government more than any, and this Government—will see to it that in air strength and air power this country shall no longer be in a position inferior to any country within striking distance of our shores [4]

Well, Sir, I accepted that solemn promise, but some of my friends, like Sir Edward Grigg and Captain Guest, wanted what the Minister for the Co-ordination of Defence, in another state of being, would have called "further and better particulars," and they raised a debate after dinner, when the Prime Minister, then Lord President, came down to the House and really showed less than his usual urbanity in chiding those Members for even venturing to doubt the intention of the Government to make good in every respect the pledge which he had so solemnly given in the afternoon I do not think that responsibility was ever more directly assumed in a more personal manner. The Prime Minister was not successful in discharging that task, and he admitted with manly candor a year later that he had been led into error upon the important question of the relative strength of the British and German air power.

No doubt as a whole His Majesty's Government were very slow in accepting the unwelcome fact of German rearmament. They still clung to the policy of one-sided disarmament. It was one of those experiments,

[4] See p. 103

we are told, which had to be, to use a vulgarism, "tried out," just as the experiments of non-military sanctions against Italy had to be tried out Both experiments have now been tried out, and Ministers are accustomed to plume themselves upon the very clear results of those experiments They are held to prove conclusively that the policies subjected to the experiments were all wrong, utterly foolish, and should never be used again, and the very same men who were foremost in urging those experiments are now foremost in proclaiming and denouncing the fallacies upon which they were based. They have bought their knowledge, they have bought it dear, they have bought it at our expense, but at any rate let us be duly thankful that they now at last possess it.

In July 1935, before the General Election, there was a very strong movement in this House in favor of the appointment of a Minister to concert the action of the three fighting Services. Moreover, at that time the Departments of State were all engaged in drawing up the large schemes of rearmament in all branches which have been laid before us in the White Paper and upon which we are now engaged. One would have thought that that was the time when this new Minister or Co-ordinator was most necessary. He was not, however, in fact appointed until nearly nine months later, in March 1936. No explanation has yet been given to us why these nine months were wasted before the taking of what is now an admittedly necessary measure. The Prime Minister dilated the other night, no doubt very properly, on the great advantages which had flowed from the appointment of the Minister for the Co-ordination of Defence. Every argument used to show how useful has been the work which he has done accuses the failure to appoint him nine months earlier, when inestimable benefits would have accrued to us by the saving of this long period.

When at last, in March, after all the delays, the Prime Minister eventually made the appointment, the arrangement of duties was so ill-conceived that no man could possibly discharge them with efficiency or even make a speech about them without embarrassment. I have repeatedly pointed out the obvious mistake in organization of jumbling together—and practically everyone in the House is agreed upon this—the functions of defense with those of a Minister of Supply. The proper organization, let me repeat, is four Departments—the Navy, the Army, the Air and the Ministry of Supply, with the Minister for the Co-ordination of Defence over the four, exercising a general supervision, concerting their actions, and assigning the high priorities of manufacture in relation to some comprehensive strategic conception. The House is familiar with the many requests and arguments which have been made to the Government to create a Ministry of Supply. These arguments have received powerful reinforcement from another angle in the report of the Royal Commission on Arms Manufacture.

The first work of this new Parliament, and the first work of the Minister for the Co-ordination of Defence if he had known as much about the subject when he was appointed as he does now, would have been to set up a Ministry of Supply which should, step by step, have taken over the whole business of the design and manufacture of all the supplies needed by the Air Force and the Army, and everything needed for the Navy, except warships, heavy ordnance, torpedoes and one or two ancillaries. All the rest of the industries of Britain should have been surveyed from a general integral standpoint, and all existing resources utilized so far as was necessary to execute the program.

The Minister for the Co-ordination of Defence has argued as usual against a Ministry of Supply. The arguments which he used were weighty, and even ponderous—it would disturb and delay existing programs; it would do more harm than good; it would upset the life and industry of the country; it would destroy the export trade and demoralize finance at the moment when it was most needed; it would turn this country into one vast munitions camp. Certainly these are massive arguments, if they are true One would have thought that they would carry conviction to any man who accepted them. But then my right hon. Friend went on somewhat surprisingly to say, "The decision is not final." It would be reviewed again in a few weeks. What will you know in a few weeks about this matter that you do not know now, that you ought not to have known a year ago, and have not been told any time in the last six months? What is going to happen in the next few weeks which will invalidate all these magnificent arguments by which you have been overwhelmed, and suddenly make it worth your while to paralyze the export trade, to destroy the finances, and to turn the country into a great munitions camp?

The First Lord of the Admiralty in his speech the other night went even farther. He said, "We are always reviewing the position." Everything, he assured us, is entirely fluid. I am sure that that is true. Anyone can see what the position is. The Government simply cannot make up their minds, or they cannot get the Prime Minister to make up his mind. So they go on in strange paradox, decided only to be undecided, resolved to be irresolute, adamant for drift, solid for fluidity, all-powerful to be impotent. So we go on preparing more months and years—precious, perhaps vital to the greatness of Britain—for the locusts to eat. They will say to me, "A Minister of Supply is not necessary, for all is going well." I deny it. "The position is satisfactory." It is not true. "All is proceeding according to plan." We know what that means

Let me come to the Territorial Army. In March of this year I stigmatized a sentence in the War Office Memorandum about the Territorial Army, in which it was said the equipment of the Territorials could not be undertaken until that of the Regular Army had been completed. What has been done about all that? It is certain the evils are not yet removed. I agree wholeheartedly with all that was said by Lord Winterton the other day about the Army and the Territorial Force. When I think how these young men who join the Territorials come forward, almost alone in the population, and take on a liability to serve anywhere in any part of the world, not even with a guarantee to serve in their own units; come forward in spite of every conceivable deterrent; come forward—140,000 of them, although they are still not up to strength—and then find that the Government does not take their effort seriously enough even to equip and arm them properly, I marvel at their patriotism. It is a marvel, it is also a glory, but a glory we have no right to profit by unless we can secure proper and efficient equipment for them.

A friend of mine the other day saw a number of persons engaged in peculiar evolutions, genuflections and gestures in the neighborhood of London His curiosity was excited. He wondered whether it was some novel form of gymnastics, or a new religion—there are new religions which are very popular in some countries nowadays—or whether they were a party of lunatics out for an airing On approaching closer he learned that they were a Searchlight Company of London Territorials who were doing their exercises as well as they could without having the searchlights. Yet we are told there is no need for a Ministry of Supply

In the maneuvers of the Regular Army many of the most important new weapons have to be represented by flags and discs.[5] When we remember how small our land forces are—altogether only a few hundred thousand men—it seems incredible that the very flexible industry of Britain, if properly handled, could not supply them with their modest requirements. In Italy, whose industry is so much smaller, whose wealth and credit are a small fraction of this country's, a Dictator is able to

[5] This is still the case in 1938 in many regular units.

boast that he has bayonets and equipment for 8,000,000 men. Halve the figure, if you like, and the moral remains equally cogent.

The Army lacks almost every weapon which is required for the latest form of modern war. Where are the anti-tank guns, where are the short-distance wireless sets, where the field anti-aircraft guns against low-flying armored aeroplanes? We want to know how it is that this country, with its enormous motoring and motor-bicycling public, is not able to have strong mechanized divisions, both Regular and Territorial. Surely, when so much of the interest and the taste of our youth is moving in those mechanical channels, and when the horse is receding with the days of chivalry into the past, it ought to be possible to create an army of the size we want fully up to strength and mechanized to the highest degree.

Look at the Tank Corps. The tank was a British invention. This idea, which has revolutionized the conditions of modern war, was a British idea forced on the War Office by outsiders. Let me say they would have just as hard work today to force a new idea on it. I speak from what I know. During the War we had almost a monopoly, let alone the leadership, in tank warfare, and for several years afterwards we held the foremost place. To England all eyes were turned. All that has gone now. Nothing has been done in "the years that the locust hath eaten" to equip the Tank Corps with new machines. The medium tank which they possess, which in its day was the best in the world, is now long obsolete. Not only in numbers—for there we have never tried to compete with other countries—but in quality these British weapons are now surpassed by those of Germany, Russia, Italy and the United States. All the shell plants and gun plants in the Army, apart from the very small peace-time services, are in an elementary stage. A very long period must intervene before any effectual flow of munitions can be expected, even for the small forces of which we dispose. Still we are told there is no necessity for a Ministry of Supply, no emergency which should induce us to impinge on the normal course of trade. If we go on like this, and I do not see what power can prevent us from going on like this, some day there may be a terrible reckoning, and those who take the responsibility so entirely upon themselves are either of a hardy disposition or they are incapable of foreseeing the possibilities which may arise.

Now I come to the greatest matter of all, the air. We received on Tuesday night, from the First Lord of the Admiralty [Sir Samuel Hoare], the assurance that there is no foundation whatever for the statement that we are "vastly behindhand" with our Air Force program. It is clear from his words that we are behindhand. The only question is, what meaning does the First Lord attach to the word "vastly"? He also used the expression, about the progress of air expansion, that it was "not unsatisfactory." One does not know what his standard is His standards change from time to time. In that speech of the 11th of September about the League of Nations there was one standard, and in the Hoare-Laval Pact there was clearly another.

In August last some of us went in a deputation to the Prime Minister in order to express the anxieties which we felt about national defense, and to make a number of statements which we preferred not to be forced to make in public. I personally made a statement on the state of the Air Force to the preparation of which I had devoted several weeks and which, I am sorry to say, took an hour to read. My right hon. Friend the Prime Minister listened with his customary exemplary patience. I think I told him beforehand that he is a good listener, and perhaps he will retort that he learned to be when I was his colleague. At any rate, he listened with patience, and that is always something. During the three months that have passed since then I have checked those facts again in the light of current events and later knowledge, and were it not that foreign ears listen to all that is said here, or if we were in secret Session, I would repeat my statement here. And even if only one half were true I am sure the House would consider that a very grave state of emergency existed, and also, I regret to say, a state of things from which a certain suspicion of mismanagement cannot be excluded I am not going into any of those details. I make it a rule, as far as I possibly can, to say nothing in this House upon matters which I am not sure are already known to the General Staffs of foreign countries; but there is one statement of very great importance which the Minister for the Co-ordination of Defence made in his speech on Tuesday. He said:

> The process of building up squadrons and forming new training units and skeleton squadrons is familiar to everybody connected with the Air Force The number of squadrons in present circumstances at home today is eighty, and that figure includes sixteen auxiliary squadrons, but excludes the Fleet Air Arm, and, of course, does not include the squadrons abroad.[6]

From that figure, and the reservations by which it was prefaced, it is possible for the House, and also for foreign countries, to deduce pretty

[6] November 10, 1936.

accurately the progress of our Air Force expansion. I feel, therefore, at liberty to comment on it.

Parliament was promised a total of seventy-one new squadrons, making a total of 124 squadrons in the home defense force, by 31st March, 1937. This was thought to be the minimum compatible with our safety. At the end of the last financial year our strength was fifty-three squadrons, including auxiliary squadrons. Therefore, in the thirty-two weeks which have passed since the financial year began we have added twenty-eight squadrons—that is to say, less than one new squadron each week. In order to make the progress which Parliament was promised, in order to maintain the program which was put forward as the minimum, we shall have to add forty-three squadrons in the remaining twenty weeks, or over two squadrons a week. The rate at which new squadrons will have to be formed from now till the end of March will have to be nearly three times as fast as hitherto. I do not propose to analyze the composition of the eighty squadrons we now have, but the Minister, in his speech, used a suggestive expression, "skeleton squadrons"—applying at least to a portion of them—but even if every one of the eighty squadrons had an average strength of twelve aeroplanes, each fitted with war equipment, and the reserves upon which my right hon. Friend dwelt, we should only have a total of 960 first-line home-defense aircraft.

What is the comparable German strength? I am not going to give an estimate and say that the Germans have not got more than a certain number, but I will take it upon myself to say that they most certainly at this moment have not got less than a certain number. Most certainly they have not got less than 1500 first-line aeroplanes, comprised in not less than 130 or 140 squadrons, including auxiliary squadrons. It must also be remembered that Germany has not got in its squadrons any machine the design and construction of which is more than three years old. It must also be remembered that Germany has specialized in long-distance bombing aeroplanes and that her preponderance in that respect is far greater than any of these figures would suggest.

We were promised most solemnly by the Government that air parity with Germany would be maintained by the home defense forces. At the present time, putting everything at the very best, we are, upon the figures given by the Minister for the Co-ordination of Defence, only about two-thirds as strong as the German air force, assuming that I am not very much understating their present strength. How then does the First Lord of the Admiralty [Sir Samuel Hoare] think it right to say:

On the whole, our forecast of the strength of other Air Forces proves to be accurate; on the other hand, our own estimates have also proved to be accurate.

I am authorized to say that the position is satisfactory.

I simply cannot understand it. Perhaps the Prime Minister will explain the position. I should like to remind the House that I have made no revelation affecting this country and that I have introduced no new fact in our air defense which does not arise from the figures given by the Minister and from the official estimates that have been published

What ought we to do? I know of only one way in which this matter can be carried further. The House ought to demand a Parliamentary inquiry. It ought to appoint six, seven or eight independent Members, responsible, experienced, discreet Members, who have some acquaintance with these matters and are representative of all parties, to interview Ministers and to find out what are, in fact, the answers to a series of questions; then to make a brief report to the House, whether of reassurance or of suggestion for remedying the shortcomings. That, I think, is what any Parliament worthy of the name would do in these circumstances. Parliaments of the past days in which the greatness of our country was abuilding would never have hesitated. They would have felt they could not discharge their duty to their constituents if they did not satisfy themselves that the safety of the country was being effectively maintained.

The French Parliament, through its committees, has a very wide, deep knowledge of the state of national defense, and I am not aware that their secrets leak out in any exceptional way. There is no reason why our secrets should leak out in any exceptional way. It is because so many members of the French Parliament are associated in one way or another with the progress of the national defense that the French Government were induced to supply, six years ago, upward of £60,000,000 sterling to construct the Maginot Line of fortifications, when our Government was assuring them that wars were over and that France must not lag behind Britain in her disarmament. Even now I hope that Members of the House of Commons will rise above considerations of party discipline, and will insist upon knowing where we stand in a matter which affects our liberties and our lives. I should have thought that the Government, and above all the Prime Minister, whose load is so heavy, would have welcomed such a suggestion.

Owing to past neglect, in the face of the plainest warnings, we have now entered upon a period of danger greater than has befallen Britain since the U-boat campaign was crushed; perhaps, indeed, it is a more grievous period than that, because at that time at least we were possessed of the means of securing ourselves and of defeating that campaign Now we have no such assurance. The era of procrastination, of half-measures, of soothing and baffling expedients, of delays, is coming to its close In its place we are entering a period of consequences. We have entered a period in which for more than a year, or a year and a half, the considerable preparations which are now on foot in Britain will not, as the Minister clearly showed, yield results which can be effective in actual fighting strength, while during this very period Germany may well reach the culminating point of her gigantic military preparations, and be forced by financial and economic stringency to contemplate a sharp decline, or perhaps some other exit from her difficulties. It is this lamentable conjunction of events which seems to present the danger of Europe in its most disquieting form We cannot avoid this period; we are in it now. Surely, if we can abridge it by even a few months, if we can shorten this period when the German Army will begin to be so much larger than the French Army, and before the British Air Force has come to play its complementary part, we may be the architects who build the peace of the world on sure foundations.

Two things, I confess, have staggered me, after a long Parliamentary experience, in these Debates. The first has been the dangers that have so swiftly come upon us in a few years, and have been transforming our position and the whole outlook of the world. Secondly, I have been staggered by the failure of the House of Commons to react effectively against those dangers. That, I am bound to say, I never expected. I never would have believed that we should have been allowed to go on getting into this plight, month by month and year by year, and that even the Government's own confessions of error would have produced no concentration of Parliamentary opinion and force capable of lifting our efforts to the level of emergency. I say that unless the House resolves to find out the truth for itself it will have committed an act of abdication of duty without parallel in its long history.

Replying to Mr. Churchill in this debate, Mr. Baldwin said.

"I want to speak to the House with the utmost frankness. . . . The difference of opinion between Mr. Churchill and myself is in the years 1933 onwards. In 1931-32, although it is not admitted by the Opposition, there was a period of financial crisis. But there was another reason. I would remind the House that not once but on many occasions in speeches and in various places, when I have been speaking and advocating as far as I am able the democratic principle, I have stated that a democracy is always two years behind the dictator. I believe that to be true. It has been true in this case. I put before the whole House my own views with an appalling frankness. You will remember at that time the Disarmament Conference was sitting in Geneva. You will remember at that time there was probably a stronger pacifist feeling running through this country than at any time since the War. You will remember the election at Fulham in the autumn of 1933, when a seat which the National Government held was lost by about 7000 votes on no issue but the pacifist.... My position as the leader of a great party was not altogether a comfortable one. I asked myself what chance was there—when that feeling that was given expression to in Fulham was common throughout the country—what chance was there within the next year or two of that feeling being so changed that the country would give a mandate for rearmament? Supposing I had gone to the country and said that Germany was rearming and that we must rearm, does anybody think that this pacific democracy would have rallied to that cry at that moment? I cannot think of anything that would have made the loss of the election from my point of view more certain."

THE LAGGING PROGRAM

January 27, 1937

Private Motion of Mr. Oliver Simmonds calling attention to the inadequacy of British air defense

1936

November 25 The German Ambassador in London (Herr von Ribbentrop) flies to Berlin and signs the German-Japanese Anti-Comintern Pact.

December 10. Abdication of King Edward VIII.

1937

January 2 Gentleman's agreement "concerning assurances with regard to the Mediterranean" signed in Rome by Count Ciano and Sir Eric Drummond.

January 23. Trial opens in Moscow of Radek, Sokolnikov, and others accused of being "Trotskyist terrorists, wreckers, murderers and spies."

January 27. Sir Thomas Inskip makes a "frank statement" about the progress of the Royal Air Force expansion scheme Of the 124 squadrons projected for home defense, 100 will have been formed by the end of March; 22 of these 100 are on a one-squadron basis He expresses the hope that the remainder will be formed, though not necessarily at full complement, by July.

THE LAGGING PROGRAM

WE ARE indebted to the hon Member for Duddeston [Mr. Simmonds] for introducing the Debate which has called forth the important Ministerial statement to which we have listened. As regards the figures which the hon. Gentleman gave of air strength, although I have had no conversation with him on this matter, I had, curiously enough, possessed myself of the Air Force List in order to ascertain the official statement of the progress that is being made. One knows that between 70 and 80 squadrons figure in this List and that a very large number of them have only three or four officers apiece. Here we are within nine weeks of the 31st March, by which time we were promised 124 squadrons When that promise was made it meant, one supposed, 124 squadrons complete in all respects, with all their flights and the reserve machines which they ought to have—the reserves in the case of our squadrons differing from those in other countries. They were to be completed by 31st March, and now we have the figures which the right hon. Gentleman, with perfect candor and courtesy to the House and convenience to the country, has given us this afternoon. There will be, he hopes, on 31st March 100 squadrons instead of 124, and of these 22 will consist of only one flight each.

[SIR T. INSKIP: To the best of my recollection no date was given in the White Paper for the completion of the expanded scheme, which is the present one. The date 31st March was the date in the original scheme, what I call the absorbed scheme, of 124 squadrons.]

As to what is in the White Paper I cannot charge my memory, but certainly we have been told, not once but a hundred times, that 124 was the figure which was being aimed at by 31st March.

[SIR T. INSKIP: Is now aimed at.]

Then there is no difference between us. The fact remains that out of the 124 squadrons there will be only 100. Of these 22 will consist only of one flight each, and I suppose others will consist of only two flights each. These squadrons are formed very much in the way in which we are assured the human race was originally formed. A rib is taken from one body and starts out on an independent existence of its own. But 22 squadrons consisting of only one flight each really cannot bear their part as complete squadrons. They are not in a condition to take part in fighting. They are only nuclei around which are built up new drafts and semi-trained personnel. If we take 22 from 100 it leaves 78, and that is the number which we shall have on 31st March in place of 124. That is to say, we shall be 46 short of the promised total.

Now, 46 out of 124 is a considerable proportion, and it must be remembered that when the first program was mentioned in March 1935 we already had 52 or 53 squadrons. So we have actually had 25 or 26 squadrons in 20 months and we shall be 46 short of what we hoped to have on 31st March. In order to be punctual in the fulfillment of the program outlined we should require to do in nine weeks nearly double what we have done in 20 months. It is clearly a serious deficiency. There is no good in pretending that it is a comparatively small falling short. It is an enormous percentage of deficiency. Even if you were to assume that all the squadrons which are supposed to be completed were fully equipped, not only in personnel but in machines, even if you were to assume that all of these squadrons were equipped with modern machines, there would still be a great falling short. And even if the full program of 124 had been completed by 31st March it would still not have given us parity with the German strength at that date, or anything like it.

We have been most solemnly promised parity. We have not got parity. Would the right hon. Gentleman rise in his place and say he could contend that we had parity at the present time with this Power which is in striking distance of our shores in first-line strength? I say that we have not got the parity which we were promised. We have not nearly got it, we have not nearly approached it. Nor shall we get it during the whole of 1937, and I doubt whether we shall have it or anything approaching it during 1938. I feel bound to make these statements.

Mr. Simmonds spoke also of the strength of the German air force, and I am very glad to see the Prime Minister [Mr. Baldwin] in his place when I refer to this matter. I hope he will allow me to say that I think he will find that he has again been misled by his advisers in the statement which he made in the Debate in November about German air strength. I suggested that as a minimum—and I laid stress on the fact that it was a minimum—German air strength then was 1500 front-line machines. Of course, they have increased it since. My right hon. Friend then said that he was advised by his experts—and naturally he could not be expected to ascertain the figures for himself—that that was a very considerable over-statement, and that the actual number was substantially less. Now I continue to assert the truth of my figures and to repeat that at the very least they had at that date 1500. They have considerably more now. Actually, the Germans are believed to possess at least 150 formed squadrons.

I wonder whether the difference between the Government and me upon this point is that I have always counted twelve German machines to the squadron. That is the calculation adopted in France and other countries. The fact, of course, is that the German squadron is organized on the basis of three flights of three machines each, with three machines in reserve. But the three machines in reserve are not reserve machines in the sense that they belong to a different status of efficiency from the other machines. They are in the same class as the other machines, with the same class of pilots. They are absolutely the same as the pilots of the other machines in value and capacity. If, for the purposes of calculation, for what I may call Parliamentary purposes and for making a good show, you count those squadrons at nine machines to the squadron, you get rid of no fewer than 450 machines which are perfectly serviceable machines with first-rate pilots, machines of a modern type, organized in squadrons. They are wiped out as if they did not exist. That makes the figures look better. Whether it has the slightest effect upon the realities the House can judge for itself.

If you take the basis of 150 squadrons at 12 machines to each squadron, it would give a figure of something like 1800 front-line machines at the present time. I notice that figure is very much the same as the figure quoted in the French Chamber yesterday, and not in any way challenged or disputed, of 2000 machines for the German first-line. If you add to that the squadrons of Luft-Hansa machines which could be made available immediately, then the figure of 2000 machines would be reached. It is clear that our figure, when 100 squadrons are completed, will be barely half that, and when 124 squadrons are completed, of course, the German figure will have advanced as their program proceeds. Therefore, when I said in November last that we had not got two-thirds of their strength,

I made, as I have always done on these occasions, a very deliberate understatement. I think one half would be a far truer guide to the relative strength than the figure which I then quoted. Well, that is not parity.

The hon. and gallant Member for Erdington [Wing-Commander Wright] raised a point of importance. He was bringing some succor to the Government and saying how he rejoiced about the years which the locusts had eaten, but his actual point of substance was one of the most disquieting that could be raised. He said that the one kind of aircraft which we required above all others was the long-range bombing machine. If that were to be adopted as the test, then the question of parity would recede to a very remote distance, because there is no branch of our service in which the relative comparison is more unfavorable to us than that which the hon. and gallant Gentleman selected as the most important and decisive of all.

I do not intend to detain the House any longer at present, except to say that I hope the Government are taking what steps they can to ascertain all the information which comes to hand about air fighting in Spain. Very valuable and instructive events are occurring in those scenes of horror. It is said that German anti-aircraft guns in groups, electrically controlled, have produced extraordinarily good results upon hostile aviation. At any rate, the whole of that matter requires to be most carefully studied, because anything which can increase our defense against air attack would be of enormous advantage. For my part, I believe that the day will come when the ground will decisively master the air and when the raiding aeroplane will be almost certainly clawed down from the skies in flaming ruin. But I fear that perhaps ten years, ten critical and fateful years, will pass before any such security will come, and that in the interval only minor palliatives will be at our disposal.

THE DEFENSE LOAN

March 4, 1937

Third Reading of the Defense Loans Bill

January 30 Hitler declares·

"There can be no humanly conceivable object of dispute between Germany and France. The German Government have further assured Belgium and Holland that they are prepared at any time to recognize and guarantee these States as inviolable neutral territories."

February 6. Sir Thomas Inskip, addressing the Fareham Conservative Association, says·

"It has cost tens of millions of pounds to re-equip the country in haste I hope we shall never again as a nation make the mistake of allowing our defenses to fall into a state of disrepair."

February 11. Mr Neville Chamberlain tells the House that the Government propose to seek legislative powers to raise capital, or use realized budget surpluses, for defense expenditure, up to a sum not exceeding £400,000,000 spread over a period of not exceeding five years.

Sir Samuel Hoare, First Lord of the Admiralty, speaking at the Birmingham Conservative Club, says:

"We have learned a lesson. We are determined that this state of affairs shall never recur. We intend in future that our strength shall be proportionate to our responsibilities."

February 16. Publication of a White Paper on Defense envisaging a total expenditure of £1,500,000,000.

March 3. Navy estimates published; gross total of £105,065,000, an increase of £23,776,000 over 1936.

March 4. Army Estimates published, gross total of £90,120,000, an increase of £26,000,000.

THE DEFENSE LOAN

THE INTRODUCTION OL tnis Bill aoes not imply alteration in the Government's policy or add anything in principle to what was already known about that policy. We knew more than a year ago, when the first White Paper was produced, that the Government were convinced that it was their duty to spend upon rearmament every penny in their power without—as they so limited themselves, and I think wrongly—interfering with the normal trade and life of the country. The Chancellor of the Exchequer more than a year ago told us that this spending would substantially exceed the revenue from taxes.

That was the position a year ago, and it is the same position now. All that has happened is that a forecast has been made of Defense expenditure for a period of five years, which amounts to £1,500,000,000, £1,100,000,000 of which is to be raised by taxes, and £400,000,000 by loan, and permission is sought from the House of Commons to make the necessary borrowing as the occasion arises. The mention of these prodigious sums has made a profound impression, and the reactions upon the whole have been highly favorable to the Government and to this country. The official Opposition have once again allowed themselves to be maneuvered off-side on a great national question on which they are as convinced, or almost as convinced, as Members on this side. His Majesty's Government have also placed themselves in a very favorable position against critics who, like myself, have for a long time been urging more active and timely measures. The great majority of the House will no doubt feel that the Government are doing everything that the situation demands, or at any rate everything that could be reasonably asked for, and they will feel inclined to silence critics with the remark, "If you are not satisfied with £1,500,000,000 being spent on armaments, nothing in reason will ever

content you." The Parliamentary position of the Government is, therefore, as strong as it could possibly be. The Opposition attack half-heart-
edly a policy which everyone knows is essential to our safety, and critics
from the opposite angle are easily disposed of by reference to the grandiose
figures which are involved.

But there are other, broader advantages which flow from the Government's declaration. Nothing is more important for British policy than
clarity and continuity. The fact that the British Government are coming
forward with a five-years plan of armaments on this scale, the evidences
of our great financial strength, the very general acceptance of this policy
by all parties in the nation, the welcome which it has received from so
many countries, particularly small countries, in all parts of the world—all
these give to our Dominions and to foreign countries a chance of walking
in step with us. I have felt during the last few years, and especially now,
that Great Britain has only to pursue a set course, uninfluenced by the
shifting gusts of incident and opinion, for a definite period, to find
herself moving along in a great company. We are the head of an Empire
of free Dominions. We are also looked to with friendly, appealing eyes
by a large number of peace-seeking nations. We do not give them a
chance of adjusting their policy and their outlook to ours if we swing
to and fro in accordance with the minor and superficial variations which
take place from year to year.

We have now got a policy in foreign affairs based upon the Covenant
of the League of Nations and upon special agreements with France,
which in any temper but that of partisanship would be recognized generally as carrying with it what the great mass of the nation as a whole
desire; and now, in addition to a foreign policy, we have a policy upon
Defense which, if we pursue it resolutely for four or five years, should
so long a period be granted to us, and if we do not vary or weaken
our course, may well leave us in a far safer and more agreeable position
than any which we have occupied since German rearmament began in
earnest. Time passes quickly. Everything is in constant change When the
first beginnings of evil which may subsequently challenge peace and freedom and even the life of the State make their appearance on the hori-
zon, it is right then to sound the alarm and to try, even by frantic exertions,
to arouse somnolent authority to novel dangers; but once we are in the
danger zone, once everybody can see that we are marching through that
long, dark valley of which I spoke to the House two years ago, then
a mood of coolness and calmness is enjoined.

There is another aspect. When the perils are distant, it is right to dwell upon defects and deficiencies, so that they may be made good in time; but when they come much nearer, it is perhaps natural, and also prudent and healthy, to dwell, in public at any rate, upon resources rather than upon defects, and to take a fair stock of our strength no less than of the hazards of our position. We must remember that we are for the time being no longer entirely masters of our own fate. That fate no longer depends altogether on what we decide here or on what the Cabinet settle in Downing Street. It depends on what may happen in the world, on what other countries do, for good or for ill. It may be hard for our island people, with their long immunity, to realize this ugly, unpleasant alteration in our position. We are an undefeated people. Nearly a thousand years have passed since we were subjugated by external force. All our outlook for several generations has been influenced by a sense of invincible, inexpugnable security at home. That security is no longer absolute or certain, and we must address our minds courageously, seriously, to the new conditions under which we have now to dwell, and under which Continental nations have always dwelt.

Of course, the question turns entirely upon whether the air arm is regarded as a decisive weapon. In France it is not so regarded, and in Germany, I believe, it is not so regarded At the Brest-Litovsk Conference Trotsky uttered the following sentence when the full German demands were made known: "The destiny of great nations is not to be determined by the temporary condition of their technical apparatus." That was a profound truth. If it failed to be true in respect of any country in the world, that country would be this island, so artificial in the character of its strength and wealth, and so different from that of the great self-contained or self-supporting populations which inhabit the continent of Europe.

Mere declarations of readiness to spend money over a five-year period do not affect the realities through which we shall have to live in 1937, 1938, and 1939. It has been obvious for some time past that the Government desire to spend as much money as they possibly can upon rearmament, getting value for their money, but neither the readiness of Ministers to place orders nor the readiness of the House of Commons to vote enormous sums is the limiting factor which governs our position today. The sole question of interest from the point of view of security is not the amount of money which Ministers will ask or which Parliament will vote, but what the contractors can earn in the next two years, and the only proof of our increasing security, the only measure of the steps which are taken to regain our security, is the weapons which we actually put in the hands of trained units from month to month. I tried to bring this idea to the notice of the House a year ago. I know of no factors which are now apparent which were not apparent a year ago, and of no vital factors which were not apparent two years ago and even earlier.

There is nothing in this situation that the House has not long ago been apprised of. The Minister for the Co-ordination of Defence, ever since he found out what to do, has been placing orders, endeavoring to stimulate the expansion of skilled labor, the manufacture of machine tools, the erection and adaptation of very large plants. All that process, so tardily begun, is now going forward, is now gradually acquiring momentum. No foreigner will underrate the power and flexibility of British industry, and I certainly think that we ourselves should not do so; but the only figure of real interest in this enormous proposal of £1,500,000,000, from the point of view of security, is the amount which can be spent in 1937 and 1938 That figure we do not yet know. I should be agreeably surprised and reassured if, proceeding on the present lines, more than £60,000,000 or £70,000,000 were required to be borrowed in the next twelve months. Surely the City of London has shown itself somewhat adrift from Parliamentary and political realities by recording a fall in gilt-edged stocks because of borrowing which, during the next year, cannot possibly amount to any serious burden upon the great movements of the money market.

The Minister for the Co-ordination of Defence told us of a large number of important subjects upon which plans have been made or even actual preparations begun. He spoke of food supply, of the accumulation of raw materials, the gathering of projectiles and the production of cannon, and above all of preparation for air defense. But nowhere was there any quantitative statement, nowhere was there any date given by which particular progress-points were to be reached. Nowhere was there any distinction drawn between the paper plans of committees and the elaborate organization of personnel required to make them work—nowhere any assurance that the programs would be carried out punctually, or in good time. How could there be when, except for the air program, no dates for the completion have been assigned to any of the numerous programs, nor even in most cases their dimensions?

For instance, take shells for the Army. Without knowing what is to be the scale of the Army it is impossible for the House to judge whether the arrangements made are or are not adequate. An Army with three or four divisions is one thing, but an Army of fifteen divisions, as we had in the first six months of the War, is an entirely different problem. We know nothing on the point. There is no means by which the House can check these provisions except by a secret Select Committee with power to send for persons and papers. Take the defense of London. Everything that has emerged from the Spanish business shows the importance of anti-aircraft guns. We know that Germany has thirty regiments of mobile anti-aircraft artillery, or about 250 to 300 batteries with 1500 modern aircraft guns, in addition to the whole of their static artillery for anti-aircraft defense. It is perfectly true that we do not need to have a large Army like Continental nations, but we do need to have an effective and adequate anti-aircraft defense. There is no alteration in the scale for us on that point. How long will it be before we have 1500 good modern anti-aircraft guns with trained crews and all the necessary equipment?

It is the same with the Air Force, although there we had a point, the 31st March, by which a certain measure of defense was to be reached. We know that this program is grievously in arrears. The Minister spoke in these debates of our anti-aircraft defense being the "best that could be devised." I should like the House to note the use of the word "devised." I wonder how long the interval will be before what is being devised will be translated into what we actually have. Take the re-equipment of the Territorials of which we spoke a year ago. Is that going to be completed in 1938 or 1939, or in 1940? We shall know in time, because people all over the country will see exactly the state of these forces when they turn out to drill; the truth must become known when schemes emerge in realities. But we shall not be the only people to know.

There is a serious issue, which I am bringing forward on another occasion, raised by the presence in this country of the large number of foreigners who are all held together by bonds of Nazi or Fascist organization. That is a new feature, and it is a matter which certainly will have to be considered. In my view there are any number of facts about which we have no good information in this House, but on which probably foreign General Staffs are perfectly well informed. When the Fleet went to the Mediterranean a year and a half ago the movements of every ship were printed in every paper on the Continent. The only country which was unable to form any opinion on the matter was the one which was vitally interested. I must say that I am astounded at the wave of optimism, of confidence, and even of complacency, which has swept over Parliament and over public opinion. There is a veritable tide of feeling that all is well, that everything is being done in the right way, in the right measure and in the right time.

When a whole Continent is arming feverishly, when mighty nations are laying aside every form of ease and comfort, when scores of millions of men and weapons are being prepared for war, when whole populations are being led forward or driven forward under conditions of exceptional overstrain, when the finances of the proudest dictators are in the most desperate condition, can you be sure that all your programs so tardily adopted will, in fact, be executed in time? At any rate, His Majesty's Government would surely be prudent to shorten this dangerous passage through the valley by every means in their power and bring to an end the period of insecurity to which we should never have been exposed. I have dealt with the good effects of this Defense Loans Bill throughout the Empire and Europe, but probably all the reactions abroad have not been equally beneficial.

I do not set too much store by the declarations of the Italian Dictator, which are no doubt addressed to our account. Italy has for a long time, under the inspiration of that extraordinary man, been held at a very high pitch of tension. I seem to have read a year ago that even quite young children were being taught to fire with the rifle. I expect they have been doing all that they can for a long time back. In Germany too the strain is very great. One wonders whether the peoples of these countries have a spirit so much uplifted above all other races as to enable them to support hardships and perform prodigies which are beyond the normal vigor of mankind. I do not believe that either of these great Dictators can do much more than they have been doing for a long time past But let us not ignore what they are doing. They are welding entire nations into war-making machines at the cost of the sternest repression of all the amenities and indulgences of human existence. I cannot understand, in the face of all these facts and so many others that are known to all of us, how His Majesty's Government can imagine they can meet and ward off the armed menace of nations already at full strain and overstrain merely by going along in the present comfortable manner without any decisive impingement upon private trade or profit-making or demanding any temporary sacrifices of comfort and changes in our way of living in order that we may preserve ourselves in freedom. Financial sacrifices alone will not suffice; the whole nation must pull together.

Having felt bound to strike a somber note this afternoon, I am most anxious not to omit the other side of the case before I sit down. First of all there is the Navy, which, even today, is far stronger, relatively to any navy in Europe, than it was in 1914. When we see the enormous program included in this Bill, which Parliament will so gladly vote this year, we may well feel assured that, so far as Europe is concerned, not only will the supremacy of the Navy be maintained, but it will become increasingly preponderant. I am glad to think that the menace of the submarine is no longer comparable to what it was in the Great War. Everything we have heard from the Spanish war seems to enforce the Admiralty view that it is not so easy to annihilate warships by aeroplanes as some people have been making out. We must not under-value the enormous power and security which we should derive from the British Navy in any quarrel in which the goodwill of the United States was not withdrawn from the British Empire.

In the second place, I rest my comfort and my reassurance upon our association with our closest neighbor, the French Parliamentary democracy. What has come to pass is, undoubtedly, a virtual defensive alliance between these two countries against any unprovoked act of aggression towards either of them. I feel that the companionship of these two countries, who have no other aim than the peace and freedom of all States and races in Europe, is one of the greatest guarantees for our common safety, for a continuance of peace, for, at the very worst, our joint survival.

Finally, I think we ought to place our trust in those moral forces which are enshrined in the Covenant of the League of Nations. Do not let us mock at them, for they are surely on our side. Do not mock at them, for this may well be a time when the highest idealism is not divorced from strategic prudence. Do not mock at them, for these may be years, strange as it may seem, when Right may walk hand in hand with Might. Let us, therefore, do everything in our power to add to our own strength and use that strength for the purpose of helping the gathering together of the nations upon the basis of the Covenant of the League Upon the rock of the Covenant many nations great and small are drawing constantly and swiftly together. In spite of the disappointments of the past, in spite of many misgivings, difficulties and ridiculings, that process is continuing, and these nations are welding themselves into what will some day be a formidable yet benignant alliance, pledged to resist wrong-doing and the violence of an aggressor.

THE CIVIL WAR IN SPAIN

April 14, 1937

Labor Party's Motion on the Situation at Bilboa

March 5 Air Force Estimates published, gross total of £82,500,000, an increase of £32,883,000 over 1936.

March 15. Sir Philip Sassoon, introducing Air Estimates, says:
"As regards adequacy, the Government has many sources of information open to it. Many of these sources in the nature of things cannot be available to private individuals. The information from these sources is correlated, and it is upon this information that the program must be based All the information that reaches the Government is constantly under the review of the Committee of Imperial Defence and the Government, and the program is based on that knowledge."

March 22. King Leopold of Belgium pays a private visit to England, in the course of which he discusses with Mr Eden the Belgian desire for a more effective safeguarding of her neutrality

April 11. Mr. Baldwin, speaking at Bewdley, announces his intention of retiring from the premiership after the Coronation.

THE CIVIL WAR IN SPAIN

I HAVE tried very sincerely to adopt a neutral attitude of mind in the Spanish quarrel; I refuse to become the partisan of either side I will not pretend that, if I had to choose between Communism and Nazi-ism, I would choose Communism. I hope not to be called upon to survive in the world under a Government of either of those dispensations.

[Mr. MAXTON: You would not.]

It is not a question of opposing Nazi-ism or Communism, but of opposing tyranny in whatever form it presents itself; and, as I do not find in either of these two Spanish factions which are at war any satisfactory guarantee that the ideas which I care about would be preserved, I am not able to throw myself in this headlong fashion into the risk of having to fire cannon immediately on the one side or the other of this trouble. I have found it easier to maintain this feeling of detachment from both sides because, before we give any help to either side we ought to know what the victory of that side would mean to those who are beaten. I can understand a British subject espousing the cause of General Franco or Señor Caballero, but what would be that man's remorse if he found that, after contributing to the victory of either side, a horrible vengeance was wreaked, perhaps for years, upon the vanquished? Certainly I do not feel that the House of Commons ought to take any decisive action either way without knowing what the consequences would be to those who were conquered as the result of any intervention in which we engaged. I cannot feel any enthusiasm for these rival creeds. I feel unbounded sorrow and sympathy for the victims, but to give a decisive punch either way, without making sure that the result of it would not be to make ourselves responsible for a subsequent catalogue of foul atrocities, would be a responsibility which no one in the House ought willingly to accept.

There is another reason for neutrality: the even balance of the forces fighting in Spain. The Leader of the Liberal party speaks of the Government and rebels. He seems to think that all Governments must be infallible and all rebels must be vile. It all depends on what is Government, and what are rebels. To make out that this civil war in Spain is a struggle between a bland, sedate, authoritative, liberal and constitutional régime on the one hand and a few mutinous generals on the other is not to portray the facts. Before the fighting began in Spain, as fighting might begin in any country where such a situation arose, the Conservative party, even at an election in which the tide went against them, polled actually more votes than, or practically as many votes as, all the combined parties on the other side—2,500,000 either way. If we look at territory, the larger part of Spain is in the hands of the rebels. My opinion is that the vast majority of Spaniards if they could speak would like the whole thing stopped, so that they could get on with their work and enjoy life like other people. I expect there are others who think it abominable that foreigners should be intervening on either side, feeding the fires and hustling the Spanish people forward towards the furnace.

I am going to give my vote on this occasion to the Foreign Secretary. I think he has done very well not only as regards our defensive alliance with France, which is our only means of safety in these years of tardy preparation, but in the Non-Intervention Committee. I expect that the Non-Intervention Committee is full of swindles and cheats; anyhow it falls far short of strict interpretation and good faith, but it is a precious thing in these times of peril that five great nations should be slanging each other round a table instead of blasting and bombing each other in horrible war. Is it not an encouraging fact that German, French, Russian, Italian, and British naval officers are officially acting together, however crankily, in something which represents, albeit feebly, the concert of Europe, and affords, if it is only a pale, misshapen shadow, some idea of those conceptions of the reign of law and of collective authority which many of us regard as of vital importance? The man who mocks at the existence of the Non-Intervention Committee I put on the same level as the man who mocks at the hopes of Geneva and the League of Nations. Even if you tell me that it is vitiated by humbug, we should not be daunted. Hypocrisy, it is said, is the tribute which vice pays to virtue. I am not sure that virtue can afford to do without any tributes which are going about. I say frankly that I would rather have a peace-keeping hypocrisy than straightforward, brazen vice, taking the form of unlimited war.

I should not like to sit down without indulging for a few minutes in a day-dream. Alas, it is only a day-dream! Still, as an independent member whose utterances are sometimes noticed abroad, I should like to unfold this day-dream to the House. We have been talking about non-intervention, which is a policy to which we should adhere. But suppose all the great Powers were willing to abandon the policy of non-intervention in favor of a policy of combined intervention in Spain. Suppose some of them stopped pouring petrol on Spanish flames and poured cold water and good sense instead. Suppose a voice went out from Britain—and whose better than that of the Prime Minister?—which said, "Comrade Stalin"—or "Mr. Stalin"; I do not know what is the exact term—"we understand that you are not seeking the establishment of a militant Communist Government in Spain. All you want now is that there shall not be a Nazi or a Fascist Spain. Is that so?" Suppose he said, as I expect he would say, "That is so." Then suppose the voice said to Hitler, "You have rescued the German people from despair and defeat. Now will you not be the Hitler of peace? We understand that the Russian Government is not insisting upon the setting up of a Communist Government in Spain. Will you not also say that if the German people were sure that this would not happen, they would not insist upon the Spaniards adopting a Nazi régime?" Might not Signor Mussolini also hearken to these words of good sense and good faith? Might he not say, "I will not tolerate a Red Bolshevik State in Spain, but I am quite content to see the Spanish Peninsula settle down upon some Spanish basis which is neither one thing nor the other." Then might not the Liberal democracies of the West, France and Britain, and the British Empire, too, come along and say, "Well, if that is so, cannot the people of the middle view, the live-and-let-live people, have a chance? Cannot something be arranged which represents a purely Spanish solution and does not spell the triumph of any highly colored ideology?"

I make bold to say that that is what nineteen-twentieths of the Spanish people want. They do not want to go on killing each other for the entertainment of foreigners. War is very cruel. It goes on for so long. What about some such meeting as Lord Rosebery once suggested, at "a wayside inn,"[1] which would give Spain the chance at least of peace, of

[1] Lord Rosebery's advice, in a speech at Chesterfield in 1902, on the way to end the Boer War.

law, of bread, and of oblivion? I trespass upon the indulgence of the House in uttering such day-dreams, but if they will bear with me, I should like to carry them one step farther and try to cast sentiment into a mold. Of course, neither of the two Spanish sides can afford to say that it would tolerate the idea of a settlement. They are fighting for life; they are desperate men, and all their lives are at stake. They dare not show the slightest sign of weakness, but they have their seconds, they have their friends in these Great Powers who are in close touch with them. Is it not the time when this horrible duel might for the moment be considered by the seconds and not necessarily only by the principal parties, and when the seconds could decide, as they often did in private duels, that honor is satisfied, or, if you like to put it more truthfully, that dishonor is gorged?

Suppose those five Great Powers, whose fleets are now acting nominally on a common policy, after agreeing secretly among themselves, were to propose to the Spaniards a solution on the following lines—a period of six years, in three stages. The first stage would give little more than peace, order, and time to cool down, with no vengeance, no executions except for common murderers on either side. The second stage would be a kind of compromise, a hybrid Government of elements in Spain that have not been involved in the ferocity of this struggle. Let hon. Members opposite not throw away this idea without considering it. If you wish for a truce to this cruel war, you must be bold enough to consider novel and even fanciful propositions. The third stage would see the revival of those Parliamentary institutions which, in one form or another, it is my firm belief that nineteen out of twenty Spaniards never dreamed of losing or meant to see destroyed. Proud as they are, it might well be that the Spaniards, in their distress and agony, would not refuse outside help in putting the locomotive back upon the rails or pulling their wagon out of the ditch.

When millions of people are lacerated and inflamed against each other by reciprocal injuries, some element of outside aid and even of outside pressure is indispensable, and if these five Great Powers were agreed upon a plan, they might say, "If both of your factions refuse our proposals, well, then, go on with your war, and much good may it do you. But if one accepts and the other refuses, then we will all of us unite to give our favor and support, and that would be decisive, to the side which accepts the means of peace." If that course were adopted, it would show that we at any rate possess a leverage, a great leverage, in these matters, and it might well be that a result would come which would be acceptable to the mass of the Spanish people. There is fear in all Spanish hearts, even in districts which are apparently quite tranquil. They know that the turn of the wheel may send a new force into that area by which all their actions will be regarded as guilty; and it is the same on both sides. I cannot conceive that it is not a supreme object of endeavor to give them reassurance. If we try and fail, what is the loss? It is nothing worse than what all suffer anyhow. If we try and succeed, then what is the prize? The prize is far greater than any issue now at stake in Spain. It may be that the peace and glory of Europe would reward the valiant, faithful effort of the Great Powers.

We seem to be moving, drifting, steadily, against our will, against the will of every race and every people and every class, towards some hideous catastrophe. Everybody wishes to stop it, but they do not know how We have talks of Eastern and Western Pacts, but they make no greater security. Armaments and counter-armaments proceed apace, and we must find something new. Worry has been defined by some nerve-specialists as "a spasm of the imagination." The mind, it is said, seizes hold of something and simply cannot let it go. Reason, argument, threats, are useless. The grip becomes all the more convulsive. But if you could introduce some new theme, in this case the practical effect of a common purpose and of co-operation for a common end, then indeed it might be that these clenched fists would relax into open hands, that the reign of peace and freedom might begin, and that science, instead of being a shameful prisoner in the galleys of slaughter, might pour her wealth abounding into the cottage homes of every land.

AIR RAID PRECAUTIONS

November 16, 1937

Second Reading of the Air Raid Precautions Bill

1937

April 25.   Franco-British declaration issued relieving Belgium of her Locarno obligations while continuing in force the French and British guarantees of her safety.

May 28..   Mr. Baldwin resigns. Mr. Neville Chamberlain becomes Prime Minister, Sir John Simon becomes Chancellor of the Exchequer; Sir Samuel Hoare leaves the Admiralty for the Home Office; Mr. Duff-Cooper goes to the Admiralty; Mr. Hore-Belisha becomes Secretary of State for War.

May 30.   Spanish Government aeroplanes bomb German battleship *Deutschland* at Iviza, in the Balearics

May 31   German warships shell Almeria Germany and Italy withdraw from naval supervision in Non-Intervention agreement.

June 12.   Marshal Tukhachevsky and seven other Russian generals executed on charges of treason and of spying "on behalf of an unfriendly state."

June 19   Mr. Eden and the French, German and Italian Ambassadors consider the matter of the alleged attempts of the Spanish Government to torpedo the German cruiser *Leipzig* France and Britain refuse to accede to Germany's demand for a joint four-power naval demonstration off Valencia.

June 21   German Government announces cancellation of Baron von Neurath's visit to London to discuss Anglo-German relations.

July 30   Mr Chamberlain comes to a decision regarding the Fleet Air Arm.

August 17   British Government declares itself to be seriously perturbed at the increasing number of attacks upon shipping in the Mediterranean and the extension of the area in which the incidents are taking place.

August 28   Japanese aeroplane bombs and machine-guns the British Ambassador to China, Sir Hughe Knatchbull-Hugessen.

September 11 Opening of Nyon Conference Britain and France agree to undertake joint patrol as a deterrent to piracy

November 5.   Publication of text of Air Raid Precautions Bill

November 16   Lord Halifax sets out on hunting trip to Berlin at invitation of General Goering. During the trip he visits Herr Hitler at Berchtesgaden.

AIR RAID PRECAUTIONS

I THINK the Government were right not to lead the country into a vast expenditure upon bomb-proof shelters against large armor-piercing or semi-armor-piercing projectiles. Perhaps it was not an easy decision to take, but upon the whole I think they were right not to take responsibility for affording complete immunity by passive defense to the population against air attack. It is beyond the power of any organization to do that. But these large A-P or S-A-P projectiles are not the ones which would be used against the civil population They are used to attack warships, perhaps to attack power-stations or docks, or possibly to disorganize the water-supply and electric mains of great cities; but as a weapon to attack the general civil population they would be obviously unsuitable. Only five such bombs can be carried to a ton. Raiders are not likely to fly all the way across the sea and land to carry the best part of a ton of steel in projectiles when they can effect incomparably greater damage by bringing, for instance, twenty-five times as many 20-lb. high-explosive bombs in the same manner.

The statement which was made that it took twenty to twenty-four feet of concrete to give protection against high-explosive bombs must, of course, be qualified by the fact that these particular armor-piercing bombs would not be used against the civil population, and that for all practical purposes much lighter structures give a considerable measure of immunity; and although I agree with the Government that it would be wrong to consume an undue proportion of our limited resources upon what is, after all, the most extreme form of passive defense, the question is not disposed of by the treatment it has received from the Home Secretary. More study should be given to the provision of immunity from high-explosive bombs which are in thin containers and have no great penetrative power, but have enormously destructive power when flung among ordinary houses.

I was very glad to hear from the Home Secretary [Sir Samuel Hoare] that he is alive to the danger of incendiary bombs. He said yesterday:

> I am inclined to think that in the past we have not given sufficient attention to the dangers of the incendiary bomb—that is to say, the small bomb that can start a very large number of fires.

I hope my right hon. Friend will forgive me if I turn to the records of the House. Exactly three years ago, in November 1934, in the Debate on the Address I said:

> The most dangerous form of air attack is the attack by incendiary bombs Such an attack was planned by the Germans for the summer of 1918, I think for the time of the harvest moon. The argument in favor of such an attack was that if in any great city there are, we will say, fifty fire brigades, and you start simultaneously one hundred fires and the wind is high, an almost incalculable conflagration may result [1]

Since those days the incendiary thermite bomb has become far more powerful than any used in the late War. I presume that it was of the thermite bomb that the Home Secretary was speaking yesterday. I am assured by persons who are acquainted with science that it will in fact go through a series of floors in a building, igniting each one simultaneously. I am naturally glad to find that my right hon. Friend is in agreement with me in feeling that insufficient attention has been given in the past to the dangers of this attack, and I earnestly trust that it will be the subject of continuous study. It is quite true that apparently it has not manifested itself as at all decisive in the fighting at Madrid, but you cannot tell what may be the reasons for the non-employment of this weapon against that city.

It is, however, of the more general aspects that I wish to speak today. In the same speech, three years ago, I said:

> Not less formidable than these material effects are the reactions which will be produced upon the mind of the civil population. We must expect that under the pressure of continuous air attack upon London at least 3,000,-000 or 4,000,000 people would be driven out into the open country around the Metropolis. This vast mass of human beings, numerically far larger than any armies which have been fed and moved in war, without shelter and without food, without sanitation and without special provision for

[1] See p. 142.

the maintenance of order, would confront the Government of the day with an administrative problem of the first magnitude, and would certainly absorb the energies of our small Army and of our Territorial Force Problems of this kind have never been faced before. Then there are the questions of the docks of London and the estuary of the Thames. Everyone knows the dependence of this immense community, the most prosperous in the whole world, upon the eastern approaches by water.

I ask that at some time or other we may receive assurances that these aspects of the problem are being dealt with by His Majesty's Government, and when I say "dealt with" I do not mean merely that a committee has been set up and has written out a paper scheme, but that definite, drastic, concrete steps have been taken in the appointment of individuals in the different localities, so that if, which heaven avert, trouble should come upon us, there will be a practical scheme by which an immense and tortured population may be defended.

No doubt hon. Members have heard that there is talk sometimes of what is called a nine days' war. That is a war which is so short that the scarcity of food and of raw material would not prevent an aggressor from striking down his victims and gaining a final result before the shortages became effective. It is an attempt, which this Bill seeks to face, by an act of mass terror to inflict such a slaughter on the women and children and the helpless population that they would make the Government surrender the rights, possessions and freedom of the country. That is a most hideous form of attack, and without the provisions contained in this Bill we are certainly not capable of resisting it. This is an indispensable part in our method of resistance. How should such an attack be met? It can certainly not be met by any system of passive defense. It can only be met by well-directed counter-attacks against military objectives. I believe there is no doubt that if one side in an equal war endeavors to cow and kill the civil population, and the other attacks steadily the military objectives, the focal points on which the opponent's war-making capacity depends, victory will come to the side, all other things being equal, which avoids the horror of making war on the helpless and weak.

[Mr. BELLINGER: What does the right hon. Gentleman mean by "other things being equal"?]

If the forces are equal, if the spirit is equal, if the loyalties are equal. But time will be needed for any effects of this kind to manifest themselves, and meanwhile the resisting power—the minimizing of slaughter, together with the capacity for enduring punishment with fortitude on the part of the civilian population—will be a vital factor. If it is thought that they can be made to give in or to make their Government give in before the regular operations of war can get to work, then this odious and frightful form of warfare is much more likely to be employed. The way to prevent it is to be obviously well organized, so as to make the crime not worth committing.

Therefore our defense precautions, although only subsidiary to the general problem, may nevertheless make the difference not only between victory and defeat but, what is even more important, between the thing being tried or not tried at all; may make the difference between the peace being broken and the peace being preserved The vulnerable character of Great Britain and its great cities, particularly London, not only constitutes a danger of profound preoccupation to ourselves, but is one which, if it is not remedied by comprehensive and well-conceived precautions, may well draw down upon the whole world the onrush of a measureless catastrophe.

The next milestone in this story is the circular of the 9th July, 1935. By that time we had moved on. It was found, contrary to the expectation and the figures at the disposal of the Government, contrary to the hope they had expressed, that Germany had a large organized air force. This circular issued to local authorities contained these words:

> Developments in the air have made it possible for air attacks on a large scale to be delivered, and delivered suddenly, on many parts of this country; and despite the steps which the Government are taking to increase the Air Force for home defense and the ground anti-aircraft defenses, it is impossible to guarantee immunity from attack ...So long as the possibility of attack exists, it is necessary to create organizations to minimize the consequences of attack, and, as it would not be possible to improvise effective measures on the spur of the moment in time of emergency, preparation must be made in time of peace.

That is July 1935, and, of course, this Bill is a child of the circular. Its birth-throes appear to have been severely protracted; in fact, when I took up this admirable Bill and began to look at it, I thought there must be some misprint, and that November 4, 1937, should surely have been November 4, 1935. There is nothing whatever relevant to this Bill that is known now which was not known then. There is no reason why this Measure should not have been brought before Parliament when we reassembled in the autumn of 1935. Up to the present we have received no adequate explanation of the hiatus of two years which seems to have intervened in carrying forward the negotiations with local authorities and presenting a Bill to the House, and a very serious responsibility rests upon all or any, whether they be national or local authorities, who have contributed in any way to this delay. I trust that it is not typical. I earnestly hope that what we have seen before us in this matter of air raid precautions, which necessarily comes under the public eye, is not . representative of what has been going on in other branches of our defense.

I do not like to think how the advocates of totalitarian dictatorships will grin when they read this sad story. How those persons who think that democracy is played out, and that Parliamentary Governments cannot make effective preparations for war or a policy of defense, will plume themselves upon the superiority of their institutions! With them orders can be given on a gigantic scale and are instantly obeyed throughout communities of 50,000,000 or 60,000,000 people, and the entire community is organized, by every kind of pressure, into one obedient instrument. The only chance for the defenders of liberty and democracy in a world like this is to substitute for the many advantages which despotic authority gains in the field of action a lively comradeship and association which enables them, by the co-operation of all sorts and kinds of citizens, to produce not merely an equally fine but a more flexible and more durable organization. The fact that nearly three years have passed in this squabble without any practical agreement is a reproach to the system of free government which we enjoy, love, and seek to preserve.

DICTATORS AND THE COVENANT

December 21, 1937

Debate on the Adjournment

1937

November 29. M. Chautemps, French Prime Minister, and M. Delbos, Foreign Minister, visit London to discuss political matters of common interest with the British Cabinet.

December 3. Mr Hore-Belisha reorganizes the Army Council Resignation of the Master-General of the Ordnance, Lieutenant-General Sir Hugh Elles.

December 6. Mr. Chamberlain defends Lord Swinton in the House of Commons

"As regards the attack on my noble Friend, some day perhaps justice will be done to him It is not possible for the public to know everything that has gone on in the Air Ministry since my noble Friend took charge. When it is realized, as it will be some day, with what speed and rapidity and with what efficiency he has built up a magnificent Air Force in this short space of time, unequalled in the world in the keenness and spirit of the men and equipped with machines of a power and fighting force undreamed of before my noble Friend came into office, he will earn and will receive the gratitude of the country rather than the carping criticism of the hon. and gallant Gentleman [Lieutenant-Commander Fletcher]."

DICTATORS AND THE COVENANT

I MUST candidly confess that I was personally anxious about Lord Halifax's visit to Germany. We had invited Baron von Neurath over here; he accepted, and at the last moment was unable to come. We renewed our invitation, but he did not renew his acceptance. It is unusual for a Great Power in circumstances like that to proffer a mission or a visit, however it arises, of a very important Minister, a visit which could not fail of world-wide significance; but still, diplomacy is meant to keep peoples in a good temper, and we must not be too touchy about points of diplomatic etiquette. If the only function of diplomacy is to give occasions for people to take offense, the less we have of it the better. We are strong enough, and we have a history which enables us, to say that we do not see offense where none is meant. We can lay down the proposition that the Angel of Peace is unsnubbable. There is a great advantage in convincing everybody, not only in this country but abroad, that we are really very earnest indeed for peace and that we are not looking for petty causes of quarrel or seeking opportunities for attitudinizing On the contrary, we should continue to preserve in face of rebuffs, in order to maintain and improve, easy, friendly relations with all countries, and especially with Germany.

A visit of this kind has a valuable educative effect. When we are asked whether we will grasp the proffered hand of German friendship, I think we should all answer "Yes," but at the same time one wants to know what happens after that. Often when these conversations begin they go nicely for a certain time, and then it appears that what the Germans want is that peace and goodwill should be translated forthwith into tangible and solid immediate benefits to themselves. Very often it is suggested that we should promise to do something, or give something, or, what is perhaps even more difficult, stand by and see something or other

369

done that may not be desirable. When the conversations reach that point, they become halting and embarrassed.

We must remember how very sharp the European situation is at the present time. The Prime Minister warned us rightly not to think of having blocs formed this way or that way. I agree, but the facts must not be ignored. There are at present several very important countries of secondary rank whose decision is hanging in the balance whether they should join the dictator totalitarian Powers or whether they should stand by the Covenant of the League of Nations. It is not merely their international affiliations which are involved, but the internal régime to be adopted in those countries. These countries all over Europe look to Great Britain, not to fight their battles—for we plainly cannot undertake to do that—but to keep the flag flying in the interests of peace, freedom, democracy and Parliamentary government. If it were thought that we were making terms for ourselves at the expense either of small nations or of large conceptions which are dear, not only to many nations, but to millions of people in every nation, a knell of despair would resound through many parts of Europe.

It was for this reason that Lord Halifax's journey caused widespread commotion, as everyone saw, in all sorts of countries to whom we have no commitments other the commitments involved in the Covenant of the League; but His Majesty's Government very wisely and promptly redressed the balance and restored the equilibrium of Europe by the great cordiality with which the Prime Minister and the Foreign Secretary welcomed the chief Ministers of the French Republic, and also by the consolidation of British and French policy which resulted from those extremely valuable conversations. If we take the Halifax visit and the visit of the French Ministers to this country together, as we ought to do, it seems to me clear that the final result is not only any improvement in the understanding between Great Britain and Germany that may have resulted, but a reaffirmation of British and French solidarity for mutual safety and for the discharge of our duties under the Covenant. Therefore, it seems to me that we have no reason to be dissatisfied with what happened.

I attach the greatest significance to the relations which we have with France. Those relations are founded upon the power of the French Army and the power of the British Fleet. They are also founded on the known and proved desire of both these countries to keep out of war and, to the best of their ability, to help others to keep out of war. Any separation between France and Great Britain would bring danger very near to both. I do not pretend that I do not feel anxious, but I comfort and fortify myself with the conviction that France and Britain together, with all their world-wide connections, in spite of their tardiness in making air preparations, constitute so vast and formidable a body that they will very likely be left undisturbed, at any rate for some time to come.

We have heard that since Lord Halifax's return the Government of Germany have raised questions connected with the restoration of war conquests. By this they mean conquests made from Germany and her allies in the late War. We are not called upon to express any opinion upon this until a specific request is formally made to us, but if and when that request is made, it would seem that the answer is obvious Of course, we should say that we are ready to discuss in a friendly spirit the restoration of war conquests, provided every other country, or the bulk of the countries, that made such conquests is ready to join with us and discuss the situation on equal terms. If my memory serves me, the French made important war conquests, and so did Rumania and Belgium. Poland, Yugoslavia, and Czechoslovakia owe their national existence—which I trust they may long preserve—to war conquests in which British, French, and, let us not forget, Russian soldiers played their part, and all of which were confirmed by the much-abused Treaty of Versailles and the much more justly abused Treaty of Trianon. Italy, which could hardly have won the War by itself, gained great territorial advantages in the Tyrol and the Adriatic. I am told that some of the Italian conquests correspond no more to the wishes of the local populations than we are assured some of the Germans in Czechoslovakia relish the form of government under which they have to live. The Islands of the Dodecanese, which were taken partly from Turkey and partly from Greece, are very important islands from the strategic point of view, and these are war conquests of Italy. Lastly, Japan has acquired under the mandate of the League of Nations, with an undertaking not to fortify them, islands in the Pacific whose ultimate destiny is probably more important to the United States than it is to Great Britain.

If this question of the restoration of War conquests is to be raised, and if sacrifices are to be made to lay the ghost of hatreds arising out of the late War, I say that these sacrifices should be made all round, and that all the Powers who profited in territory by the victory of the Allies should be prepared to consolidate their victory by sharing in and contributing to any measure of appeasement to those who were defeated.

There must be no singling out of Great Britain to be the only Power invited to make these sacrifices. We have heard a lot about the return of the former German colonies Although there are a large number of people in this country who would be willing to make sacrifices to meet German wishes about the colonies if they could be assured that it meant genuine lasting peace to Europe, none of them would yield one scrap of territory just to keep the Nazi kettle boiling.

There are other matters besides these on which His Majesty's Government, and in particular the Foreign Secretary, deserve the compliments of this House; one is the Nyon Conference Let me recall the ugly situation which existed before the Nyon Conference. Eight or nine pirate submarines were loose in the Mediterranean, sinking ships from one end of it to the other, and leaving crews to drown with the most atrocious inhumanity. All of a sudden Great Britain and France decided that these outrages must be stopped, and stopped if necessary by armed force. Anyone could feel, although it was not expressed in words, the stiffening and surge of resolution which accompanied the summoning of that Conference. That was a great responsibility for our Foreign Secretary to take, but he was able to take it, and the results were most satisfactory. From that moment not a single torpedo has been fired by any submarine in the Mediterranean at any ship carrying any cargo under any flag. The success of these measures should be recognized even by those who criticize the course which the Government have pursued, but I must pay my tribute to Signor Mussolini, who joined in the common exertions of the Mediterranean Powers, and whose prestige and authority—by the mere terror of his name—quelled the wicked depredations of these marauders. Since the days of Caesar himself there has been no more salutary clearance of pirates from the Mediterranean.

We have heard it said that the departure of Italy from the League of Nations is a death-blow to the League. I think we ought to be able to get over that. We have been told both by the Leader of the Opposition and by the head of the Government why it is probably not quite so bad as it sounds. It reminds me of the old story of the boy who was asked, "Is your father a Christian?" The boy replied, "Yes, sir, but he has not been doing much at it lately." I do not see why the League should be weakened by the departure of a country which has, to put it as politely as I possibly can, broken every engagement into which it has entered, and whose spokesmen have rejoiced in mocking and insulting every principle on which the League is founded. On the contrary, I agree with the Leader of the Opposition that the League may be strengthened.

It is of the utmost consequence to the unity of British national action that the policy of adhering to the Covenant of the League of Nations shall not be weakened or whittled away. I read in the *Times* a few days ago a letter in which a gentleman showed that these ideas of preventing war by international courts and by reasonable discussion had been tried over and over again. He said they had been tried after Marlborough had defeated Louis XIV, and after Europe had defeated Napoleon, but, he said, they had always failed. If that is true it is a melancholy fact, but what was astonishing was the crazy glee with which the writer hailed such lapses from grace. I was told the other day, though I have not verified it, of a sentence of Carlyle's in which he describes "the laugh of the hyena on being assured that, after all, the world is only carrion."

I look upon the League as a great addition to the strength and to the safety of our country, and I appeal to some of my hon. Friends who, I know, do not quite take that view to bear with me for a few moments upon this. Since when can we afford to ignore the moral forces involved in the public opinion of the world? Moral force is, unhappily, no substitute for armed force, but it is a very great reinforcement, and it is just that kind of reinforcement which may avoid and prevent the use of armed force altogether. For five years I have been asking the House and the Government to make armaments—guns, aeroplanes, munitions—but I am quite sure that British armaments alone will never protect us in the times through which we may have to pass.

By adhering to the Covenant of the League we secure the goodwill of all the nations of the world who do not seek to profit by acts of wrongful and violent aggression. We secure a measure of unity at home among all classes and all parties, which is indispensable to the efficiency of our foreign policy as well as to the progress of our defensive preparations. We consecrate and legitimize every alliance and regional pact which may be formed for mutual protection. Strict adherence to the Covenant of the League and to the Kellogg Pact will win for us a very great measure of sympathy in the United States. That sympathy may have an effect upon the interpretation put upon the laws of neutrality which, in certain circumstances, might be of enormous practical consequence to us. Can we be sure that even in the dictator countries these principles do not find an echo in many hearts? Can we be sure that even the dictators themselves may not, from one reason or another, respond to some extent to them ? Nothing could be more improvident or more imprudent than for the Western democracies to strip themselves of this great addition to their means of self-preservation, or to blot out from the eyes of their peoples ideals which embody the larger hopes of mankind.

MR. EDEN'S RESIGNATION

February 22, 1938

Debate on Foreign Affairs

1938

February 3.   Signor Mussolini introduces the goose-step into Italy.

February 5.   German Army crisis. Dismissal of Field-Marshal von Blomberg and General von Fritsch. Herr von Ribbentrop becomes Foreign Minister. General Goering becomes a Field-Marshal.

February 12.   Herr Hitler summons Dr. Schuschnigg to Berchtesgaden.

February 16.   Dr. Schuschnigg reorganizes the Austrian Cabinet. Seyss-Inquart becomes Minister of the Interior and Security.

The *Times* says: "No one but a fanatic will be persuaded that Nazism, as it may be practiced and justified in Germany, can spontaneously take strong and useful roots in Austrian soil, or that Austria could ever become under duress a convinced and willing partner in a system not her own."

The *Volkischer Beobachter* asks: "Can there be a better answer to the international Press agitation against the Reich and the rumors of a putsch in Austria than this new joint contribution to the peace of Central Europe?"

February 20.   Resignation of Mr. Eden.

MR. EDEN'S RESIGNATION

It is with sorrow that I rise today to take part in this Debate. Since my right hon. Friend became Prime Minister, I have tried my best to give him disinterested and independent support I know what his difficulties are, and we all know the dangers by which we are encompassed; yet I could not sit silent here this afternoon without expressing in good faith and in sincerity my disagreement with the course which he has taken, and my increasing concern for the consequences attendant upon it. There is one thing, however, that I will not do; I will not say one word willingly to exacerbate the differences which have arisen between the late Foreign Secretary and his former colleagues. No man, with the best will and sense of detachment in the world, can resign from a Government without wounds given and taken. My hope is that those wounds will not rankle or fester into personal differences, however serious the political issues upon which the men are divided.

This is a moment to celebrate the achievements of the former Foreign Secretary. They ought not to be overlooked at this time. They have been remarkable For a year and a half we have followed his policy of nonintervention in Spain, and even those who have been most irritated by many of its aspects must have admired the extraordinary tenacity of purpose and steadiness of aim with which he has maintained a central course, without undue bias on either side. And at the end of all this, with all the shifting scenes of the Spanish war, we are found to be the country most trusted by both sides, and the only country, perhaps, which still possesses some eventual power of merciful mediation.

Then there was the Nyon Conference. Here was the only occasion I know of where Britain and France together definitely stood up to the outrages that were being committed. The Prime Minister said that certain incidents had occurred in the Mediterranean. Those "certain incidents" were eight or nine submarines—and where, I should like to know, could they have come from?—sinking ships all over the Mediterranean and leaving the crews to drown. But when, at Nyon, England and France acted together it was seen that there is a strength behind these two countries, and almost all the other countries in the Mediterranean resorted to them. On the very next day that odious form of warfare came to an end, and, with one exception, has never been employed since. I tell that story because it seems to me that we should not set ourselves unduly against the duty which sometimes falls upon nations and individuals of standing up boldly in defense of the right, even though that may not be unattended with risk. In the last place, no one at the Foreign Office has been so successful as my right hon. Friend in establishing that relationship of goodwill and sympathy with the United States which must forever play a leading part in all our affairs.

I thought I might recite these incidents to the House because it is only right that we should recognize that his tenure of the Foreign Office has been not only distinguished, but memorable. We had yesterday the conventional and official account by both sides of the differences that led to this series of misfortunes. For the first time we can form a clear picture of what happened. Evidently there were divergences, marked no doubt by goodwill and all the courtesies of Cabinet association, between the Foreign Secretary and the new Prime Minister. These divergences extended principally, first, to their conception of the present condition of the League of Nations and its Covenant; and, secondly, to the attitude which we should adopt towards the dictator Powers

Coming to the merits of the actual dispute, it would seem to many people that this was an inopportune time for negotiations with Italy. In the first place, all these acts of bad faith which have been described to the House are fresh in everyone's mind In the second place, the dictator Powers of Europe are striding on from strength to strength and from stroke to stroke, and the Parliamentary democracies are retreating abashed and confused. On the other hand, behind this fine façade there was every sign that the Italian Dictator, at any rate, was in a very difficult position· the industrious, amiable Italian people long over-strained; everything in the country eaten up in order to augment the magnificence of the State; taxes enormous, finances broken; officials abounding, all kinds of indispensable raw materials practically unpurchasable across the exchange; Abyssinia a curse, a corpse bound on the back of the killer; Libya and

Spain, perhaps 400,000 men overseas, all to be maintained by a continuous drain on the hard-driven, ground-down people of Italy. One would have thought that these corrective processes upon external arrogance and ambition might have been allowed to run their course for a while; or, otherwise, how are the healing processes of human society to come into play?

I believe myself that we might have left this scene alone for a time. The Italian Dictator would soon have been compelled to bring many of his troops home from Libya, and some, at any rate, of his troops home from Spain, where they have given little satisfaction either to himself or to General Franco. We know that large numbers of people who have gone to Abyssinia in the hope of some Eldorado will be soon coming back to Italy, disillusioned Many questionings were arising in Italian bosoms which were natural and legitimate and could not be suppressed or ignored. All this was in the interest of peace, and also, I might add, what is an even greater cause than peace, freedom. It is sometimes wise to allow natural processes to work, and crimes and follies to be paid in coin from their own mint. The internal condition of Italy certainly causes its Dictator grave anxiety. He stood in need of an external success. It is quite easy to understand why Signor Mussolini should have instructed Count Grandi to encourage talks with Great Britain. But it is less easy to understand why we should have hurried so eagerly to the rescue. Here was a case where we ought to have allowed time to play its part.

However, as I reconstruct the story, the Cabinet, from the usual vague, well-intentioned desire for peace and friendship, enjoined the Foreign Secretary to have these talks. It is quite clear that he was reluctant to do so, and, in my opinion, he was right. The talks proceeded very unenthusiastically for a number of days, and no doubt Count Grandi reported to Rome that the progress made was small. At any rate, at this point—on the 11th of February—the following statement is made in the Italian Press—an inspired statement on the authority of Signor Farinacci, which carries with it the decision and authority of the Italian Government:

> Our opinion will not change until London's foreign policy ceases to be directed by Mr. Eden. In many speeches and on many occasions he has shown his poisonous attitude of mind towards Italy....

And then there is a good deal of further abuse. This was a very serious article. No such expression of opinion could have appeared in that country unless it had been approved by the dictator. It amounted to this, that there was a demand that the Foreign Secretary should go, and that unless he went there could be no progress in these talks. I therefore read with very much concern in the London evening newspapers of the following Friday, February 18, that the Prime Minister had taken the negotiations into his own hands, and had invited Count Grandi to conduct discussions with him and the Foreign Secretary, not at the Foreign Office but at No. 10 Downing Street.

I think that the House must see that this was clearly the episode which brought these divergences, which have not been concealed, to a definite head. Here is the Foreign Secretary attacked by a foreign Government through their controlled Press, his own papers filled with rumors that he will resign, and the Prime Minister coming in on this peculiar and difficult situation and taking charge of the discussions himself. Of course, he has a perfect right to do so; and, if he feels the urge, he has an inevitable duty to do so. But what was the position of the Foreign Secretary in this situation? I am trying to apply my mind to that, with some experience of the ways of Cabinets and Ministers. What degree of authority, what sphere of usefulness, would be left to the Foreign Secretary in these Italian discussions after what had occurred? Clearly, he and they had been taken charge of by his superior, and taken charge of at a time when his dismissal was being loudly demanded by a foreign country with which this country was in negotiation This is a bald statement of fact which everybody can get from the newspapers.

What is remarkable, I think, is that the Prime Minister should have been surprised on that second Friday when the Foreign Secretary began to talk about resignation and say he would not agree to this, that, or the other. I think that shows that the Prime Minister, acting entirely within his rights and from the best of motives, had taken a step the consequences of which he did not fully apprehend but which are now obvious to us all. Some people think the Foreign Secretary ought to have stayed on longer in a state of what can only be described as public chaperonage. It has been generally agreed that these are questions which a man can only judge for himself. Speaking about this memorable episode of his resignation, I am bound to say that in my view, as a Member of this House, I believe he acted absolutely rightly, and I think the responsibility for that event, for what has happened, and for what is going to happen, rests for good or ill upon the Prime Minister, who was also acting entirely within rights.

The Prime Minister yesterday, speaking of the future, said that we must look forward, and not unduly look back. The Prime Minister has assumed the whole responsibility. He has taken control of foreign affairs, and of this decisive sphere of those affairs, into his own hands. The House, by a large majority, is, I am convinced, willing that he should do so. Whatever my views may be as to the wisdom or unwisdom of a particular course, I am not going to fail in the wish and hope that he may be rightly guided, and his efforts crowned with success. I will not attempt to predict the course of the negotiations with Italy to which we are now committed, but I must say that their initiation appears untimely and their outlook bleak. We shall certainly be asked to give a lot, and there is very little we can receive in return, except the discontinuance by Italy of wrong and unneighborly action in which she has long indulged.

There is, however, one consideration which I fully admit would throw a different light on this scene. Even at the risk of being accused of some illogicality in my argument, I would say that if it were possible for Italy to discharge her duty in aiding Great Britain and France in defending the integrity and independence of Austria, for the sake of that I would go as far as any man in making concessions. It would not be possible without some new service rendered by Italy to the general cause of European peace and appeasement. But here I was disappointed to read last week that my noble Friend Lord Halifax had said in another place that there could be no question of our trying to have the Rome-Berlin axis altered in any way. Then it does seem to me that this is very disconcerting. It is difficult to see what serious advantage can inure to Great Britain in the Mediterranean, beyond expressions of goodwill and temporary relief from wrongful annoyances to which we have been subjected.

This last week has been a good week for dictators—one of the best they ever had. The German Dictator has laid his heavy hand upon a small but historic country, and the Italian Dictator has carried his vendetta to a victorious conclusion against Mr. Eden. The conflict between the Italian Dictator and my right hon. Friend has been a long one. There can be no doubt whatever who has won. Signor Mussolini has won. All the might, majesty, power and dominion of the British Empire have not been able to secure the success of the causes which were entrusted to the late Foreign Secretary by the general will of Parliament and of the country. So that is the end of this part of the story—namely, the complete defeat and departure from power of the Englishman whom the British nation and the British Parliament, reinforced by the mandate of a General Election, entrusted with a certain task; and the complete triumph of the

Italian Dictator at a moment when success was desperately needed by him for domestic reasons.

What has happened since the resignation was announced? All over the world, in every land, under every sky and every system of government, wherever they may be, the friends of England are dismayed, and the foes of England are exultant. Can anybody who reads the reports which come in hour by hour deny that? We have a heavy price to pay for all this. No one can compute it. Small countries in Europe balancing which way to turn, to which system to adhere, liberal or authoritarian—those countries are more inclined to move to the side of power and resolution. It will be universally believed that it is Signor Mussolini's superior power which has procured the overthrow of the British Foreign Secretary. I cannot myself contemplate the arrival of the British envoy at Rome to make a pact which, if it is successful, will involve the recognition of the conquest of Abyssinia without a pang of bitter humiliation, which I am sure will be felt in millions of cottage homes throughout this country.

But what has happened in the United States of America? There havoc has resulted from this event. I do not say that it cannot be repaired, but millions of people there who are our enemies have been armed with a means to mock the sincerity of British idealism, and to make out that we are all Continental people tarred with the same brush. That is the propaganda which has been given an enormous impetus, while our friends, those who are steadily working for the closer co-operation of the two countries on parallel lines, are downcast, baffled and bewildered.

The resignation of the late Foreign Secretary may well be a milestone in history. Great quarrels, it has been remarked, arise from small occasions, but seldom from small causes. That there was a complete divergence between the former Foreign Secretary and the Prime Minister is too plainly apparent. The former Foreign Secretary adhered to the old policy which we have all followed for so long. The Prime Minister and his colleagues have entered upon another and a new policy.

The old policy was an effort to establish the rule of law in Europe and build up through the League of Nations, or by regional pacts under the League of Nations, effective deterrents against the aggressor. That is the policy which we have followed. Is the new policy to come to terms with the totalitarian Powers in the hope that by great and far-reaching acts of submission, not merely in sentiment and pride, but in material factors, peace may be preserved? I earnestly hope that I may be reassured, and that Ministers will take occasion to explain their policy more fully. It may be that when the new directors of our foreign policy study the grim face of Europe and the world at this moment, when they have studied it with direct responsibility and with full information from day to day, they will come back to the old conclusions. But then it may be too late. The situation may have vitally changed. Many forces now favorable may have disappeared. Many friends in Europe may have entered into new combinations. Many sources of strength, moral and physical, upon which we might now rely, may be gone.

I was glad to hear the Prime Minister say that our association with France was unchanged and unbroken, but let there be no mistake about it. Our own safety is bound up with that of France. We have our Navy, but that is no protection against the air. The peace of Europe rests today upon the French Army. That army at the present time is the finest in Europe, but with every month that passes its strength is being outmatched by the ceaseless development of the new formations into which the vastly superior manhood of Germany is being cast. Almost any foreign policy is better than duality or continual chops and changes. It is strange that the British people, who have such a reputation for stability in other matters, should have been in the last few years pursuing a foreign policy so baffling by its shifts and twists that foreign countries have been unable to keep step with us, while the little nations who are indirectly affected by our changes are thrown into the utmost bewilderment and confusion.

The other day Lord Halifax said that Europe was confused. The part of Europe that is confused is that part ruled by Parliamentary Governments. I know of no confusion on the side of the great Dictators. They pursue their path towards somber and impressive objectives with ruthless consistency and purpose. They know what they want, and no one can deny that up to the present at every step they are getting what they want. When I look back upon the last five or six years I discern many lost chances when we could have made a stand, a united stand, against the dangers, and when by an act of generosity and magnanimity following upon the marshaling of material strength we could have perhaps prevented the evils which are now upon us.

The grave and perhaps irreparable injury to world security took place in the years 1932 to 1935 in the tenure of the Foreign Office of the present Chancellor of the Exchequer [Sir John Simon]. In those days I ventured repeatedly to submit to the House the maxim that the grievances of the vanquished should be redressed before the disarmament of the victors was begun. But the reverse was done. Then was the time to make concessions to the German people and to the German rulers. Then was the time when they would have had their real value. But no such attempt was made. All that was done was to neglect our own defenses and endeavor to encourage the French to follow a course equally imprudent. The next opportunity when these Sibylline Books were presented to us was when the reoccupation of the Rhineland took place at the beginning of 1936. Now we know that a firm stand by France and Britain with the other Powers associated with them at that time, and with the authority of the League of Nations, would have been followed by the immediate evacuation of the Rhineland without the shedding of a drop of blood, and the effects of that might have been blessed beyond all compare, because it would have enabled the more prudent elements in the German Army to regain their proper position, and would not have given to the political head of Germany that enormous ascendancy which has enabled him to move forward. On the morrow of such a success we could have made a large and generous settlement.

Now we are in a moment when a third move is made, but when that opportunity does not present itself in the same favorable manner. Austria has been laid in thrall, and we do not know whether Czechoslovakia will not suffer a similar attack. Let me remind hon. Members when they talk about Germany's desire for peace that this small country has declared that it will resist, and if it resists that may well light up the flames of war, the limits of which no man can predict. It is because we have lost these opportunities of standing firm, of having strong, united forces, a good heart, and a resolute desire to defend the right and afterwards to do generously as the result of strength, that, when our resources are less and the dangers greater, we have been brought to this pass. I predict that the day will come when at some point or other, on some issue or other, you will have to make a stand, and I pray God that when that day comes we may not find that through an unwise policy we are left to make that stand alone.

THE ANNEXATION OF AUSTRIA

March 14, 1938

Supply (Foreign Affairs considered in Committee)

1938

February 25. Lord Halifax becomes Foreign Secretary.

March 2. Publication of White Paper announcing a speeding up of defense measures.

March 8. Publication of Cadman Report criticizing the state of civil aviation.

March 9. Dr Schuschnigg announces that a plebiscite will be held on March 13 to approve a "free and German, independent and social, Christian and united Austria."

March 11. Herr Hitler sends an ultimatum to Dr Schuschnigg demanding postponement of plebiscite. Subsequent ultimatums demand Schuschnigg's resignation and the appointment of Seyss-Inquart as Chancellor Schuschnigg resigns. German troops cross the Austrian frontier.

March 11. Lord Winterton, Chancellor of the Duchy of Lancaster, joins the Cabinet and is appointed to be an additional member of the Air Council.

March 12. Herr Hitler flies to Linz.

March 13. Federal State of Austria dissolved and annexed to German Reich.

March 14. France and Russia renew their pledges of aid to Czechoslovakia in the event of aggression. Field-Marshal Goering assures the Czechoslovak Government of Germany's determination to respect the territorial integrity of Czechoslovakia. Great Britain takes formal note of this assurance.

THE ANNEXATION OF AUSTRIA

THE SPEECH OF the Prime Minister overshadowed the Debate and dominates all our minds. I do not know when in my lengthening experience of the House of Commons I have heard—certainly not since the War— a statement so momentous, expressed in language of frigid restraint but giving the feeling of iron determination behind it. I am sure in all quarters of the House we heard with the greatest pleasure his affirmation of the rights and interest and duty of Great Britain in Central Europe. He has said that there must be no hasty decision, and everybody will feel that while our minds are under the immediate influence of this painful and lamentable event is not the best time to take fresh resolves, provided that nothing is lost by delay.

I listened with great pleasure to the speech of the Member for Sparkbrook [Mr. Amery]. I found myself ready to respond to the appeal which he made that we should pool our opinions and efface differences as far as possible. Above all, I agree with him in his statement that the policy to be declared, within a reasonably short time, by this country must be clear and precise, so that it can be understood, for good or ill, by all countries and all parties. Everyone remembers the controversy, which has dragged on for many years, about whether we could have stopped the Great War in 1914 if Sir Edward Grey had made plain declarations a week before hand. I myself am of opinion that he did all that it was possible for him to do in the circumstances, and I doubt very much whether the event would have been averted even if he had made such a declaration. But still there is a weight of historic judgment piling up that in all these matters of international strife and danger it is most necessary that nations should declare plainly where they stand, and of all the nations which should so declare itself our country, with her insular characteristics still partially remaining to her, has an obligation to give a perfectly plain statement of what she will or will not do in certain contingencies when those contingencies approach the threshold of reality. Long delay would be harmful. Why should we assume that time is on our side? I know of nothing to convince me that if the evil forces now at work are suffered to feed upon their successes and upon their victims our task will be easier when finally we are all united. Not only do we need a clear declaration of the Government's policy, but we require to set to work to rally the whole country behind that declared policy, in order that there may not be shifts and changes, as well as that there may not be any doubt or hesitation. It will certainly be no easier for us to face the problems with which we are confronted a year hence than it is today. Indeed, we might easily delay resistance to a point where continued resistance and true collective security would become impossible.

The gravity of the event of the 11th of March cannot be exaggerated Europe is confronted with a program of aggression, nicely calculated and timed, unfolding stage by stage, and there is only one choice open, not only to us, but to other countries who are unfortunately concerned—either to submit, like Austria, or else to take effective measures while time remains to ward off the danger and, if it cannot be warded off, to cope with it. Resistance will be hard, yet I am persuaded—and the Prime Minister's speech confirms me—that it is to this conclusion of resistance to overweening encroachment that His Majesty's Government will come, and the House of Commons will certainly sustain them in playing a great part in the effort to preserve the peace of Europe, and, if it cannot be preserved, to preserve the freedom of the nations of Europe. If we were to delay, if we were to go on waiting upon events for a considerable period, how much should we throw away of resources which are now available for our security and for the maintenance of peace? How many friends would be alienated, how many potential allies should we see go, one by one, down the grisly gulf, how many times would bluff succeed, until behind bluff ever-gathering forces had accumulated reality? Where shall we be two years hence, for instance, when the German Army will certainly be much larger than the French Army, and when all the small nations will have fled from Geneva to pay homage to the ever-waxing power of the Nazi system, and to make the best terms they can for themselves?

We cannot leave the Austrian question where it is. We await the further statement of the Government, but it is quite clear that we cannot accept as a final solution of the problem of Central Europe the event which occurred on March 11. The public mind has been concentrated upon the moral and sentimental aspects of the Nazi conquest of Austria —a small country brutally struck down, its Government scattered to the winds, the oppression of the Nazi party doctrine imposed upon a Catholic population and upon the working-classes of Austria and of Vienna, the hard ill-usage of persecution which indeed will ensue—which is probably in progress at the moment—of those who, this time last week, were exercising their undoubted political rights, discharging their duties faithfully to their own country. All this we see very clearly, but there are some things which I have not seen brought out in the public Press and which do not seem to be present in the public mind, and they are practical considerations of the utmost significance.

Vienna is the center of all the communications of all the countries which formed the old Austro-Hungarian Empire, and of all the countries lying to the south-east of Europe. A long stretch of the Danube is now in German hands. This mastery of Vienna gives to Nazi Germany military and economic control of the whole of the communications of south-eastern Europe, by road, by river, and by rail. What is the effect of this upon the structure of Europe? What is the effect of it upon what is called the balance of power, such as it is, and upon what is called the Little Entente? I must say a word about this group of Powers called the Little Entente. Taken singly, the three countries of the Little Entente may be called Powers of the second rank, but they are very vigorous States, and united they are a Great Power. They have hitherto been, and are still, united by the closest military agreement. Together they make the complement of a Great Power and of the military machinery of a Great Power. Rumania has the oil; Yugoslavia has the minerals and raw materials. Both have large armies; both are mainly supplied with munitions from Czechoslovakia. To English ears, the name of Czechoslovakia sounds outlandish. No doubt they are only a small democratic State, no doubt they have an army only two or three times as large as ours, no doubt they have a munitions supply only three times as great as that of Italy, but still they are a virile people; they have their treaty rights, they have a line of fortresses, and they have a strongly manifested will to live freely.

Czechoslovakia is at this moment isolated, both in the economic and in the military sense. Her trade outlet through Hamburg, which is based upon the Peace Treaty, can, of course, be closed at any moment. Now her communications by rail and river to the south, and after the south to the south-east, are liable to be severed at any moment. Her trade may be subjected to tolls of an absolutely strangling character Here is a country which was once the greatest manufacturing area in the old Austro-Hungarian Empire. It is now cut off, or may be cut off at once unless, out of these discussions which must follow, arrangements are made securing the communications of Czechoslovakia. She may be cut off at once from the sources of her raw material in Yugoslavia and from the natural markets which she has established there. The economic life of this small State may be practically destroyed as a result of the act of violence which was perpetrated last Friday night. A wedge has been driven into the heart of what is called the Little Entente, this group of countries which have as much right to live in Europe unmolested as any of us have the right to live unmolested in our native land.

It would be too complicated to pursue the economic, military, and material reactions, apart from moral sentiments altogether, into the other countries. It would take too long, but the effects of what has happened now upon Rumania, upon Hungary, upon Bulgaria, upon Turkey, must be the subject of the closest possible study, not only by His Majesty's Government, but by all who aspire to take part in the public discussion of these matters By what has happened it is not too much to say that Nazi Germany, in its present mood, if matters are left as they are, is in a position to dominate the whole of South-east Europe. Over an area inhabited perhaps by 200,000,000 of people Nazidom and all that it involves is moving on to absolute control. Therefore, I venture to submit to the House that this Nazi conquest of Austria cannot remain where it is, and that a patient, determined, persevering discussion of it ought to take place and to be pushed forward, first of all, no doubt, through the Chanceries and by the diplomatic channels, but also and ultimately it should be pushed forward in the natural place for such discussions at Geneva—under the League of Nations. We are not in a position to say tonight, "The past is the past." We cannot say, "The past is the past," without surrendering the future. Therefore, we await further statements from His Majesty's Government with the greatest possible interest.

The serious nature of our affairs is realized and apprehended in all parts of the House. I have often been called an alarmist in the past, yet I affirm tonight that there is still, in my belief, an honorable path to safety and, I hope, to peace. What ought we to do? The Prime Minister today has made a declaration upon the subject of defense.

There is to be a new effort of national rearmament and national service. We shall have to lay aside our easy habits and methods. We shall have to concentrate on securing our safety with something like the intensity that has been practiced in other countries whose excesses we may desire to restrain. I think the House will be grateful to the Prime Minister for that declaration, and I am certain that he may rely upon all those strong forces in every party throughout the country to second the efforts of the Government to place us in a position where we shall not feel ourselves liable to be blackmailed out of our duties, out of our interests and out of our rights.

It seems to me quite clear that we cannot possibly confine ourselves only to a renewed effort at rearmament. I know that some of my hon. Friends on this side of the House will laugh when I offer them this advice I say, "Laugh, but listen." I affirm that the Government should express in the strongest terms our adherence to the Covenant of the League of Nations and our resolve to procure by international action the reign of law in Europe. I agree entirely with what has been said by the Leaders of the two Opposition parties upon that subject; and I was extremely glad to notice that at the beginning and in the very forefront of his speech the Prime Minister referred to the League of Nations and made that one of the bases of our right to intervene and to be consulted upon affairs in Central Europe. The matter has an importance in this country. There must be a moral basis for British rearmament and British foreign policy. We must have that basis if we are to unite and inspire our people and procure their wholehearted action, and if we are to stir the English-speaking people throughout the world.

Our affairs have come to such a pass that there is no escape without running risks. On every ground of prudence as well as of duty I urge His Majesty's Government to proclaim a renewed, revivified, unflinching adherence to the Covenant of the League of Nations. What is there ridiculous about collective security? The only thing that is ridiculous about it is that we have not got it. Let us see whether we cannot do something to procure a strong element of collective security for ourselves and for others. We have been urged to make common cause in self-defense with the French Republic. What is that but the beginning of collective security? I agree with that. Not so lightly will the two great liberal democracies of the West be challenged, and not so easily, if challenged, will they be subjugated. That is the beginning of collective security. But why stop there? Why be edged and pushed farther down the slope in a disorderly expostulating crowd of embarrassed States? Why not make a stand while there is still a good company of united, very powerful countries that share our dangers and aspirations? Why should we delay until we are confronted with a general landslide of those small countries passing over, because they have no other choice, to the overwhelming power of the Nazi régime?

If a number of States were assembled around Great Britain and France in a solemn treaty for mutual defense against aggression; if they had their forces marshaled in what you may call a Grand Alliance; if they had their Staff arrangements concerted; if all this rested, as it can honorably rest, upon the Covenant of the League of Nations, in pursuance of all the purposes and ideals of the League of Nations; if that were sustained, as it would be, by the moral sense of the world; and if it were done in the year 1938—and, believe me, it may be the last chance there will be for doing it—then I say that you might even now arrest this approaching war. Then perhaps the curse which overhangs Europe would pass away. Then perhaps the ferocious passions which now grip a great people would turn inwards and not outwards in an internal rather than an external explosion, and mankind would be spared the deadly ordeal towards which we have been sagging and sliding month by month. I have ventured to indicate a positive conception, a practical and realistic conception, and one which I am convinced will unite all the forces of this country without whose help your armies cannot be filled or your munitions made. Before we cast away this hope, this cause and this plan, which I do not at all disguise has an element of risk, let those who wish to reject it ponder well and earnestly upon what will happen to us if, when all else has been thrown to the wolves, we are left to face our fate alone.

THE DANUBE BASIN

March 24, 1938

Third Reading of the Consolidated Fund Bill

THE DANUBE BASIN

THE PRIME MINISTER, in what I think it is not presumptuous for me to describe as a very fine speech, set before us the object which is in all our minds—namely, how to prevent war. A country like ours, possessed of immense territory and wealth, whose defenses have been neglected, cannot avoid war by dilating upon its horrors, or even by a continuous display of pacific qualities, or by ignoring the fate of the victims of aggression elsewhere. War will be avoided, in present circumstances, only by the accumulation of deterrents against the aggressor. If our defenses are weak, we must seek allies; and, of course, if we seek allies, alliances involve commitments. But the increase of commitments may be justified if it is followed by a still greater increase of deterrents against aggression.

I was very glad to hear the Prime Minister reaffirm in such direct terms our arrangements for mutual defense with the French Republic. Evidently they amount to a defensive alliance. Why not say so? Why not make it effective by a military convention of the most detailed character? Are we, once again, to have all the disadvantages of an alliance without its advantages, and to have commitments without full security? Great Britain and France have to stand together for mutual protection. Why should not the conditions be worked out precisely and the broad facts made public? Everyone knows, for instance, that our Air Force is tripled in deterrent effectiveness if it operates from French bases, and, as I pointed out in the House three weeks ago, the fact that an attack upon this country would bring the attacker into conflict with the French Army is another great security to us here. We are obliged in return to go to the aid of France, and hitherto we have always been better than our word.

Here, then, is the great security for the two countries. Do not conceal it. Proclaim it, implement it, work it out in thorough detail. Treat the defensive problems of the two countries as if they were one. Then you will have a real deterrent against unprovoked aggression, and if the deterrent fails to deter, you will have a highly organized method of coping with the aggressor. The present rulers of Germany will hesitate long before they attack the British Empire and the French Republic if those are woven together for defense purposes into one very powerful unit. Having gone so far, there is no safe halting-place short of an open defensive alliance with France, not with loose obligations, but with defined obligations on both sides and complete inter-staff arrangements. Even an isolationist would, I think, go so far as to say, "If we have to mix ourselves up with the Continent, let us, at any rate, get the maximum of safety from our commitments."[1]

Then we come to the case of Czechoslovakia. There has been a lot of talk about giving a guarantee, but I should be sorry if the grave issue now open in Europe were to turn solely on that point, cardinal though it be. Far wider decisions are called for; far larger interests are at stake. I listened with the utmost attention to all that the Prime Minister said about our relations to Czechoslovakia, and it seems to me that he has gone a long way in making a commitment. First, I was very glad to hear him reaffirm his adherence and that of the Government to the obligations of the Covenant of the League. Under the Covenant of the League we are not obliged to go to war for Czechoslovakia. But we are obliged not to be neutral, in the sense of being indifferent, if Czechoslovakia is the victim of unprovoked aggression. The Prime Minister seemed to me to go farther than those mere obligations of the League, and to indicate how very real was the interest which we took in affairs in that part of the world. Lord Halifax, speaking in another place, used language which is particularly important coming from the head of the Foreign Office. He said he had asked Field-Marshal Goering to repeat to him the assurances which he had given to the Prime Minister of Czechoslovakia, and that this had been done by the German Government; and then Lord Halifax said:

"By those assurances, solemnly given and more than once repeated, we naturally expect the German Government to abide, and if indeed they

[1] The Government acted in this sense and a month later invited M. Daladier and M. Bonnet to London to discuss methods of concerting the defensive arrangements of the two countries. These are now being elaborated by the Staffs.

desire to see European peace maintained, as I earnestly hope they do, there is no quarter in Europe in which it is more vital that undertakings should be scrupulously respected "

We not only have, therefore, the general obligations of the Covenant of the League, but we have this particular reference to special assurances given and received and noted There is a third aspect We have our agreement, which I have described, and of which the Prime Minister has reminded us, with France, and if France is attacked by Germany for going to the rescue of Czechoslovakia, no one can say that we shall not be involved—not legally, not as a matter of bond, but by the force of events. The Prime Minister used language which undoubtedly had the effect of making it perfectly plain that the course of war once started could not be limited, that no one could tell what would happen, that other countries would be drawn in, and he mentioned especially France and Great Britain as two countries which might be involved.

Taking all these points together, I cannot doubt that we have considerable commitments, and personally, I am very thankful for any words that have been used which sustain that point of view. But this seems to be another case, if I may say so, of making very considerable commitments without gaining the full proportion of deterrent value. We are not taking the fullest steps in our power to stop the event occurring, and yet we are liable to suffer from it if it occurs. We are liable not only to be drawn in, but to be drawn in, perhaps, late in the day, and very likely in unfavorable circumstances. It is really for consideration whether, having gone so far, the bolder course might not be the safer. All attempts to bridge a twelve-foot stream by an eight-foot plank are doomed to failure, and the plank is lost. It is a concession, no doubt, to bring forward a nine-foot plank, but again that may be lost. The great point in view is to achieve the object, and to produce the effect of an adequate deterrent.

The question does not turn upon an automatic permanent pledge. What I should be inclined to ask if these matters could be at any time reconsidered is not that a permanent or automatic pledge should be given, but that now, on this present occasion, in the circumstances which surround us at the moment, with the rape of Austria before our eyes, Great Britain should say, "If the Germans march in upon this State of Czechoslovakia without even waiting for an impartial examination, perhaps by a commission of the League of Nations, or some other body, into the position of the Sudeten Deutsch and the remedies offered for their grievances—if in those circumstances an act of violent aggression were committed upon that country, then we should feel, on this occasion, and in this emergency, bound to act with France in resisting it." Such a declaration, although limited to this particular emergency, although limited until a tribunal has examined the position and until the negotiations now proceeding have reached their conclusion—such an assurance would, I believe, do a great deal to stabilize the position in Europe, and I cannot see that it would very seriously add to our risks.

I must say that I myself have not felt during this crisis that there is an immediate danger of a major land war breaking out over Czechoslovakia. I know it is very rash to make such a statement, but when there is so much natural, but misdirected, alarm in the country, now on one point and now on another, one must run some risks in stating one's honest opinion. At any rate, that is the assumption on which I base my argument this afternoon, and I will give my reasons to the House. The first reason is that, in the opinion of many good judges, Germany is not ready this year for such an ordeal as a major land war. The second reason carries more conviction to me, because obviously the first is based upon facts which one cannot measure and secrets which one cannot probe It is that I cannot see that it would be to the interest of the rulers of Germany to provoke such a war.

Are they not getting all they want without it? Are they not achieving a long succession of most important objectives without firing a single shot? Is there any limit to the economic and political pressure which, without actually using military force, Germany will be able to bring to bear upon this unhappy State? She can be convulsed politically, she can be strangled economically, she is practically surrounded by superior forces, and unless something is done to mitigate the pressure of circumstances, she will be forced to make continuous surrenders, far beyond the bounds of what any impartial tribunal would consider just or right, until finally her sovereignty, her independence, her integrity, have been destroyed. Why, then, should the rulers of Germany strike a military blow? Why should they incur the risk of a major war?

Moreover, I think it is to be considered that there are other, even more tempting lines of advance open to Germany's ambitions. A serious disturbance among the Hungarian population in the Rumanian province of Transylvania might offer a pretext for the entry of German troops, at a Hungarian invitation or without it. Then all the possibilities of the oil and food of Rumania would be open. Here, again, force may be avoided and virtual annexation may be veiled in the guise of a compulsory alliance. In the meantime the control of Vienna enables the economic fortunes of all the States of the Danubian Basin to be manipulated, exploited and controlled so as to favor German designs, and for the benefit of German finance, trade and arms. Why, then, should Germany go to the one place where she would encounter the veto of France, and of Russia, which has also made definite assurances? I do not think the Government would have run very much risk if they had added the full force of Great Britain to the French declaration about Czechoslovakia. They would not greatly have increased their commitments and they would have made assurance double sure.

But the story of this year is not ended at Czechoslovakia. It is not ended this month. The might behind the German Dictator increases daily. His appetite may grow with eating. The forces of law and freedom have for a long time known nothing but rebuffs, failures and humiliations. Their influence would be immensely increased by any signs of concerted action and initiative and combination. The fact that Britain and France combined together at such a moment in such a cause would give them the strength and authority that they need in order to convince wavering States that they might find a good company of determined people to whom they might join themselves upon the basis of the Covenant and in accordance with its principles. On the morrow of such a proof of unity as could be given between Great Britain and France we might be able to make such an arrangement, or begin to make it, for the effective fulfillment of the Covenant. We might have a group of Powers, as it were Mandatories of the League, who would be the guardians of civilization, and once this was set up strong and real it would liberate us, at least over a long period, from the torments of uncertainty and anxiety which we now have to endure. Joint action on this occasion would make easier and safer the problem of dealing with the next occasion. If successful, it would certainly pave the way to more effective joint action in the enforcement of the non-intervention policy in Spain. Nations that have joined together to meet one particular emergency may well find, when they look around, that they have assembled forces sufficient to deal with other emergencies not yet before us, and thus we may gather an ever-growing company, ranged under standards of law and justice, submitting themselves to principles that they are ready to enforce: and thus, by military and moral means combined, we may once more regain the ascendant and the initiative for the free peoples of the world and throughout the Empire.

Do not let anyone suppose that this is a mere question of hardening one's heart and keeping a stiff upper lip, and standing by to see Czechoslovakia poleaxed or tortured as Austria has been. Something more than that particular kind of fortitude will be needed from us. It is not only Czechoslovakia that will suffer. Look at the States of the Danube Basin First and foremost there is Yugoslavia. That is a most powerful and virile State, three-quarters of whose martial people are undoubtedly in the fullest sympathy with the democracy of France and Great Britain, and are animated by an ardent hatred of Nazi or Fascist rule. They have a rooted desire to maintain themselves in their independence. Is nothing being done to ascertain what Yugoslavia would do, assuming that Great Britain and France were prepared to interest themselves in the problems of the Danube Basin? Yugoslavia might well be gained, and I am told that the effect of that on Bulgaria would probably be to draw her into the same orbit. Then there is Rumania, so directly menaced by the potential German movement to the East. These three countries if left alone, and convinced that there is no will power operating against the Dictators, will fall one by one into the Nazi grip and system. What then will be the position of Greece and Turkey?

I ask these questions, hoping that they may be carefully considered Is it not possible that decided action by France and Great Britain would rally the whole of these five States as well as Czechoslovakia, all of whom have powerful armies, who together aggregate 75,000,000 of people, who have several millions of fighting men already trained, who have immense resources, who all wish to dwell in peace within their habitations, who individually may be broken by defeat and despoiled, but who, united, constitute an immense resisting power? Can nothing be done to keep them secure and free and to unite them in their own interests, in French and British interests and, above all, in the interests of peace? Are we really going to let the whole of these tremendous possibilities fall away without a concerted effort of any kind? If we do, let us not suppose for a moment that we shall ourselves have escaped our perils. On the contrary, we shall have multiplied our perils, for a very obvious reason. At present Germany might contemplate a short war, but, once she has laid hands on these countries and extended her power to the Black Sea, the Nazi régime will be able to feed itself indefinitely, however long war may last, and thus we may weaken the deterrent force against war of that blockade to which the hon. Member who has just spoken referred. We should have removed another of the deterrents that stand between us and war. The Nazification of the whole of the Danube States is a danger of the first capital magnitude to the British Empire. Is all to go for nothing? Is it all to be whistled down the wind? If so, we shall repent in blood and tears our improvidence and our lack of foresight and energy.

I have set the issue before the House in terms which do not shirk realities. It has been said by almost all speakers that, if we do not stand up to the Dictators now, we shall only prepare the day when we shall have to stand up to them under far more adverse conditions. Two years ago it was safe, three years ago it was easy, and four years ago a mere dispatch might have rectified the position. But where shall we be a year hence? Where shall we be in 1940? In these next few months all these substantial countries will be deciding whether they will rally, as they would desire to do, to the standards of civilization which still fly over Geneva, or whether they will be forced to throw in their lot and adopt the system and the doctrines of the Nazi Powers. The Prime Minister spoke about the negotiations with Italy. I forbear to comment upon them, because I prefer to await the results when they are presented to us. I know no more effective means of aiding those negotiations than the creation of a Danubian block, and nothing that would make it more likely that any engagement entered into would bear fruit and be effective in the hour of serious need. I trust that the Government will do their utmost. If it is too late, the evil is upon us, but do not let any chance be thrown away of endeavoring to save this great area from being overrun, exploited and despoiled.

I now come to the second aspect of the deterrents which we are assembling against aggression—namely, national defense. I welcome very much the announcement that the Prime Minister has made in this respect, and particularly his decision to consult the trade unions. I know that he is averse from hasty decisions. No one can say that this is a hasty decision in the third year of rearmament.[2] I was very glad also to hear the reassurance that drastic action will be taken to augment the speed of our air program, of our air raid precautions system and of our anti-aircraft artillery. It is only a fortnight ago that my right hon. Friend told us he was satisfied that we were making the best and the most effective use of our resources. However, it appears that there

[2] See p. 272 n.

were other resources not being used which now will be used in a greater effort. I regret very much that these additional resources have not been applied during the last two years, when the air program was seen to be trailing so far behind. Not only did we start two years too late, but the second two years have been traversed at only half-speed. The Minister for the Co-ordination of Defence said a fortnight ago in rebuking me:

> I detected in Mr Churchill's demands a fundamental difference of opinion with the Government, for he contemplates a great deal more interference with industry than has hitherto taken place.

I was sorry to be told I was in fundamental difference with the Government, and I am glad to know from the Prime Minister's statement that this particular fundamental difference is likely very soon to be removed. However, I must say I do not feel sure even now, after this latest decision, that the problem of rearmament is being dealt with on right lines. Is the method of organization to be employed adapted to a nation-wide effort? Ought there not to be created, however tardily, a Ministry of Supply? Ought there not to be created a far more effective Ministry of Defence? Are there not problems pressing for solution which can be handled only by a Minister of Defence? Ought there not to be a Defence of the Realm Act giving the necessary powers to divert industry, as far as may be necessary, from the ordinary channels of commerce so as to fit our rearmament in with the needs of our export trade and yet make sure that rearmament has the supreme priority?

I will venture to echo the question which was posed by Mr. Amery last week Is our system of government adapted to the present fierce, swift movement of events? Twenty-two gentlemen of blameless party character sitting round an overcrowded table, each having a voice—is that a system which can reach decisions from week to week and cope with the problems descending upon us and with the men at the head of the dictator States? It broke down hopelessly in the War. But is this peace in which we are living? Is it not war without cannon firing? Is it not war of a decisive character, where victories are gained and territories conquered, and where ascendancy and dominance are established over large populations with extraordinary rapidity? If we are to prevent this bloodless war being turned into a bloody war, ought not His Majesty's Government to adopt a system more on a level with the period of crisis in which we live?

Let me give a warning drawn from our recent experiences. Very likely this immediate crisis will pass, will dissipate itself and calm down. After a boa constrictor has devoured its prey it often has a considerable digestive spell. It was so after the revelation of the secret German air force. There was a pause. It was so after German conscription was proclaimed in breach of the Treaty. It was so after the Rhineland was forcibly occupied. The House may recall that we were told how glad we ought to be because there would be no question of fortifying it. Now, after Austria has been struck down, we are all disturbed and alarmed, but in a little while there may be another pause. There may not—we cannot tell. But if there is a pause, then people will be saying, "See how the alarmists have been confuted; Europe has calmed down, it has all blown over, and the war scare has passed away." The Prime Minister will perhaps repeat what he said a few weeks ago, that the tension in Europe is greatly relaxed. The *Times* will write a leading article to say how silly those people look who on the morrow of the Austrian incorporation raised a clamor for exceptional action in foreign policy and home defense, and how wise the Government were not to let themselves be carried away by this passing incident.

All this time the vast degeneration of the forces of Parliamentary democracy will be proceeding throughout Europe. Every six weeks another corps will be added to the German army. All this time important countries and great rail and river communications will pass under the control of the German General Staff. All this time populations will be continually reduced to the rigors of Nazi domination and assimilated to that system. All this time the forces of conquest and intimidation will be consolidated, towering up soon in real and not make-believe strength and superiority. Then presently will come another stroke. Upon whom? Our questions with Germany are unsettled and unanswered. We cannot tell. What I dread is that the impulse now given to active effort may pass away when the dangers are not diminishing, but accumulating and gathering as country after country is involved in the Nazi system, and as their vast preparations reach their final perfection.

For five years I have talked to the House on these matters—not with very great success. I have watched this famous island descending incontinently, fecklessly, the stairway which leads to a dark gulf It is a fine broad stairway at the beginning, but after a bit the carpet ends. A little farther on there are only flagstones, and a little farther on still these break beneath your feet. Look back over the last five years. It is true that great mistakes were made in the years immediately after the War. But at Locarno we laid the foundation from which a great forward movement could have been made. Look back upon the last five years—since, that is to say, Germany began to rearm in earnest and openly to seek revenge. If we study the history of Rome and Carthage, we can understand what happened and why. It is not difficult to form an intelligent view about the three Punic Wars; but if mortal catastrophe should overtake the British Nation and the British Empire, historians a thousand years hence will still be baffled by the mystery of our affairs. They will never understand how it was that a victorious nation, with everything in hand, suffered themselves to be brought low, and to cast away all that they had gained by measureless sacrifice and absolute victory—gone with the wind!

Now the victors are the vanquished, and those who threw down their arms in the field and sued for an armistice are striding on to world mastery. That is the position—that is the terrible transformation that has taken place bit by bit. I rejoice to hear from the Prime Minister that a further supreme effort is to be made to place us in a position of security. Now is the time at last to rouse the nation. Perhaps it is the last time it can be roused with a chance of preventing war, or with a chance of coming through to victory should our efforts to prevent war fail We should lay aside every hindrance and endeavor by uniting the whole force and spirit of our people to raise again a great British nation standing up before all the world; for such a nation, rising in its ancient vigor, can even at this hour save civilization.

CPSIA information can be obtained at www.ICGtesting.com
Printed in the USA
LVOW04s1558240914

405675LV00018B/850/P